Jazz Age
Jews

MICHAEL

ALEXANDER

Jazz Age
Jews

PRINCETON UNIVERSITY

PRESS

Library of Congress Cataloging-in-Publication Data

Alexander, Michael, 1970–
Jazz Age Jews / Michael Alexander.
p. cm.
Includes bibliographical references and index.
ISBN 0-691-08679-6 (alk. paper)
1. Jews—United States—Biography. 2. Jews—United States—Social life
and customs. 3. Jews—United States—Politics and government—20th century.
4. Jews—United States—Identity. 5. Rothstein, Arnold, 1882–1928. 6. Frankfurter,
Felix, 1882–1965. 7. Jolson, Al, d. 1950. 8. United States—Ethnic relations. I. Title.
E184.37 .A13 2001
305.892′.4073—dc21   2001019853

British Library Cataloging-in-Publication Data is available

This book has been composed in Caledonia
Designed by Jan Lilly
Composed by Eileen Reilly

Printed on acid-free paper. ∞

www.pup.princeton.edu

Printed in the United States of America

10 9 8 7 6 5 4 3 2 1

TO MY PARENTS—

"I love the old folks at home!"

CONTENTS

CONTENTS

Jazz Age
Jews

By the 1920s a new generation of Jewish children had grown up in America. Many had migrated from Eastern Europe in the great transatlantic waves of 1882, 1891, 1904, and after. Others, though born in the United States, had immigrant parents. Either way, their fathers and mothers had suffered hunger, humiliation, and pogroms in Europe, but this was not the children's experience. Generally they went to American public schools and colleges, found white-collar jobs, escaped the urban ghettos of first settlement for greener places, and entered the middle class. Along the way they built Jewish neighborhoods with their own religious schools and community centers. They established thriving Jewish businesses and even entire industries. They formed a tangible voting block and helped shape public opinion and policy. They also contributed substantially to American cultural production, from popular entertainment to academia. In short, these children were making it in America. Moreso, they were participating in a host society as their ancestors in Galicia, Romania, or the Russian Pale never had.[1]

For these Jews in America, in any way calculable by socioeconomic statistics, five hundred years of alienation had ended. At least so it would seem. Yet as this generation took its place among other middle-class groups in American society, some of its members displayed a peculiar behavior that did not correspond to their new social positions: They acted as though they were increasingly marginalized. What is more, many identified themselves with less fortunate individuals and groups, people who remained in America's economic, political, and cultural margins. Jews did this by imitating, defending, and actually participating in the group life of marginalized Americans. I call this behavior *outsider identification*, and it is a paradox in the psychology of American Jewry. As Jews moved up, they identified down. Addressing the origins, influences, and consequences of this exceptional Jewish liberalism is the focus of this book.[2]

1

I explore the paradox of outsider identification through three titanic events—the Black Sox scandal, the trial of Sacco and Vanzetti, and the release of the first talkie, *The Jazz Singer*. Though these events are linked by their close company in the ocean of headlines, song refrains, and movie reels by which Americans knew the Jazz Age, they are even more closely connected by the public identification with marginalized Americans made by three children of the great Jewish migration. More important, the wider Jewish community agreed with these children and celebrated them.

Arnold Rothstein, gangster and alleged fixer of the 1919 World Series, is our first subject. While most Jews entered the worlds of law, medicine and pharmacy, dentistry, finance and accounting, social work, education, fashion, and entertainment—all legitimate and re-spectable industries—some, such as Rothstein, charted an alternate path. They invented the modern business of gambling and rationalized the structure of modern organized crime. Professional gambling was illegal, and worse, it carried a nasty social taint. Yet some Jews chose to run that business despite the other, legitimate choices newly and increasingly available to them. Of course numerous Americans, immi-grants and not, participated in illicit behavior in the 1920s. What is remarkable is not only the prominence of Jews in gambling and orga-nized crime, but their warm-hearted reception by many of their law-abiding fellow Jews. Why did upstanding Jewish citizens defend their brethren for being gamblers, even while they themselves tried to forge trusting relationships with gentiles in the legitimate business world?

Next comes politics. Felix Frankfurter, immigrant to the Lower East Side of New York City, had risen about as high in the American aristocracy as anyone could. He was full professor of law at Harvard—and had been since he was thirty-one—and had had the ear of every liberal president since Theodore Roosevelt. He was the closest of friends with both Justice Brandeis and Justice Holmes of the U.S. Supreme Court. Nevertheless, Frankfurter did something that Har-vard professors just did not do. He defended two convicted murder-ers, the anarchists Sacco and Vanzetti, in the face of evidence even Justice Holmes considered ample to justify the convictions. Frank-furter argued that the judge and jury could not have adjudicated fairly because an atmosphere of racial and political prejudice pervading

America during the Red Scare of 1920 had created a condition of regular judicial bias in Massachusetts. While this kind of argument is commonplace today, then it was not. Indeed, Frankfurter may have been the first to make it. Meanwhile, every public voice of the Jewish community supported Frankfurter's position, while none upheld the view of the Commonwealth of Massachusetts, that the two anarchists had been fairly convicted. The case of Sacco and Vanzetti divided America but not American Jews. Like no other ethnic group, why did Jews categorically take as their own cause two Italian anarchists?

The third case considers the career of Al Jolson, jazz singer and blackface entertainer. At a time when African-American migration was dividing northern American cities, and as the white middle class defined itself against this new presence, Jews became fascinated by African-American culture or at least their own version of it. On Broadway, along Tin Pan Alley, and in Hollywood they showed off their new attraction and proclaimed themselves to be, if anywhere in the conflict between black and white, decidedly on the side of American blacks. As a group not widely accepted as white themselves, why did Jews take this risky position?

Each case describes an episode in a long career of self-marginalization on the part of children of the great migration, each climaxes in a famous display of outsider identification, and each culminates in epidemic expressions of approval of that behavior by much of the Jewish community. Together, they cover three sociological realms—economics, politics, and culture—in which Jews were making it in America but nevertheless were identifying with those who were not.[3]

From where did this proclivity for self-marginalization and outsider identification come? Perhaps we should consult the religion, culture, and worldview of Jews as they lived in Eastern Europe for the roots of outsider behavior in America. After all, Jewish Americans were not created ex nihilo.

By the time of their great migration to America, Jews had lived in Eastern Europe for half a millennium. For most of that time they had been estranged from native society. Take, for example, the Russian case. According to Eli Lederhendler, scholar of Eastern European Jewry, 95 percent of the Russian and formerly Polish Jewry at the turn of the century lived in the Pale of Settlement, the westernmost area of Russia between the Baltic and Black seas in which Jews were legally bound to reside. Non-Jewish Russians made up less than 5 percent of the Pale's urban population. In 1897, 96.5 percent of Russian Jews stated that their mother tongue was Yiddish. In 1898, 54 percent of all Jewish children in the empire attended traditional Jewish elementary schools rather than Russian schools. A separate Jewish social order existed within the confines of the Pale. Jews were alienated from Russia with respect to language, culture, religion, economy, education, geography, demography, and citizenship.[4]

The situation of Jews in Russia was typical of Eastern Jews generally. To explain their systemic alienation from host societies, Jews turned to their sacred texts. They invoked the Exodus account of Jewish slavery to explain how a wandering nation—a people in exile—would inherit the promise of the covenant. As Jews had been enslaved in Egypt, so they were exiled in Europe. As the Israelites had returned home with the commandments, so the current keepers of God's covenant would also be returned home. Through the doctrines of exile and covenant, Jews told themselves that humiliation and alienation were signs of being God's chosen people.

Exile and covenant became core components of Ashkenazic (Central and Eastern European) Jewish culture. According to Jacob Katz, historian of European Jewry, the twin concepts were "embodied in and permeated all the primary sources on which Jewish education was founded. They were not only formulated in words, but also expressed in ceremonial performed both by the individual and by the congregation." In time, Jews came even to embrace their places on the margins of host societies to prove their special status. Jewish communities would sometimes institute their own social policies of "exclusiveness and tolerance" for the surrounding communities among which they lived, and circumscribe how they interacted with the gentile world by cultivating economic, political, and cultural models of "self-conscious distinctiveness."[5]

So soundly did Jewish communities mark themselves off from their neighbors, both theologically and socially, and so thoroughly did their neighbors return the exclusion, that Jewish identity fused with outsider status. In turn, Jewish identity became threatened by perceived social integration. To halt such integration, Jewish communities revitalized their social distinctions from time to time, *intentionally* impairing their economic, political, and cultural relations with gentiles.[6] This is rather similar to what happened in the cases of Rothstein, Frankfurter, and Jolson, who marked themselves off from American society and were celebrated by their Jewish peers for doing so.

But Europe—particularly Eastern Europe—differed greatly from America. In late-nineteenth-century Eastern Europe, such traditional institutions of Jewish authority as the rabbinate and *kehilla* were being destroyed by antisemetic policies of the tsars. As the agrarian order of Eastern Europe slouched in the face of the emerging industrial economy of the West, Eastern governments increasingly blamed their misfortune on the "alien" Jews who lived among them. This oppression devastated institutional aspects of Jewish life. Nevertheless, the same official oppression also unwittingly helped maintain Jewish identity. Many Jews remained within their Jewish communities, not for religious reasons, but because the policies of oppression included segregation. Thus the definition of Jews as outsiders and aliens was reinforced.

As they were in Eastern Europe, Jewish institutions of authority were weak in America. It was not government oppression, however, but religious freedom that caused the erosion. The United States had no official policy of segregation concerning Jews. Conversely, it refrained from endorsing a Jewish church, or any church for that matter. To the government, naturalized Jews were simply citizens, not to be distinguished from other Americans. Jewish religious institutions were allowed to thrive or dissolve by the will of the Jewish population alone, without the intervention of government. The American separation of church and state allowed the Jews who came during the great wave of immigration around the turn of the twentieth century to integrate into American society in one short generation. But religious liberty and social acceptance also had drawbacks, which amounted to a double blow against traditional Jewish life: the absence of strong, entrenched institutions of Jewish authority, and the lack of governmental policies of segregation and oppression. What, then, remained to define Jewish identity?

Social acceptance and success in America threatened the status of Jews as outsiders; therefore, Jewish identity was also threatened. At this moment, in the 1920s, while the descendents of the Eastern European migration were finally moving into the mainstream of a host society, they began to identify down. In America, when Jews were not being marginalized, they identified with those who were. Explicitly, the larger community of Jews linked the outsider identification of people like Rothstein, Jolson, and Frankfurter to traditional Jewish identity by *invoking the language of exile* to explain, and finally to praise, their behavior. Thus Jews met the obligation of their self-definition as an exiled people. With the help of outsider identification, at least one foundation of Jewish identity survived in America.

AMERICAN Jews had not always thought this way. Eighteenth- and nineteenth-century migrations from Western Europe had also brought Jews to America. Unlike children of the great Eastern European migrations, descendents of these earlier immigrants tended more readily to adopt the social views of the American establishment and of the communities in which they settled. During the Civil War, for instance, Jewish opinion was split according to locale, with Southern Jews (Confederate Secretary of State Judah P. Benjamin among them) supporting the secessionists, and Northern Jews favoring abolition. Ordinarily, the earlier Jewish immigrants tried to emulate the social graces of America's old guard; indeed, even their behavior in synagogue reflected nuances of Protestant worship. When Western European Jews in America acted philanthropically, as they often did, the pattern of their charity was not to identify themselves with the downtrodden but rather to teach poorer peoples to conform to mainstream American conduct, just as they had.

That is to say, when earlier waves of immigrant Jews had come to America they identified up, not down. The routine of upward conformity paralleled Jewish behavior in Western Europe where, unlike Eastern Europe, throughout the nineteenth century Jewry had been emancipated and permitted to join host societies. Jewish acceptance in Western Europe entailed a distressing compromise, however, for the emancipation of Jews as individuals in the body politic meant that Jewish culture, traditionally organized around group life, diminished.

With political emancipation in Western Europe, Jews were expected to quit their separate Jewish nation and conform to the manners and worldview of the society-at-large. Western Jews accepted the condition attached to political equality and brought it with them to America. Even in America, where Jewish emancipation was unqualified, descendents of Western European Jewry still shunned ethnic markers of Jewish difference and looked to mainstream society to define their conduct.[7]

Yet at the turn of the twentieth century the last large wave of Jewish immigrants did not come predominantly from emancipated lands; neither did it bring traditions of acculturation and conformity. Thus the children of the great migration saw little conflict between their Americanization and Jewish group life. Even those who chose to eschew religious practice in America felt no need to lessen other ties to their people.[8] For Arnold Rothstein, Felix Frankfurter, and Al Jolson, ethnic identity and outsider identification comfortably replaced observance of the Law. For those who saw these three secular Jews as Jewish heroes, models, and exemplars of right Jewish behavior in America, ethnicity and outsider identification complemented religious observance. Neither being Jewish nor being marginalized excluded one from being American, they thought. Rather, they imagined that being marginalized was the most American way to be.

In this sense the stories of Rothstein, Frankfurter, and Jolson are about Americanization. Less about assimilation or the desire to acculturate, the behaviors of these three men and the reactions to them by the bulk of American Jewry are about marking oneself as different—by using a language familiar from centuries of being different—and imagining that you are a better American for doing so.[9]

THESE new American Jews from Eastern Europe, outnumbering the descendents of all previous Jewish migrations to America nearly nine to one, in effect became American Jewry. Within a generation their perspective of Americanization-through-difference trickled through the alleys of America's ghettos, along the parkways of second settlement, and finally into broad Jewish-American consciousness. Often the attitude of Jewish difference came to persuade the descendents of earlier Western European migrations as well, as happened in the case of American Zionism (discussed in chapter 9). American Jewish identity had been turned on its head. Increasingly, as Jews found themselves succeeding in the American social order and thereby wandering from an identity based on centuries of marginalization, they identified with outsiders to even the balance. As gambling, radical politics, and black music grew chic among the smartest, jazziest cliques, even gentile Americans could participate in the course of difference. In the grand, decade-long showdown between the old and the new that characterized the Jazz Age, descendents of the great Jewish migration found themselves in the middle of the fray. Their tendency to identify themselves with the causes of outsiders had flung them there.

Still, it is sensible to consider the role of antisemitism in helping to forge outsider identification. Indeed, antisemitism did surge in the jazz age, and at many levels of American society. As the Ku Klux Klan rode strongly for the first time in fifty years and Henry Ford appealed to a burgeoning popular spirit of antisemitism in the *Dearborn Independent*, Eleanor Roosevelt expressed her race feelings, privately, after her husband, Franklin Roosevelt, invited Felix Frankfurter home to lunch in 1918. "An interesting little man," Eleanor wrote of her guest, "but very jew." Her sentiment was typical of an age some have described as tribal and others have recognized as systemically antisemitic, anti-Catholic, and anti-immigrant. Certain business and law firms remained closed to Jews; certain positions in government could not be reached; certain neighborhoods were simply inaccessible. Undoubtedly, this affected Jewish behavior.[10]

Nevertheless, Jews were not the only group to face discrimination. But they were the only group that, as a group, identified with people more marginalized than themselves. The same cannot be said of Italians, Irish, or African-Americans.[11] Nor can these associations be described principally as strategic alliances from which Jews benefited. When Jews took the side of ethnic gangsters, anarchists, and African-Americans, they thwarted their own upward mobility. Why? This book posits that their theological belief in perpetual Jewish difference, paired with their understanding of Jewish history as the history of exile—both of which their culture and real social circumstances had engrained in them for centuries—gave them ample reason for doing so.

Here, then, are three Jewish stories behind three larger American ones. The events described in these pages were the stuff of conversation and controversy throughout America. Their Jewish fomenters were sometimes hated, sometimes loved, often imitated and caricatured, but they were not ignored. Their deeds helped shape the consciousness of the entire nation and the identity of their own people. More important, though, these Jews stand for something else. The stories of Rothstein, Frankfurter, and Jolson are about making it but thinking you haven't. They are about being there but believing you are held back. My foremost aim, then, is to explore an antilogy of success in America, among Jews primarily but perhaps also among those other Americans who, despite evidence of their own success, understand themselves best by identifying with those who have least.

With this in mind, let us turn to the story of Arnold Rothstein.

Jazz Age Economics

FOR SOME TIME before the 1920s, Americans had been honing their formula for the creation of wealth. Centralized production, scientific management, a national communications infrastructure, an international distribution network, corporatization, equity capital— none of this was new, not even in Europe. But only after the Great War, as both the Allies and Central Powers looked for a model with which to rebuild their nations, did Europeans finally realize the change—their former colonies were now the colonizers. By the time the war ended, the Allies had borrowed seven billion dollars from Americans and added another three billion dollars to the bill by November 1920. "We were the most powerful nation," F. Scott Fitzgerald remembered thinking at the time. "Who could tell us any longer what was fashionable and what was fun?"[1]

By 1920, investment in manufacturing had caused the gross value of manufactured products to grow to triple that of agriculture. The 1920 census reported that town and city dwellers (in communities of 2,500 or more) were America's newest majority. Concurrently, American exports rose 333 percent above the 1913 output, to 8.25 billion dollars. Rationalized mass production was the new economic miracle, though it was really nothing new. Henry Ford and Frederick W. Taylor had proven before the war that when one coordinated a worker's every motion with scientific precision, production levels rose and cost fell. On December 10, 1915, the millionth Ford automobile put on the road all but proved it.[2]

Manufacturing efficiency intrigued Americans, but how could a young entrepreneur without family wealth use the lesson? Prewar capital had been scarce, held in the hands of a few bankers and robber barons. But during the war, money became easier to find. The federal

11

government, looking to stimulate armament production, took out massive loans by issuing Liberty Bonds, and continued to do so after the fighting had ended. Government spending, far outrunning tax revenues, flooded the economy with more cash and, thereby, more credit. Using that capital to make matériel for the war and for returning soldiers became the fashionable way to procure a fortune. Among those who benefited from the burst of war production were immigrant Jews who, by the 1920s, had taken their profits from clothing and uniform manufacture and, as a group, had shifted from working as wage laborers to being mostly self-employed.[3]

Some observers wondered what would happen to the rate of government consumption in peacetime. Others were more concerned about when the government would pay off its war debt and remove that money from the economy. Who would remain with enough cash to buy things? Policymakers such as Secretary of Commerce Herbert Hoover began talking of "stimulating consumption," and advertising soon displaced manufacturing as the newest of the practical sciences. The slogan and the logo, promoting such products as *Lucky Strike* cigarettes, *Coca-Cola*, and *Gulf* gasoline, became as common as road signs.[4]

But consumption remained a secondary matter. Americans were coming to realize that selling things was not the only way to make money. Because the corporation, with its cadre of professional managers, had come to replace the family-based enterprise, companies could sell their own equity to create capital. Purchasing stocks and bonds soon became as interesting to Americans as manufacturing. Still, there was something sinister about making money without producing anything. Populists, using the most derisive tone, equated stock markets with gambling dens and labeled brokers as speculators.

But to speak of stock markets, speculation, and gambling forges too far into the world of Arnold Rothstein. It is sufficient here to conclude, again with the words of Fitzgerald, that America had embarked upon "the most expensive orgy in history," and few thought much about when the revelry would end.[5]

PART I

"Biznez Iz Biznez": The Arnold Rothstein Story

I have been victimized more than once
simply because of the business that I was
in and the peculiar moral code which
governs it. . . . It is not pleasant to be what
some may call "a social outcast."

Arnold Rothstein

Arnold Rothstein

IN 1919 THE biggest bookmaker in America was Arnold Rothstein. He could cover any bet—on horse races, casino games, cards, billiards, and for every sport, professional or amateur. He swindled stocks. He corrupted politicians. He ran four illegal casinos. He trained Lucky Luciano and Meyer Lansky in the ways of illicit finance and the organization of crime. And he was never convicted of a single crime, except in the newspapers.

From the moment the American press learned that the 1919 World Series had been fixed, it has been the public consensus that Rothstein fixed it. Newspapermen such as Damon Runyon began to call him the Brain, the Big Bankroll, the Big Jew Uptown. Some simply called him "A.R." For the remainder of his career Rothstein's name was synonymous with the victimless crime that battered the nation.

Americans had hoped the World Series of 1919 would welcome home from the Great War victorious soldiers and signal that everyone might settle back into routines of normalcy, isolationism, and contentment. By 1919 baseball was considered America's sport, pure as any children's sandlot game. In this World Series the Chicago White Sox faced the Cincinnati Reds. The Sox had a long roster of colorful, provincial characters, starting with "Old Roman" Charles Comiskey, the self-made owner of the team and whisper-campaign candidate for governor of Illinois. There was Eddie Cicotte, the team's starting pitcher, ladies' man, and dapper Midwestern style-setter. And, of course, there was one of America's most beloved baseball personalities, the illiterate "Shoeless" Joe Jackson, a man so homespun that Comiskey had to guard against his hopping some train back to South Carolina to trade the complicated city life of the baseball star for his old job at the mill.

These were the good guys. This was a home team. For them, the children of Chicago wagered pennies earned scrounging for foul rags and coal. And it was the children better than anyone who intuited the meaning of the fix when the news broke. The *Chicago Tribune* reported that as the White Sox left the courtroom after appearing before the first Grand Jury, a small boy tugged at Shoeless Joe's sleeve.

"Say it ain't so, Joe," the boy pleaded. "Say it ain't so."

"Yes, kid," Jackson replied, "I'm afraid it is."

"Well," the boy said, "I never would've thought it."[1]

Someone, somehow, had smuggled the cynicism of Europe and the Great War into the United States and had succeeded in corrupting the premier symbol of American purity. Who might have done it? Was it Old Roman Comiskey, the man who had spent twenty years building the good name of the team he had founded? Were the players not as innocent and fresh-off-the-farm as they appeared? The media quickly decided, and baseball's weekly periodical, the *Sporting News*, declared what was on the mind of many a patriotic American: "A lot of dirty, long-nosed, thick-lipped, and strong-smelling gamblers butted into the World Series—an American event, by the way."[2]

The Black Sox fix was just one of many unfortunate events that some explained as the work of a Jewish conspiracy in America. While the Black Sox scandal flooded the mainstream papers, Henry Ford circulated his own *Dearborn Independent*, which claimed, repeatedly and inelegantly, that Jews had provoked the Great War for the purpose of profiteering, and continued to dupe honest working Americans through dirty politics, banking, and even jazz. As for the Black Sox, the ballplayers had become yet another variety of pawn in a world increasingly determined by internecine politics, mysterious power, and deception.[3] Somehow a vague, foreign enemy had made his way from the battlefields of Europe to the ballpark in Chicago. Standing behind the enemy was Arnold Rothstein.

Any history of gambling and financial crime in the 1910s and 1920s must pay some attention to the history of Jews in America. Jews pioneered the modern business of gambling and heavily participated in the closely related business of stock market bucketeering. Those are facts.[4] Without question, other ethnic groups also demonstrated similar proclivities for these fields, most notably Irish Americans. (The

Arnold Rothstein story could not be written without reference to at least three different men named Sullivan.) Nevertheless, the histories of American gambling and gray-area finance would be told very differently without Herman Rosenthal, Sam Paul, Louis Webber, Jack Rose, Sam Schepps, Bill Cowan, Izzy Ham, Leo Mayer, Maxie Blumenthal, Sam Adler, Sol Lichtenstein, George Graham Rice (born Jacob Simon Herzig), Nick Cohen, Harry Pollak, Nicky Arnstein, "Cheeks" Ginsberg,[5] Paddy Goldberg, Harold Sonking, Phil Kastel, Jakie Fields, Hyman Turchin, Isaiah Lebow, Emil Fuchs, Joseph Shalleck, George Morton Levy, Maurice Cantor, and of course Arnold Rothstein.

The business practices of these gentlemen could—and often did—cross into the realm of crime. It may be more precise, however, to say that their pursuits resided in the margins, in the gray area, of the legal American economy. Though bookmaking was sometimes legal, the business of gambling consistently raised suspicions of social taint. Similarly, sometimes practices of double-dealers in the securities business defied the law, and sometimes they rested comfortably within the law's loopholes. In all cases, however, these crafts carried the stigma of ignobility in the larger economic order, despite the fact that Americans called for these services. In these gray areas and within this contradiction—between the services Americans wanted and the social (and sometimes legal) proscription of their providers—Arnold Rothstein and his associates made their livings.

Thus the Arnold Rothstein story, with its wayward Jews and suspicious money, must describe the uncomfortable territory where stereotype and fact converge. One need hardly mention that the business world of Arnold Rothstein did not constitute a significant portion of the larger Jewish economy. For Jewry in America, the 1910s and 1920s brought unusual economic opportunity and success in perfectly respectable businesses. In the ghettos of Eastern Europe in the nineteenth century, Jews had been estranged from the predominant economy. In America just the opposite was true. Within a generation working-class Jews rapidly (though not easily) entered the middle class, while other Jews gained an economic stature unprecedented in their American history. While Rothstein ran his gambling, loansharking, and bucket-shop operations from his reserved tables at Reuben's

and Lindy's delicatessens (both legitimate and successful Jewish restaurant businesses), Adolph Zukor, Carl Laemmle, William Fox,
Louis B. Mayer, and the Warner Brothers headed their Hollywood
studios; E. A. Filene, Nathan Straus, and Julius Rosenwald ran their
department stores; Paul Warburg sat on the Federal Reserve Board;
Oscar Straus became Secretary of Commerce under Theodore Roosevelt; and Bernard Baruch appeared as the genius who helped Woodrow Wilson convert the American peacetime economy for war, and
then back again. As American business emerged as the preeminent
economic power on the world scene, American Jews strode forth,
often leading the way.[6]

Although Rothstein and his kind straggled far behind the legitimate
Jewish business world in sheer numbers, their presence in the Jewish
imagination was large. The Jewish people understood that a separate,
successful economy existed in the underworld and that Jews were not
strangers to it. For the Yiddish press, as for much of America, Arnold
Rothstein became the underground economy personified. The Black
Sox scandal and the murder of Rothstein in 1928 provided moments
when Jewry in America could comment on this other Jewish economy
in which the most ancient stereotypes of Jews and money seemed to
agree with fact. This convergence did not disturb them. Rather, they
embraced it.

The story of Arnold Rothstein helps us understand the strange proclivity that certain Jews in America had for gray-area business at a
time when legitimate business was opening to them. Also, Rothstein's
story has a larger point. Jewish reactions to Rothstein's business and
public behavior explain why the larger community of Eastern European Jews in America accepted and welcomed its controversial brethren precisely for working along the margins of the American business
world at a time when so many Eastern Jews were rising higher in the
legitimate economy than they had for centuries.

Gambling in the Time of
Rothstein's Youth

IN THE summer of 1898, a sixteen-year-old delinquent wandered into a poolroom on the Bowery and found a home. There among members of the most crass and dissolute culture in New York City, Arnold Rothstein learned the business of low-stakes gambling. His mentor was Big Tim Sullivan, proprietor of the East Side's largest lottery. Unemployed or grossly underpaid Bowery residents loitered in Tim Sullivan's poolhalls shooting billiards while they waited for the late-night drawing of the house lottery, or "pool," for which the halls were named. Some of these men were chronic gamblers, some were drunks who consumed flat beer by the pitcher, and some simply wanted to avoid their decrepit tenements and boarding houses for as long as possible after a twelve- to sixteen-hour workday.[1]

Tim Sullivan ran more than just a few poolhalls. The chesty Irishman also ran the entire East Side of Manhattan. True, he was the New York state senator from the East Side, where his illegal lottery was safely located, but more importantly he was the Tammany boss of the Bowery and therefore a major power in New York City politics. His power came from his extraordinary talent for bringing in Democratic ballots. When Sullivan acquired the Bowery district in 1893, neither the Italians west of the Bowery nor the Jews to the east were well organized. Four years later, in the municipal election of 1897, the Tammany candidate for the D.A.'s office beat the incumbent progressive Republican by pitting working-class pride against the dull mores of the Protestant ruling class with the simple slogan "To Hell with Reform." The same campaign brought the crooked Robert Van Wyck to the mayor's office. In both instances Big Tim's district had swung the immigrant vote to the Democrats, where it remained more or less permanently.[2]

Around the time Arnold Rothstein wandered into the poolroom, Sullivan was just learning how to use his political connections for personal profit. He organized what became known to muckrakers as the "gambling commission," which also included "Big" Bill Devery, chief of the New York City Police Department. Sullivan's gambling commission offered poolrooms and gambling parlors an even trade: money for political protection. As long as Big Tim and Big Bill were paid, the police refrained from raiding. A muckraker for the *New York Times* estimated that over eleven hundred poolrooms and casinos in New York City paid the gambling commission around three million dollars a year.[3]

A brigade of youths hovered around Tim Sullivan's places, and they introduced Arnold to the finer points of back-alley gambling. Arnold roamed the East Side, straggling behind older mates such as "Beansy" Rosenthal, a chubby and dim-witted rambler, and "Monk" Eastman, the bouncer of the New Irving Dance Hall who would soon become savage leader of the Eastmans, the gang that shook down the Jewish ghetto.

As Arnold wandered about downtown, he compulsively collected the odds for every game he came across. Soon he recognized in himself a unique talent: numbers seemed to talk to him. Like no subject he had ever studied at Boy's High School before he dropped out, the probabilities of a pair of dice held him spellbound. Arnold could instantly calculate the true odds of throwing a hard four in a game of craps (each die showing two pips—odds at eight to one). He also knew always to fade the shooter (bet against the dice roller), because the "Don't" bettor has a slight edge. Fractions, figures, and schemes accumulated in his head.

Arnold experimented with different games on the streets of the Bowery. Like every amateur, he won occasionally; more often he lost. But all the while, he was learning to master the hidden percentages. He found out how much each game paid its winners, and then he calculated the real chances of winning. In Arnold's quick-witted circles, the mathematical difference between these two numbers was known as a "sure thing." Gambling taught Arnold how to recognize the opportunities that lie in these gray areas.

Beansy, Monk, and Arnold occasionally ran a low-stakes game of craps for the truants who called the streets around Sullivan's saloons their home. Sam Paul lived in the area. So did Louis Webber, "Bald" Jack Rose (not yet bald), and Sam Schepps, each of whom would own casinos in the following decade. Although craps had not yet been yoked for casino play, the boys' street games enchanted Sullivan. Unlike the elaborate card game faro, which was the staple of most gambling parlors (and notorious as a fixed game), or compared even with stuss (*shtuss*: Yiddish for "folly"), which was faro's Lower East Side equivalent, craps played *fast*. Money changed hands at a fantastic rate, sometimes five or six times a minute.[4]

Sullivan admired how the boys mastered the odds. They seemed to make money while most adults lost what meager wages they might have brought home. After a successful round with the dice, the boys would gloat and wave their thick bankrolls around the poolhalls. Sullivan didn't mind. He affectionately called Arnold and his friends the "smart Jew boys."[5] Their enthusiasm encouraged more bets from lottery customers.

Also in the summer of 1898, while Arnold introduced himself to low-stakes gambling downtown, the rest of New York City noticed workmen resuscitating the old brownstone two doors from Delmonico's Restaurant on 44th Street and Broadway. Workmen peeled out its rickety floors and replaced them with teakwood. They stripped paint off the walls to make way for Spanish leather and white mahogany paneling. One day deliverymen hustled a shipment of Chippendale furniture up the front stoop. Another day they distributed a sea of tapestries, Barye bronzes, and Chinese porcelains. Some suspected that a robber baron was moving in, but word soon spread that 5 East 44th Street was the latest business enterprise of Mr. Richard Canfield. Every sporting man knew what that meant: Another Canfield casino was going up.[6]

Richard Canfield patterned the place after his successful casinos in Saratoga Springs and Newport Beach, where the wayward children of America's aristocracy came to play. The casinos were all elegant, exclusive, and deliciously illegal. Ten people were the most ever to be seen around Canfield's hickory roulette wheels, and then only when Reggie Vanderbilt brought a group of his friends from Yale. Canfield named his chic New York casino the Saratoga Club, but nobody ever called it that. To anyone in the know, it was "the place next to Del's."[7]

Arnold learned about Richard Canfield from the Bowery residents in Sullivan's saloons. With an average wage of $500 a year, these men could hardly afford to patronize Richard Canfield's establishments. But talk was cheap, so from late afternoon to well into the night, Bowery poolhalls were filled with exquisite imaginings of what Canfield's gambling palace might be like. In life these disheveled men played penny stuss in the cafes along the Lower East Side, but in dreams they all wagered to the limit at Canfield's: $5,000 bets on the roulette wheel and $1,000 hands of faro. In life they hustled billiards for nickels and dimes while they waited for the lottery drawing; in dreams they taunted the likes of playboy John W. "Bet-a-Million" Gates in no-limit poker in the private gaming rooms of Canfield's palace, and sent out for full meals from Delmonico's, compliments of the casino.[8]

Rothstein watched Sullivan's lottery sales increase in proportion to the gossip about Canfield's. He could see that people gambled for many reasons. Some liked to display their economic status; others tried to buck the increasingly "ordered economic rationality" they faced every day at work;[9] perhaps, in their own way, they even enacted and circumscribed a cultural system.[10] But while the dice flew, as the white ball on the roulette wheel began to stagger, during the final stretch, to all these diverse people gambling delivered one singular human emotion: hope. In Big Tim's poolhall, young Arnold learned the most important lesson of his life: professional gambling is the sale of hope packaged in favor of the house.

Richard Canfield had also learned this lesson as a young man. Born in New Bedford, Massachusetts, ten years before the Civil War, Canfield claimed he was "half Puritan and half Quaker," and boasted of ancestors who arrived on the Mayflower. In his youth Canfield traveled the Northeast as a professional gambler in search of a fair hand of faro, which he never found. Eventually he learned that the house is the only professional because only the house enjoys the vigorish, a predetermined statistical advantage. After managing several casinos in New York and then establishing his own in Saratoga Springs and Newport, Canfield opened his club next to Delmonico's and came to represent, rather misleadingly, the American myth of the millionaire self-made through a life of lucky cards and shrewd bets.[11]

Richard Canfield found that his riches and social status grew concurrently. He became friendly with the likes of Senator Edward Wolcott of Colorado, Iowa governor John Drake's son, and Wall Street financier Jesse Lewisohn. He also catered to Percival S. Hill, president of the American Tobacco Company; Julius Fleischmann, the yeast manufacturer; Alfred G. Vanderbilt; and Payne Whitney. They were all inveterate gamblers, known in the lingo of the casino as "plungers" because of their dizzying losses. When they lost, Canfield comforted these gentlemen in his private offices on the fourth floor of the club. There, after some highfalutin talk of literature, he would wave at the minor James McNeill Whistler masterpieces on his walls and remark nonchalantly that the artist was presently composing Canfield's own portrait. Just before Whistler died, he titled his last painting "Richard A. Canfield, or His Reverence." Canfield saw no irony in the title.[12]

Canfield became Arnold's ideal, according to Arnold's wife, and Tim Sullivan became his adoptive father. Sullivan showed Arnold an ethnic pattern of criminal upward mobility and empowerment, while Canfield suggested a final destination, entrance into society life that in 1898 was still mainly Protestant. Together, Canfield and Sullivan provided Rothstein with both an end and a means of economic success. Rothstein would come to accept neither model without his own particularly Eastern Jewish modifications, although he seemed to favor both over the utterly legitimate ends and means embodied by his own father, Abraham.[13]

Abraham Rothstein and his wife, Esther, presided over their upper-middle-class family of five children on East 79th Street. Abraham Rothstein had established a thriving cotton-conversion business and involved himself in the politics of the Orthodox community, including the formation of the Jewish Center. He also held a vice-presidency of Beth Israel Hospital. Through the Bessarabian Landsmanschaft, an immigrant social group comprised of those who came from the same area of the Russian Pale, Abraham met Esther. The elder Rothstein had such Jewish communal attachment that he vigorously participated in Landsmanschaft meetings although both he and Esther had been born in America.[14]

Compared to most Jewish Americans, Arnold's father was unusually tradition minded, not only orthodox but also orthoprax. He was "an intensely religious man," according to Arnold's widow, Carolyn, and reports from the Yiddish newspapers tended to agree with her.[15] Abraham required all his sons to take extracurricular orthodox religious training in a traditional *cheder*, while Arnold could scarcely sit through his public school classes.

Abraham Rothstein expected Arnold to enter the family business, but Arnold was not interested. Arnold respected his father, was even "proud of his father."[16] Yet something pushed the two apart that must have been distinct from Arnold's economic ambition. After all, the father had gained success and had done so legitimately. In later years Arnold suggested that gambling had been his way to rebel against his father's authority. On the verge of his fortieth birthday and hounded by the press over the Black Sox fix, Arnold became uncharacteristically reflective about his career, confiding to reporters: "Maybe I gambled just to show my father he couldn't tell me what to do."[17] In so believing, Rothstein repeated a theme—of generational conflict and escape from traditional authority, particularly through transgression—that pervades contemporary documents of the Jewish imagination.[18] Deborah Dash Moore demonstrated twenty years ago that most Jewish behavior in this period defied the imagined rebellion because Jews were actually integrating themselves into the middle class while they maintained and transformed the institutions of Jewish community.[19] Nevertheless, the power of the imagined conflict between parents and children—Jewish authority and release therefrom—was tangible enough to have acted more than as a mere category of the Jewish imagination or a theme in literature, but as a force in the behavior of some of this generation, including Arnold Rothstein.

Gambling itself was a particularly rebellious behavior. More precisely, professional dice playing had been prohibited in the Talmud, not once, but twice. According to Jewish law, a dice player cannot act as a witness. The reasons suggested in the tradition are several, including the notions that gambling is tantamount to robbery and that a gambler wastes time and money instead of tending to the "welfare of the world." Moreover, as the rabbis teach in the great ethical tract "*Avot*," "Human hope is but a worm." If hope in things mortal is founded upon vanity, how much moreso its sale.[20] Hmmm ...

Besides the opposition Arnold Rothstein faced from his father and from within his own tradition, he also encountered the values of the Progressive Era and its reformers. By century's turn these reformers began to upset the way New York operated. Gambling was technically illegal in New York, yet ever since 1860 when Democratic Party chairman William March Tweed established his social club, the Society of St. Tammany (Tammany Hall), as the center of all enforceable law in the city, gambling infractions had been overlooked, even glorified. Canfield could cater to members of the American economic aristocracy who considered an expensive game of faro capped with cigars and champagne an adequately pleasant Saturday night. That it was illegal added danger but no moral burden. After all, who was hurt?

Dr. Charles H. Parkhurst, reverend and muckraker, and his social gospel congregation helped change this attitude. Parkhurst argued that gambling was tied both to reprehensibly slothful work habits and to police corruption. Because the latter seemed easier to prove, Dr. Parkhurst insisted from his pulpit at the Madison Square Presbyterian Church that police corruption be investigated by independent committees of the state legislature, and, eventually, it was. The Lexow committee started brightly in 1894 by firing the crooked Big Bill Devery, then captain of the police department's Eldridge Street Station, and making Theodore Roosevelt president of the mayor's police board. The anti-reform elections of 1897 then reversed the work of the Lexow committee, and Tammany promptly promoted Devery to chief of police. From his new position Devery teamed with Tim Sullivan to create the aforementioned "gambling commission" and prospered until the findings of the Mazet committee of 1899 convinced New Yorkers once again to vote for reform in the 1901 elections. By that time, Big Bill Devery had so artfully entangled himself in the office of chief of police that the new mayor had to abolish the position to get rid of him.[21]

The elections of 1901 proved fateful. When Tammany Hall lost, every game in New York City—from Richard Canfield's ivory poker chip extravaganzas to the penny stuss games on the Lower East Side—lost its protection from raids. On the first day of 1902, William Travers Jerome became district attorney. Jerome already had a reputation as an aggressive justice of special sessions who had personally led raids on houses of prostitution and casinos when Tammany Hall hesitated. Now, as D.A., with the support of a progressive mayor, Jerome seemed unstoppable. Canfield stared into the bitter future of gambling in New York City, tightened the corset that held his enormous middle at bay, and, on the evening before Jerome was inducted into office, announced to his patrons that the last hand of faro that evening would be the last hand ever dealt in the place next to Del's. Most casino owners in New York City followed Canfield's prudent example and closed as well. Until Jerome retired in 1910, New York City would be no place to gamble.[22]

Still, there was Saratoga Springs. It seemed there would always be gambling in Saratoga, a center for casino life ever since Ben Scribner had opened a place in an alley near the United States Hotel in 1842. In Saratoga Springs gambling took place in the open. Officially it was illegal, but in fact no one attempted to veil it. Because Saratoga was a city established around the racetrack, Saratoga officials recognized gamblers such as Canfield as full members of the city's establishment. Even graft was not necessary. Canfield bought the Club House in 1894 and refurbished it after he fled New York in 1902.[23]

Yet before the end of the 1910s, casino gaming in Saratoga would follow the gambling of New York City. After District Attorney Jerome's success in Manhattan, progressive reformers in Albany pressured Saratoga authorities to deter gambling there as well. For the first time in their history Saratoga officials humbly asked casino owners to go underground. Canfield wasn't interested. He would not operate surreptitiously, not in Saratoga. He was a millionaire several times over, a pillar of Saratoga life, and an elder of his community. Furtive measures were beneath his dignity.

Dr. Parkhurst had convinced many that rational gain was moral, and gambling corrupt. The business of hope had become socially suspect. It seemed that the reformers had won the day. In 1907 Canfield washed his hands of the gambling business and retired to his millions. He granted the newspapers one last interview, however, in which he predicted how gambling, though sophistic and merely hopeful, would forever remain to taunt the Reverend Dr. Parkhurst's Protestant ethic: "There will come a day, perhaps not in our lifetime, when gambling will be licensed," Canfield promised. "Gambling cannot be stopped."[24]

The Rise of Rothstein

THE FIRST TIME anyone remembered having seen Rothstein in Saratoga Springs was for the racing season of 1904. He was huddled in a group of three or four men, and was said to be counting some money that they all had won collectively on the day's races. Rothstein was twenty-two years old, stood five-feet seven-inches tall, had brown hair and eyes, and bounced around with what was described as pantherish quickness. The men were well dressed, but there was something rough about them. One had a broken nose. Old timers remembered the disfigured man as the reigning featherweight boxing champion, "The Little Hebrew" Abe Attell.[1]

Wagering on horse racing was legal in Saratoga Springs and had been since Patten and Cole had laid their half-mile track along Union Avenue in 1847. In late July big bettors from New York City boarded the extravagant Cavanagh Special, a deluxe train of six to eight Pullman cars, and arrived in Saratoga the Saturday night before the racing season began. Six weeks later they boarded the same train home, richer or poorer for having vacationed in Saratoga Springs.

Members of the Metropolitan Turf Association, as a group of the most reliable bookmakers in New York, also took the Cavanagh Special; regulars around New York's major racetracks knew them as the Mets. After pari-mutuel[2] betting was outlawed in New York State in 1888, all wagering had to be made with one of dozens of bookmakers who swarmed around the bleachers waiting to give odds on any race. On their lapels the Mets wore special buttons that sold like seats on a stock exchange, sometimes for similar prices. Bookmakers without buttons scrounged for low-stakes action by offering more favorable odds than the Mets, and were often stiffed by sore losers for their troubles.[3]

The Mets excluded young Rothstein, who nevertheless lived well enough for several years as a second-tier bookmaker. Soon he became engaged to Carolyn Greenwald, a showgirl in a Broadway comedy. Rothstein and Greenwald spent the summer of 1909 in Saratoga Springs with friends Margaret Powell and her fiancé Herbert Bayard Swope. A reporter for the New York *Herald*, Swope would soon dominate the New York newspaper business as city editor of the New York *World*. Rothstein and Swope were Jews; Greenwald and Powell were not, although Carolyn's father was Jewish. In a simple ceremony, which only Swope and Powell witnessed, a Saratoga justice of the peace pronounced Arnold and Carolyn husband and wife.

"No sooner were we alone together," Carolyn recalled, "he said to me: 'Sweet, I had a bad day today, and I'll need your jewelry for a few days.'"[4]

Rothstein's luck quickly changed, for the battalion of reformers that had chased Richard Canfield and illegal casino gambling from New York City and Saratoga then stormed the racetracks, and by the end of the 1909 season the Mets unwillingly disbanded. In 1908 the Agnew-Hart law ushered out the age of legal bookmaking in New York State. Consequently, the 1909 racing season was weak throughout New York, and 1910 was disastrous. Even the noblest sportsmen grew bored without a gentlemanly wager. Three great New York tracks— Gravesend, Brighton, and Sheepshead Bay—closed and never re-opened. Even Saratoga shut down for the 1911 and 1912 seasons.[5]

Rothstein thanked the progressive politicians in Albany for having eliminated his fiercest competition with the Agnew-Hart law. He and others like him, many of them Jews, then began bookmaking among the ruins of establishment gambling institutions, such as the Mets and Canfield's Club House, which had been destroyed by the progressive vision of an improved America. When the horses ran in 1909, anyone who wished to wager had to place his bet with a second-tier bookmaker who was willing either to defy the legislation or to exploit a loophole in it—the new law prevented bookmakers from publicizing odds in writing but permitted oral quotations so friends could wager among themselves.

Rothstein soon found lots of friends. So did Bill Cowan, Izzy Ham, Leo Mayer, Maxie Blumenthal, Sam Adler, and "the King of the Ring"

Sol Lichtenstein, all of whom survived the passing of the Mets and Agnew-Hart. Bookmakers who took bets orally had to have tremendous aptitude with numbers because the odds changed endlessly. Those who mastered the odds mentally acted within the letter of the law, although they knowingly transgressed its spirit. Jews had inserted themselves in the gaps left by progressive legislation. In those gray areas Jews created their own marginal business world. They did not operate with the consent of the genteel establishment, as Canfield and the Mets had. Neither were they concessions of corrupt government, like Big Tim Sullivan's poolhalls. The marginal Jewish business world operated under the auspices of no recognized authority except that of the Jewish bookmakers themselves.[6]

Even with the passing of the Mets, these were slim years at the tracks for second-tier bookmakers. They could not survive on the proceeds of summer horse racing alone. When autumn came, these gamblers turned to the underground card and casino games that still popped up around Broadway despite D.A. Jerome. During the 1909 off-season, Rothstein organized what must have been the most famous secret crap game in New York City. It met regularly in the property room of Hammerstein's Victoria, an illustrious vaudeville theater. There, an irrepressible young entertainer was performing. He danced and joked and bantered with the audience. He sang whatever song might be popular on Tin Pan Alley. He wore blackface. He was Al Jolson, although to most people that name didn't mean much. Jolson liked to start his routine by announcing who was ahead and who was behind in the backroom crap game. As soon as he finished on stage, Jolson ran off to rejoin the gamblers.[7]

Rothstein began to be seen in Broadway's most popular restaurants. Although he dressed "not in the garish style of Broadway, but in the more subdued method of Fifth Avenue," he fit in well with the ambiance of the Great White Way and became something of a celebrity.[8] For instance, the owner of Rector's knew Rothstein well. Charles Rector, "the man who had parlayed a fifteen-cent oyster stew into a million dollars," owned a restaurant on Longacre Square, "walled in mirrors from floor to ceiling, richly decorated in green and gold, lighted by sparkling crystal chandeliers." Rector's was a place to be seen by Broadway society. It became a regular stop on a path along which you "began with cocktails, dined, took in a show, had supper at Rector's and wound up your festal excursion with breakfast at Jack's."[9]

Rothstein, however, followed a slightly different pattern. He didn't like shows. In fact, in a lifetime around Broadway he went only to one. Rothstein financed several distinguished shows, however, including *Abie's Irish Rose*, a runaway hit of 1922 about Jewish inter-marriage. For less obviously personal reasons he also financed *Shuffle Along* in 1921. When pressed by his wife to explain why he backed the African-American show he replied simply, "I like to hear those people talk."[10]

Rothstein occasionally went uptown to Harlem nightclubs for os-tensibly the same reason. Eventually he even owned one. But usually he stayed downtown where he conducted business. He patronized Broadway restaurants and put together card games among the wealth-ier patrons. The games gained regularity, and soon a reliable group—which became known as the Partridge Club—began to congregate for dinner and then a night of poker. At first the gamblers met at the Fifth Avenue Hotel, but soon they moved to Delmonico's and finally to Rector's. Rothstein's newspaper friend Herbert Bayard Swope par-ticipated. According to Carolyn Rothstein, other members included "captains of finance, overlords of the business world, young men of great wealth. Among the players were Leonard Replogle, Harry Sin-clair, Commissioner John O'Brien, and the late Flo Ziegfeld."[11] By "Flo" she meant Florenz Ziegfeld, the great Jewish producer who, along with the Shubert brothers, split Broadway comedy audiences for more than two decades.[12]

In *Guys and Dolls*, his fictional memoir of his career along Broad-way, Damon Runyon approvingly remembered Ziegfeld and his *Fol-lies*: "When Mr. Ziegfeld picks a doll," Runyon thought, "she is apt to be above the average when it comes to looks, for Mr. Ziegfeld is by no means a chump at picking dolls."[13] Ziegfeld was less adept at picking gambling pals, for his friend Arnold Rothstein was growing into a successful career gambler, a man who supported his family by placing bets and finding rich suckers. "He didn't look like a gambler," insisted Rothstein's friend and fellow conman Nicky Arnstein. "His face was not impassive, but a kaleidoscope of emotion. When he played, he smiled and grunted and scowled and laughed hoarsely. He looked pleased and he looked worried. But those expressions told his opponents nothing because they told too much. Of course, if anyone had been able to read Arnold's eyes, it might have been different. But no one could read his eyes. They were always hooded."[14]

Despite Nicky Arnstein's opinion, some felt Rothstein was sometimes betrayed by "that laugh of his which everybody has agreed . . . was strangely artificial."[15] So said his wife. Carolyn also described how Arnold typically came home from playing cards at five or six o'clock in the morning after having a final meal at Jack's, which may or may not have included Jack's famous champagne breakfast of Irish ham and eggs. Although Arnold neither drank nor smoked during his late-night goings-on, without fail he rose at three o'clock the next afternoon speaking the following words: "I don't feel well."

"Then," his wife remembered (perhaps embellishing), "more likely than not he took a dose of milk of magnesia, or something of the sort. He seldom if ever consulted doctors, but he was always suffering of headache, or indigestion, and was constantly absorbing remedies which included bicarbonate of soda and ranged through most of the proprietary medicines advertised to cure headaches and indigestion."[16]

ACCORDING TO Carolyn, it was around this time that Rothstein began "to keep those little black books, about which so much was made at the time of his death."[17] A player in the Partridge Club usually wagered much more than the cash he kept with him, so Arnold took to collecting IOU slips; eventually he wrote all bets owed into his little black book. Soon those books became well enough marked with paid debits for Rothstein to open his very own casino. He ran it from the basement of his home on 44th Street, Richard Canfield's old neighborhood.

Rothstein attracted wealthy clients from his poker circles and from the clientele of the Broadway restaurants where he was well known. Occasionally Rothstein used chorus girls to steer men to his place. Within a year the basement casino could not hold the crowds his business generated, so Rothstein moved the action to the parlor of a larger brownstone on 46th Street. Arnold and Carolyn lived upstairs. Diners from nearby Jack's and Rector's dropped by routinely.

The place was "fitted with secret panels guarding recesses in the walls into which the tables, wheels and chips might be slipped during the time that possible raiders were trying to negotiate the heavily reinforced doors."[18] But Rothstein's casino was rarely raided and then only with ample warning from his paid friends at Tammany. Once District Attorney Jerome retired in 1910, New York's lax attitude toward gambling returned, and again casinos ran without fear of prosecution.

New York, however, had not returned to the age of Richard Canfield and his pompous Whistler paintings. Gambling was now a Jewish business. Many of Big Tim Sullivan's "smart Jew boys" from the Bowery had built casinos. Sam Paul's Resort had opened. "Bridgey" Webber, named after his brief marriage to a two-hundred-pound prostitute named Bridget, ran "the biggest opium joint in Chinatown," the Sans Souci Music Hall on 14th Street, and a gambling place on 44th. Harry Vallon (born Valinsky) kept opening and closing places, but he never seemed able to stay in business. Sam Schepps was the same way. "Beansy" Rosenthal started his own casino at 104 West 45th Street. "Bald" Jack Rose—born Jacob Rosenzweig in Poland and nicknamed "Bald" because he had no hair, eyebrows, or lashes—was such a Broadway personality that a cocktail is named after him: one jigger of applejack, juice of half a lemon, half an ounce of grenadine, shaken with cracked ice and strained. Together these smart Jewish boys introduced craps to the annals of American casino gambling by innovating the twenty-five cent charge for every five dollar bet. The Bowery gang had grown up. It had also founded the modern twenty-two-billion-dollar-a-year business of casino gambling.[19]

The years of Jewish control over gambling, called "The Delicatessen Decades" by those who reviled the change from the Canfield days, changed the casino business. Whereas a Canfield casino had catered to the American aristocracy (both officials of high government and capitalists), the Jewish casinos ministered to the emerging middle class and the nouveau riche with the service of smaller bets. Therefore, while Canfield had presented gambling as the leisurely pursuit of gentlemen, the Broadway Jews were less interested in the outward appearance of respectability and gentility. Newspapers wrote of their petty rivalries daily. They seemed to nurture the notoriety.[20]

The group prospered until the fall of 1909 when its Tammany protector, Big Tim Sullivan, mysteriously went insane (perhaps from syphilis). In the later stages of his delirium, Sullivan could no longer shield his boys from such graft-hungry policemen as Lt. Charles Becker, recently appointed head of the Strong-Arm Squad (now called the Vice Squad). Becker's job was to raid gambling houses, which he did ruthlessly until he and Bald Jack Rose came to an understanding. Lt. Becker hired Rose to collect graft from the old Bowery gang. Rose knew everyone in the business, and if his personal relationship with someone had become strained, Bridgey Webber or Harry Vallon could fill in. All parties benefited from the arrangement. Lt. Becker had a bagman to pick up his money, Jack Rose received part of the graft, Webber became a big shot, and Vallon finally had a steady job. Without Big Tim Sullivan around for protection, who would think to refuse them?

Of Sullivan's Bowery adoptees, Beansy Rosenthal was not the brightest. His career started when Sullivan personally consigned to him Tammany's gambling concession for the Hesper Club. Rosenthal had worked under the careful supervision of Tammany ever since. After Sullivan's demise, Rosenthal could not accept that Lt. Becker had become the new "Big Feller." When Jack Rose came to collect a payment of five-hundred dollars, Rosenthal went to see Arnold Rothstein. Would his old pal Arnold talk to some of his well-connected customers and settle the matter? Surely Beansy Rosenthal didn't have to pay graft to an inconsequential police lieutenant. Rothstein listened carefully. Then he peeled five-hundred dollars from his own bankroll, and suggested that Beansy find Jack Rose and pay him, quickly.[21]

Instead of looking up Jack Rose, Rosenthal found his friend and *World* reporter Herbert Bayard Swope. Beansy began talking—Broadway gambling, midnight raids, money drop-offs, an evil police lieutenant. And Swope listened intently. He was terribly sympathetic, of course. Would Beansy like to make an official statement to the *World*?

When the story broke on July 13, 1912, Jack Rose and the rest of the Broadway gamblers foresaw trouble. With Rosenthal talking to the press two things could happen, neither of them good for business:

Either the new and politically ambitious district attorney, Charles S. Whitman, would close down Broadway gambling using the courts, or Lt. Becker would do so using the end of his nightstick. Someone had to convince Rosenthal to keep quiet, which in Beansy's case was no easy feat. Otherwise, he simply had to disappear.

On July 15, Whitey Louis, Lefty Louie, Dago Frank, and Gyp the Blood—three of whom were Jews, and all of them well-known gunmen from Big Jack Zelig's gang—murdered Rosenthal in front of the Hotel Metropole on 43rd Street and Broadway.[22]

Before the incident, Jack Rose had romanticized his criminal career of fast money and Broadway life, but murder was just too much. Rose got drunk and went downtown to the Lafayette Turkish Baths to calm down with a *schvitz*. When he came to his senses he hid at the home of the gambler Harry Pollak, and then fled to a hideout in the Catskills. Bridgey Webber and Harry Vallon joined him there. Eventually these three turned state's evidence, which led to the executions of the four gunmen and Lt. Becker. Big Jack Zelig was shot and killed as he left his favorite East Side restaurant, Siegel's Coffee House. Nobody knew who ordered his murder, although many reporters suspected a double-cross at the behest of Lt. Becker. Herbert Bayard Swope was promoted to city editor of the *World*.[23]

In her social history of Jewish crime, Jenna Weissman Joselit captured the sentiments of the Jewish community during the messy Becker-Rosenthal affair. She recorded the chagrin of one *Yidishes Tageblat* reporter who could not help but sigh: "And for this, the Jewish people have been chosen?"[24]

The deluge barely touched Rothstein. For a brief time he closed his casino on 46th Street and started the first floating crap game, later romanticized in the annals of Damon Runyon and others. Rothstein quickly realized that the Becker-Rosenthal affair had quelled the passion of the press and government for reform. To the satisfaction of most, illegal gambling had been sufficiently curtailed. Yet Rothstein remained. Soon he opened a casino in wealthy Hewlett, Long Island. Rothstein found that in the suburbs his clientele placed larger bets and lost more graciously. He also opened a place in Long Beach, a city on the south shore of Long Island with a sunny boardwalk, then for the first time being advertised in the Jewish press (both Yiddish and English) as a summer vacation spot. He then opened the Brook Casino in Saratoga, for which Sophie Tucker provided the entertainment while Meyer Lansky and Charlie "Lucky" Luciano ran the daily operations and learned the gambling business. These two would eventually take their knowledge and found Las Vegas.[25]

In effect Rothstein had created a chain of casinos that offered moderate-stakes wagering built in major centers of the emerging middle class and nouveau riche. His multimillion dollar business was entirely illegal, of course, but that seemed to bother only the most prudish politicians who remained unsatisfied even after the grand Becker-Rosenthal house-cleaning. Everyone else just liked to gamble.

In two short years Rothstein parlayed his casino business into a fortune. For the first time in his life he became extravagant. In 1912, at the age of 30, Rothstein bought himself a dazzling set of false teeth. A year later he and Carolyn moved from the noisy heart of Broadway to 52nd Street. Two years after that they moved again, this time to the exclusive address of 355 West 84th Street.

Yet Rothstein was unsatisfied with the sizable profits from his gambling houses. He took his enormous bankroll and started to offer usurious loans to those who could not legally obtain loans. He became the bank of New York's underworld. Carolyn described her husband's business frankly: "He lent money to thieves, blackmailers, dope peddlers, bookmakers, burglars—any one from whom he thought he could get back his money with interest. He loaned into the millions to persons who couldn't get loans from banks."

"The loans went down in the little black books," she remembered, "and when they were paid, he drew a line in red ink through the paid accounts. That was the only book-keeping in the Arnold Rothstein private bank."

The passion to collect trumped all other considerations, including marital ones. "Often on my way home in a car, I would have myself driven slowly up Broadway, past Forty-seventh to Fiftieth Street," Carolyn recalled. "It might be a cold night, or a rainy one. Or it might be snowing. But, more often than not Arnold would be there. I would ask him to come home. He would shake his head and say:

"'I'm waiting to see someone to collect from. . . .'

"He would stay out hours in all kinds of weather to collect small sums, even of amounts as low as fifty dollars. Yet, he might have made thousands that same day.

"The amounts, it always seemed to me, were not what counted so much with Arnold, as the percentages.

"It is an example of his pertinacity on the subject of money owed to him that he kept names of delinquent debtors in his books even after they were dead."[26]

IN THE summer of 1915, Rothstein invested in a luxury enjoyed by many New York patricians and bought himself a stable of horses. *assimilation (?)* He named the stable Redstone (Rothstein anglicized) and began to spend more time at the increasingly popular racetracks.[27]

But neither Rothstein nor his Redstone Stables passed as anything resembling patrician. Nor did Rothstein intend to try. At the track he made enormous bets and finagled odds, both ungentlemanly practices. He played bookmakers against one another and misled his friends to make bad wagers so that the odds might change in his favor. He hounded his debtors and casually brushed off his creditors. Some said he tampered with races.

August Belmont II found Rothstein's behavior decidedly distasteful. Belmont had built the Belmont Park racetrack on Long Island in memory of his father, and when Rothstein haggled over odds in his clubhouse, Belmont felt that memory demeaned. That memory was also somewhat clarified, for August Belmont I had been born in the Rhineland as August Schönberg, a Jewish petty merchant. In America Schönberg renamed himself Belmont, succeeded in several marginal business maneuvers, married the daughter of Commodore Perry, and baptized his children as Episcopalians. So August Belmont II built the exquisite racetrack to honor the refurbished memory of his father. When Rothstein started haggling in the grandstand of Belmont Park, something touched a nerve, and Belmont II barred Rothstein from the track's clubhouse.[28]

Rothstein asked his influential friend Herbert Bayard Swope, now city editor of the New York *World*, to intervene. On September 12, 1917, Swope wrote a letter to Belmont in which he promised that

Rothstein would decrease the size of his wagers. In this note, Swope parodied the patronizing tone then typical of the relationship between Western and Eastern Jewry. "While he is a sporting man, he comes of a decent, respectable Jewish family," Swope reminded Belmont, tongue in cheek, German Jew to former German Jew, "and I am inclined to think that once his word is given he will offer no further cause for complaint."[29] Rothstein was readmitted to the prestigious Jockey Club at Belmont Park, although his presence there forever after grated on Belmont as a reminder of his assimilation and his invented heritage.

Rothstein's social position in Saratoga Springs soon grew to equal his fiscal stature. His thoroughbreds routinely raced against those of such Yale blue-bloods as Harry Payne Whitney of the Standard Oil dynasty. In one Travers competition at Saratoga, Rothstein's colt Sporting Blood raced against the filly Whitney had primly named Prudery. In that test of wills, Sporting Blood trounced Prudery. What's more, Rothstein may have fixed the race.[30]

By these means Rothstein established himself as a vibrant participant in New York's genteel sporting life, an honor closed to Jews in far more respectable businesses merely a generation before. Moreover, Rothstein appears to have accomplished this feat without deference to establishment notions of respectability. Rothstein's business was both marginal and Jewish. He hid neither of these facts and was not embarrassed by their connotations in polite society. When Rothstein went to run his illegal Saratoga casino during August, he and Carolyn generally took the Cavanagh Special and stayed at the Grand Union Hotel. The Grand Union was the finest hotel in Saratoga, so its selection seemed obvious to the millionaire and his wife. Perhaps they did not realize that thirty years before, the great German-Jewish banker Joseph Seligman had been turned away from the Grand Union for being of the "Israelite faith," thus reminding Western European Jewry in America that its attempts to assimilate had painful limits.

In the thirty years between Seligman and Rothstein, however, both America and the dominant definition of American Jewish identity had changed. The American mainstream had been sufficiently widened by the coming of immigrants that many newcomers flatly rejected the command to homogenize and assimilate. Many of these new Americans had found that to succeed in America, one did not need to assimilate. Ethnics prospered. Moreover, for Eastern Jews, assimilation had never been part of their European experience, and they found strange the call by their German-Jewish cousins to "Americanize" if that meant loss of ethnic identity or group feeling. Rothstein never shied from his ethnic identity and never lost group feeling. He and his generation knew nothing of the long shadows cast by the Jewish Question during the Enlightenment and emancipation periods of Western Europe. Nor did they fret unduly over the problems of assimilation, homogenization, and Protestant respectability as had German Jews, such as Seligman, after the Civil War. When the bellboy showed him to his suite in the Grand Union Hotel, Arnold Rothstein just complained about the accommodations.[31]

Financial Crime

IN APRIL 1917 the United States issued two billion dollars worth of Treasury Bonds in an effort to subsidize the Great War without significantly increasing taxes. The federal government had issued bonds to finance wars in the past, but never had the Treasury Department hawked bonds the way it did for what became known as the Liberty Loan program. "We went direct to the people," Secretary of the Treasury William Gibbs McAdoo proudly recalled, "and that means to everybody—to business men, workmen, farmers, bankers, millionaires, school-teachers, laborers. We capitalized the profound impulse called patriotism."[1] McAdoo advertised his bonds doggedly with a campaign of stylish posters and the appearances of stage and screen celebrities. The government marshaled Americans into acts of financial courage. "Act and act now," one pamphlet demanded. "Buy Liberty Bonds. Buy more Liberty Bonds—all the Bonds you can. Thunder an answer to Germany that will make her cower in fear."[2] Many Americans bought them, even at the measly rate of 3.5 percent interest for a thirty-year note. When their savings accounts ebbed, McAdoo encouraged citizens to "borrow and buy," suggesting that Americans use the Liberty Bonds they already owned as collateral to buy even more of them. As the pyramid of securities grew, the total money supply increased by 75 percent and the consumer price index doubled. Inflation soared, America became papered with less valuable money, and no one seemed to notice.[3]

The war ended in a fit of delusory prosperity. Having been introduced to bonds by their government, Americans became mesmerized by the fluctuations of the market. They began to invest widely and indiscriminately in all kinds of securities.

George Graham Rice was well positioned to take their money. Rice was just one suspicious character from the world of marginal finance with whom Arnold Rothstein surrounded himself during the Great War, but he was typical. Rice had been born Jacob Simon Herzig on the Lower East Side. As a boy he was more interested in Bowery poolhall life than in his father's furrier business, and like Rothstein, he entered the world of East Side gambling. Rice began to give horse racing advice for a price and soon published his own "tipster sheet," which, incidentally, is also how Moses Annenberg began his entrepreneurial career when he started publishing the *Daily Racing Form* in 1922.[4]

After a brief stint in Sing Sing for forging his father's name to checks, Rice traveled West for the Nevada gold rush of 1904. Although he found no gold, Rice discovered something more precious: Stocks in worthless mining companies could be made valuable by the illusion of advertising, particularly by mailing reams of circulars and pamphlets to a naive buying public. As sales of worthless stock certificates begat even more sales, stock prices became artificially inflated, and soon Rice organized a brokerage firm to handle all the business. He called the house B. H. Sheftels and Company and opened offices in Chicago, Philadelphia, Detroit, Boston, and Providence. It was a multimillion-dollar operation built entirely on hype, for which he eventually served ten months on Blackwell's Island in New York. How, precisely, Rice's securities promotion differed from the puffery of Liberty Bonds by Secretary McAdoo remains inscrutable.

In 1914, perhaps thinking that he had exhausted every possible financial scheme, Rice decided to become an author. He wrote an autobiography of sorts, *My Adventures with Your Money*, which he dedicated to his clientele: "To the American Damphool Speculator, surnamed the American Sucker, otherwise described herein as the Thinker Who Thinks He Knows But Doesn't—Greetings! This Book is for you!"

"Are you aware that in catering to your instinct to 'invest,' methods to get you to part with your money are so artfully and deftly applied by the highest so that they deceive you completely?" Rice asked.

"Could you imagine it to be a fact that in nearly all cases when you find that you are ready to embark on a given speculation, ways and means that are almost scientific in their insidiousness have been used upon you?"[5]

Actually, most Americans could not imagine. In the flurry of over-inflated money that whirled in the wake of the Great War, Americans invested as never before. George Graham Rice once again opened for business, this time at 28 West 57th Street, a building owned by Arnold Rothstein. He borrowed $262,000 from Rothstein and opened a bucket shop.[6]

A bucket shop was a second-tier brokerage house, and in the late 1910s and 1920s scores of them lined the streets of America's financial districts. Bucketeers such as Rice hired high-pressure salesmen and stuffed them into offices called "boiler rooms," equipped only with typewriters, telephones, and ashtrays. The salesmen would promote and sell a legitimate stock and take the money from the client but would never actually purchase the security. In other words, they would "bucket" the stock orders. If stock prices slipped, as they often did in the bear years of 1920 and 1921, the bucket shop pocketed the "lost" money. If stock prices rose, as they often did in the bull market of 1922, the bucketeers either made payments with the cash coming in from new promotions or postponed payment with a litany of legalistic jargon that the average investor was unprepared to challenge. As a last resort the bucket shop would simply pronounce bankruptcy, the firm's assets having mysteriously vanished.[7]

As an alternative scheme a bucket shop would buy loads of a penny stock, or invent a stock and have fraudulent certificates printed, and then sell the worthless security on one of the smaller stock exchanges such as the Boston Curb or the Consolidated Exchange in New York. "The object is to unload . . . a great quantity of the stock at high prices," Rice calmly explained. "Then the promoters and the whole market quietly disappear like the proverbial Arab who silently folded his tent in the night and stole away."[8]

Bucketeers promoted these worthless stocks with "tipster sheets" similar to the ones touting horses. These fraudulent financial reports were published under the guise of providing legitimate stock advice. Bucketeers would then sell the hyped securities for dollars on the cent. George Graham Rice's *Iconoclast* was the largest circulating tip-ster sheet of the time. With a pseudo-populist rhetoric that pitted the "white-collar bandits" of the New York Stock Exchange against the desire of the average American investor to get rich quick, the *Icono-clast* blasted all reasonable investments and ballyhooed everything from recently discovered emerald treasures of the Incas to abandoned mineral mines in Idaho: "Sell any stock you can and buy IDAHO COP-PER," the *Iconoclast* advised its ever-increasing mailing list of suckers. "We know what this language means AND WE MEAN IT." Rice had bought stocks of the defunct Idaho Copper Company at ten cents per share and sold them at six dollars each.[9]

The bucket shop usually posted its worthless stock on the board of a second-tier exchange, which in New York was the Consolidated Exchange. While such reputable exchanges as the New York Stock Exchange only traded in multiples of one hundred shares, the Consol-idated took multiples of ten, and while the New York Stock Exchange tried to ascertain that stocks posted on its board were legitimate, the president of the Consolidated Exchange, Jacob Fields, never felt so compelled. In fact, "Jakie" Fields often posted the worthless stocks of the bucketeers as a favor to his friend Arnold Rothstein. That the stocks were valueless or even fraudulent was not his concern. Buy or sell, loss or gain, the Consolidated Exchange received its commission, which was 1/8 of a point for every share traded, commonly known, then as now, as a "kosher eighth."[10]

Jewish ref.

Rothstein financed many bucket shops, not only those run by Jews like George Graham Rice, Harry Pollak, "Cheeks" Ginsberg, Paddy Goldberg, Harold Sonking, and "Dandy" Phil Kastel (who went on to become the gambling tsar of New Orleans), but also the houses of such men as Charles A. Stoneham, the owner of the New York Giants who controlled a chain of bucket shops, and Edward Fuller, at whose trial prosecutors revealed $331,000 worth of checks dating from 1916 to 1921—payable to Arnold Rothstein.[11]

These financial activities may have been scandalous and unethical, but they were often quite legal. Rothstein hired a squad of lawyers to advise and protect his bucket shop interests, and his bucketeers soon learned to operate within the loopholes of the paltry securities re-quirements that those lawyers steadily and assiduously loosened. The attorneys created discretionary pools and customer authorization forms that empowered the bucketeers to trade with the customer's money in nearly any way they saw fit. Rothstein's attorneys included Hyman Turchin, Isaiah Lebow, Emil Fuchs, Joseph Shalleck, George Morton Levy, George Z. Medalie, Maurice Cantor, Arthur Garfield Hays, and—most famously—the Irish criminal lawyer William J. Fallon, whose specialty in the face of overwhelming evidence was to hang juries.[12] "It seems incredible how many times Fallon accomplished a hung jury by the count of 1 to 11," his biographer noted.[13] These attorneys were all expert in navigating the gray areas of the meager securities law.[14]

But Rothstein's savvy lawyers were severely tested when the news broke that the master mind of a five-million-dollar stolen bond caper had been caught. He was "Nicholas Arnstein, alias J. W. Arnold, alias James Wilfred Adair, alias James W. Adair, alias McCormick, alias Borech and alias Brice."[15]

NICKY ARNSTEIN was a Norwegian-born Jew, a graceful man with closely set blue eyes and a moustache he always wore twisted and waxed. In 1919 he was already a Broadway legend, having been arrested in Paris, London, and Monte Carlo on various swindling charges, usually for cardsharping wealthy patrons of cruise ships and hotels. At least, this is what everyone thought. With Arnstein, it was impossible to separate truth from rumor. "Nicky Arnstein often told me that he . . . made a reputation as an international card sharp and all-around crook of the first water," remembered his friend, the reporter Donald Henderson Clarke. "I don't like to say this about Nicky because I always liked him. However, he made his reputation for himself. No one else did, despite the fact that he would have it appear that way."[16] Arnstein had a way of lying so transparently that it became charming. He even charmed the funny girl of Ziegfeld's *Follies*, Fanny Brice. "One Saturday afternoon," Brice remembered, "I was introduced to a man who stood then and forever after for everything that had been left out of my life: manners, good breeding, education and an extraordinary gift for dreaming."[17] The two married in 1912.

Sometime in the summer of 1919 Nicky Arnstein learned that, for a price, several of the messenger boys who ran errands between the firms on Wall Street were willing to "lose" the negotiable securities and bearer bonds they carried. Two of the older boys, brothers Joseph and Ira Gluck, collected the securities from other messengers and fenced them through a friend, Harry Wolf, who lived in the Bronx. For a while Wolf laundered the securities himself, but soon he became overwhelmed as the amounts the Gluck brothers stole grew into hundreds of thousands of dollars. Through a friend who gambled in circles around Hoboken, New Jersey, Wolf met Nick Cohen. Unlike Wolf, Cohen was an adult with seemingly endless connections on Wall Street. With his partner, Nicky Arnstein, Cohen promised he could unload stolen securities worth millions.

When Nick Cohen consulted his partner about the Wall Street messenger boys, Arnstein knew exactly how to turn the stolen securities into cash. Because the securities had serial numbers that might be traced, they could not be sold on the open market. Since the days of the "borrow and buy" Liberty Loan program, however, the government had simplified the use of securities as collateral for loans. Bucket shops routinely overlooked such clerkish details as serial numbers. If Arnstein used the stolen securities as collateral for loans, the securities would be safely buried in the files of scattered brokerage houses. When Arnstein defaulted on his loans, as he invariably did, those bucket shops happily considered the securities assets of their firm on which the bucket shops could now borrow. The securities had vanished, the crime untraceable.

That is, until the Gluck brothers decided to push around Murray Abramowitz, messenger boy for the Wall Street firm Parrish & Co. After having been roughed up one time too many by the Glucks, Abramowitz agreed to help the police entrap the brothers, which he did with $2,500 worth of securities.

Joseph Gluck sat in jail for ten days waiting for Arnstein to bail him out. Arnstein never came, however, because he had left town upon Gluck's arrest. Gluck then told the police the story of the securities scam. He named a broker for the Consolidated Exchange, David Sullivan, who also turned state's evidence. The *New York Times* summarized Sullivan's testimony: "How a substantial part of the $2,500,000 in securities stolen . . . were peddled in small lots at one fourth of their value so far as the return to the master crooks was concerned:

how these securities were put up by the purchasers as collateral for loans: how, to conceal the transactions from honest cashiers and clerks in the brokerage offices, fake purchases of stocks, bought under fictitious names, were recorded in the books of Sullivan & Co. and how the securities themselves changed hands in barrooms, on street corners and in hotel rooms in various cities, all form a part of the amazing recital."[18]

By the time Gluck and Sullivan finished testifying, the police had arrested Nicky Arnstein, Nick Cohen, and Harry Wolf for stealing securities. Phil Kastel, Harry Pollak (the gambler who had hidden "Bald" Jack Rose after the Becker-Rosenthal affair), "Cheeks" Ginsberg, and "Paddy" Goldberg from Cleveland were all accused of burying stolen securities in their bucket shops. Even Arnold Rothstein was called in for questioning, not unjustifiably, as he was a known associate of most of the accused. He was quickly released on grounds of insufficient evidence.[19]

District Attorney Dooling announced that a ring of "bond Fagins" (so named after Charles Dickens's master thief in *Oliver Twist*) had been discovered. The New York *World*, now under the firm leadership of Herbert Bayard Swope, was quick to print the sensational, if antisemitic, accusation. Harry Wolf, who had only been a transitory culprit, also found his profile in the *World*. Newspapers surmised that the patriotic Liberty Bonds were the prize of these bond Fagins, even though young Joseph Gluck insisted that he would never steal Liberty Bonds because he had served his country in France during the war. The papers reported the occupations of the accused sometimes as brokers, sometimes as bucketeers, and sometimes as gamblers; when one was associated with the Consolidated Exchange, those terms were interchangeable anyway. The newspapers dubbed Nicky Arnstein the mastermind of the plot against American patriotism. "Master Mind!" Fanny Brice burst out when she heard the accusation. "He couldn't Master Mind an electric bulb into a socket."[20]

Rothstein paid his lawyers to defend Arnstein and posted one hundred thousand dollars for his bail. In the end Arnstein served three years in Leavenworth Federal Penitentiary, and Fanny Brice became an international celebrity with her timely version of the song "My Man."[21]

The *American Hebrew* alerted its middle-class, English-speaking readership to the following: "We have just learned, from sources which we must regard as unimpeachable, that 'Nicky' Arnstein, the alleged 'king of the brokerage thieves,' . . . is not a Jew. He traces back his genealogy to the Dutch, and his ancestors were probably called 'Herrn Stein.' . . . Neither our race nor our religion claims 'Nicky.'"[22] The *American Hebrew* could not know that far worse was yet to come.

The Black Sox and
the Jews

IN 1919 it became Rothstein's habit to sit in Reuben's Delicatessen and pick nervously at sweet rolls. Although he had an office nearby, Rothstein spent most of the 1920s in midtown delicatessens, first Reuben's on 57th and Madison, then, when it opened in 1921, Lindy's on Broadway. Once the Reverend Dr. Parkhurst and other progressives destroyed the corrupt Irish political machine, the Jewish underworld emerged in its stead. Thus Reuben's and Lindy's filled the gap left by the Protestant destruction of Irish Catholic Tammany Hall.[1]

The Irish-American strategy of illegal empowerment had been illicitly to wield the power of government office—classic political corruption. That Irish power could enjoy public recognition was a benefit of this strategy, although this benefit was also its undoing. Since Tammany politicians were public figures, they had to court the goodwill of newspapers and voters. Moreover, Tammany could be overturned by the simple democratic process. Although the Irish machine worked desperately to manipulate both the press and the vote, ousting Irish corruption both through the press (muckraking) and through elections became the foundation of the progressive strategy to reform, including the campaigns of Parkhurst and his Presbyterian congregation. Similarly, Richard Canfield's business had been founded with the legitimating nod of the Protestant establishment he courted. When that establishment agreed to the demands of its reformers, Canfield lost his protection.

Rothstein faced no similar threats. Unlike Canfield, Rothstein neither sought nor needed the legitimating recognition of the American establishment, and unlike Irish corruption, the Jewish underworld had no pretense to public office or desire thereof. But then one would not expect participants in an Eastern Jewish culture to think to inhabit the structure of government office. Certainly no such opportunity had been available in Eastern Europe and it was not looked for in the United States. Rather, Rothstein created a counter-structure to government, one founded not on elected political power but on the power of money *to buy* political power through graft. Although Rothstein paid Tammany enormous sums, he stayed away from the building. His own headquarters consisted of the Jewish restaurants surrounding Times Square along Broadway. By taking permanent tables at Reuben's and Lindy's, Rothstein demonstrated to his business relations that the nature of power in New York had become Jewish. If one wanted Rothstein's counsel, one went to the kosher deli.[2]

From his table at Reuben's, Rothstein kept phenomenally busy in 1919. His friend Nicky Arnstein often stopped by to beg Rothstein to find more bucket shops willing to bury stolen bonds. Rothstein opened the Arnold Rothstein Realty Corporation and the insurance firm of A. L. Libman, Inc., of which he was president. Both firms had offices in Rothstein's newly purchased building at 45 West 57th Street. Rothstein also mediated the sale of the New York Giants for his Tammany acquaintance Andrew Freedman, a Jew of German background, to bucket shop millionaire and personal friend Charles A. Stoneham. Giants manager John McGraw, a poolhall operator and a longtime friend of Rothstein, became partial owner of the team, as did Magistrate Francis Xavier McQuade, who once dismissed gun charges held against Rothstein. All the while Rothstein ran four large and profitable casinos scattered between Long Island and upstate New York.[3]

Amid this snappy schedule of intrigues and legitimate business deals, Abe Attell sauntered into the deli. "The former featherweight champion, on whose fights, win or lose, Arnold never lost a bet," had a proposition.[4] He wanted Rothstein to fix the World Series.

Attell, still known as "the Little Hebrew" around Broadway, had enjoyed twelve years as featherweight champion until the New York Boxing Commission suspended his title in 1912 for throwing a fight.

In 1919 Attell was not as famous as the current Jewish lightweight champion, Benny Leonard, but he was still well enough recognized in sporting circles to pick up the latest trade gossip. One day in late September two former professional athletes approached Attell at Jamaica Racetrack with such privy information. The pair, an ex-ball-player and an ex-fighter, told Attell that the Chicago White Sox were fed up with their tightfisted owner "Old Roman" Comiskey and wanted to throw the upcoming World Series against the Cincinnati Reds. The two schemers claimed they had eight ballplayers willing to participate. The price to throw the Series? Ten thousand dollars for each of the eight players.

Attell turned to Rothstein, the only person he knew who might have eighty thousand dollars handy for such an enterprise, but Rothstein barely listened to him. Could the two has-been athletes guarantee that the White Sox would really throw the games? Could the pair keep things quiet so that the odds would remain in favor of the White Sox? Who else had the two approached for the money? Who else had the disgruntled White Sox spoken to? Attell could answer none of these questions. Rothstein would not risk his money or the legal difficulty on amateurs, even for a friend as old as the Little Hebrew. Within days of declining Attell's offer, an influential gambler from Boston approached Rothstein with practically the same proposition. Joseph "Sport" Sullivan claimed he could fix the players for eighty thousand dollars. Rothstein turned him down too.[5]

Rothstein could use the inside information to place bets without paying the players anything and without risking criminal prosecution. So Rothstein turned to his little black book. He had to put down bets for both Chicago *and* Cincinnati to provide an alibi if the fix ever became public, which he was certain it would if Abe Attell was the brain behind it.[6] Merely wagering carried no real criminal risk. Even children bet on the World Series.

His precaution worked, both when the president of the American League questioned Rothstein personally in New York just after the news of the fix became public and before the Grand Jury in Chicago when the State of Illinois decided to prosecute. There, according to popular historian Eliot Asinof, Rothstein told his version of what had happened in the fall of 1919.

Abe Attell did the fixing. . . . The whole thing started when Attell and some other cheap gamblers decided to frame the Series and make a killing. The world knows I was asked in on the deal and my friends know how I turned it down flat. I don't doubt that Attell used my name to put it over. That's been done by smarter men than Abe. But I wasn't in on it, wouldn't have gone in on it under any circumstances, and didn't bet a cent on the Series after I found out what was under way. My idea was that whatever way things turned out, it would be a crooked Series anyhow, and that only a sucker would bet on it.[7]

Surely that was a lie. Rothstein bet money on the Series with inside knowledge of the fix; it was not his business practice to bet otherwise. Nevertheless, as Rothstein left the witness stand, Maclay Hoyne, the attorney general for the State of Illinois, declared "I don't think Rothstein was involved in it," and put Rothstein's legal record to rest.[8]

The American public was not so forgiving. While eight members of the White Sox with boyish nicknames like "Buck" and "Chick," "Happy" and "Lefty," "Swede" and, of course "Shoeless Joe," sat on trial in Chicago for throwing the World Series, baseball fans blinked incredulously as Rothstein brushed off his box seat at the Polo Grounds in New York beside the president of the Giants baseball club, Charles A. Stoneham. Rothstein's bucketshop crony tried desperately to ignore any perception of impropriety. Carolyn Rothstein said that her husband never sat in the box much anyway. He was always too busy hustling bets in the stands.[9]

The attorney for "Happy" Felch, centerfielder of the White Sox, readied the public for a conspiracy of Jewish bankers when he announced, "The gambling syndicate with headquarters in the East has enlisted the services of others besides crooked baseball players; it is evident that either the offices of various stock brokers or the operators of the ticker service in some brokers' offices are in on this conspiracy to reap a fortune by destroying the game of baseball."[10]

Journalists pressured ballclub owners to restructure the business of baseball, to prosecute the Black Sox, and to appoint a baseball commissioner with totalitarian power over the owners to oversee the game. The names suggested for the new baseball commissioner position ran, according to Asinof, "like a Presidential nominating committee list for the Republican party," including General John Pershing, Senator Hiram Johnson, Major General Leonard Wood, and Judge Kenesaw Mountain Landis.[11]

The owners agreed to offer the appointment to Judge Landis of the U.S. District Court in Chicago. Landis quickly came to understand the weight of the responsibility before him. "I was sitting in my court room," he explained, "and over against the wall was the propeller of an airplane; the plane my son used in France. It came like a flash to me, thinking of my boy, what baseball meant to him when he was young; what it means to him to-day. And I knew that is what baseball means to every kid in America.

"Baseball is something more than a game to an American boy," the judge concluded. "It is his training field for life work. Destroy his faith in its squareness and honesty and you have destroyed something more; you have planted suspicion of all things in his heart."[12]

The judge was exceedingly subtle, linking the mission of the boys in France to the defense of the great American game of baseball. If Judge Landis had only implied that a foreign power was at work against the American ideals of "squareness and honesty," others were more explicit. "If fans wish to know the trouble with American baseball," Henry Ford pronounced, "they have it in three words—too much Jew."[13]

Even those who tried to remain broadminded with respect to American Jewry were stumped by the fix. When asked whether the state of Jewish criminality had improved in the past ten years,[14] Commissioner Richard Enright of the New York City Police Department made sure to explain that Jews were normal, law-abiding citizens. Jews were not particularly radical, Commissioner Enright noted. Neither were they bad drivers, because Jews tended not to drink. When speaking of the Jew as a gambler, however, the Commissioner touched upon a great weakness. "Most Jews have the sporting instinct in them," he observed. "They like to bet on horse races, boat races, baseball games—and anything where stakes can be placed. As long as the game is square, it does no particular harm. . . . The American public has always had the sporting instinct very well developed.

"However, gambling as a business is very much to be deplored, and it is unquestionably a detriment to society. The gambler is necessarily a parasite. . . . He is not a producer in any sense of the word. I regret to state that the Jews in some parts of the community have a monopoly on gambling."[15] The commissioner had summarized the paradoxical American attitude toward gambling since the wave of progressive reform; gambling itself remained permissible, even sportsmanlike, but the *business* of gambling was parasitical, morally smutted. Americans who gambled might enjoy normal social positions; those who provided the apparatus for gambling were social outcasts.

Jews had heard this sort of contradictory rhetoric before, when Pope Innocent III (r. 1198–1216) addressed the topic of Jewish usury and its necessary, but profane, place in Christendom.[16] Therefore, it is not coincidental that some of the most lucid social critics and writers of the 1920s drew their contemporary Jewish characters directly from the medieval imagination of the usurer—the exceedingly powerful parasite on innocent society. In his recounting of the baseball scandal, F. Scott Fitzgerald used the caricature of the Jewish usurer when he gasped for America through a character in *The Great Gatsby*:

> Fixed the World's Series? The idea staggered me. I remembered of course that the World's Series had been fixed in 1919 but if I had thought of it at all I would have thought of it as a thing that merely *happened*, the end of some inevitable chain. It never occurred to me that one man could start to play with the faith of fifty million people—with the single-mindedness of a burglar blowing a safe.[17]

Would that the blame could be isolated as conveniently as in fiction. For *The Great Gatsby*, Arnold Rothstein became Meyer Wolfsheim, a lampoon as graceless and crass as the living man was polished. Although Rothstein knew Great Britain, having traveled there several times for business, Meyer Wolfsheim marveled that his friend Gatsby had attended "Oggsford College in England. You know Oggsford College?"—and stumbled over the pronunciation of a language that Rothstein spoke natively. And while Rothstein dressed in the "subdued method of Fifth Avenue,"[18] Wolfsheim pointed his shirts with cuff links made of the "finest specimens of human molars."

Then again, Fitzgerald wanted less to lampoon the man than to lampoon his nose. Although Fitzgerald claimed to have met Rothstein,[19] his Wolfsheim was "a small flat-nosed Jew . . . with two fine growths of hair which luxuriated in either nostril," and when Wolfsheim felt fury it was not so much expressed by his face, but rather "his nose flashed . . . indignantly." When Edith Wharton finished reading *The Great Gatsby* she dashed off a note to Fitzgerald and specified that in Wolfsheim, Fitzgerald had created the *"perfect Jew."*[20]

With Wolfsheim, Fitzgerald represented what he imagined to be a massive and treacherous pivot in the stratification of the American social order. The Tom Buchanans of Yale had been replaced by nouveau riche Jay Gatsbys, an indistinguishable crowd with neither history nor pedigree who chase money blindly in the ever elusive search for something real. In their hopeful chase, this new class unwittingly serves the purpose of Wolfsheim, foul Jewish lord of the underworld who now wields complete power in an America with no recognizable authority.

What an ugly vision of the impact of immigration and the widening of American roads to success for those who had not gone to Princeton or Yale. How simple to imagine a content American past with baseball at its center.[21] Surely Fitzgerald had overstated purposefully, for the sake of fiction, the actual power of Rothstein and his limited coterie. Nevertheless, how telling of the American imagination that Fitzgerald drew his Rothstein character directly from the Anglo-Saxon imagination of the usurer. Or worse. Unlike Shylock, Wolfsheim does not even bleed. Perhaps that is because unlike Shylock, Wolfsheim does not falter.

"Why isn't he in jail?" Fitzgerald wondered for America.

"They can't get him, old sport," came the answer. "He's a smart man."

The Jews React

"IT MAKES sense to teach a child to play dominoes or chess," a father had written to the advice column of the *Forverts* in 1903, "but what is the point of a crazy game like baseball? The children can get crippled." Abraham Cahan, the broadminded editor of the *Forverts*, sympathized with the son, however, as well as the children of "half the parents in the Jewish quarter" who faced the same problem. "Let your boys play baseball and play it well," he advised. "Let us not so raise the children that they should grow up foreigners in their own birthplace."[1] Parents and educators of the Lower East Side came to agree with Cahan as they were introduced to the health and cultural benefits of baseball and put the game in the schools.[2]

The notion of a Jewish baseball player brought smiles mixed with irony and pride, as Irving Berlin realized with his well-received number "Jake! Jake! The Yiddisher Ball-Player," a theme far more endearing to Jewish ears than the song's original title, "Ike, Ike, Ike, You're a Regular Kike." Meanwhile, in 1908 Albert Von Tilzer, of the Jewish songwriting firm Shapiro, Bernstein, & Von Tilzer, coauthored "Take Me Out to the Ball-Game," and thereby answered any lingering question as to which sport Americans held most dear.[3]

Still, when the Black Sox scandal broke in 1920, readers of the *Yidishes Tageblat* had some new sporting vocabulary to master— *gefikst* was one new verb, *tsu betten* was another. "Fair play" and "a square deal" were some new concepts as well. When reporting on the fix, the tone of the Yiddish daily mirrored the sensationalism of the mainstream American press until sports writers began to suspect that "the Little Hebrew" Abe Attell had been involved. Soon Rothstein's name found its way into the scandal, and just as the mainstream press put the Black Sox on the front page, the *Yidishes Tageblat* lost interest in the story.[4]

Concerning the fix, most Yiddish papers followed the way of the *Yidishes Tageblat*. Yiddish newspaper coverage of the scandal dwindled while the *New York Times* and the *World* reported every traumatic rumor. The English-language Jewish press, controlled mainly by Western Jews, never picked up the Black Sox scandal at all. At the time of the fix, the English-language Jewish press maintained a policy of not reporting Jewish crime because doing so it said, "would give a distorted picture of Jewish life and attention to such reports would give the world the impression that the crimes are significant, thus placing the Jew in an unfavorable light before the world." Because putting Jews in a favorable light was the fundamental strategy of Western Jewish assimilation, the Western Jewish press rarely covered the details of Jewish criminality except to mitigate or deny them, as it had denied that Nicky Arnstein was a Jew.[5]

The *Forverts*, however, had no such policy and took a unique position concerning the fix. In 1920 the Yiddish *Forverts* had a circulation of two hundred thousand, making it the most widely read Jewish newspaper in America. It was explicitly socialist and often took stands contrary to those popular in the mainstream New York press, such as when the *Forverts* refused to support American involvement in the Great War. Although the paper had embraced baseball as the national game since the turn of the century, it took a decidedly coldhearted stand in its first article about the Black Sox, "The Swindle in 'Holy' Baseball." "What Americans have forgotten," a socialist editorialist reminded readers, "is that in the swamp of corruption created by graft and bribery, nothing can remain pure." Moreover, "a baseball player is simply an employee of a private owner or a capitalist corporation which deals in baseball for profit."[6]

The *Forverts* blamed capitalism for destroying the national game and taunted the mainstream press as the real "greenhorn" for not noticing the corporate menace. The purity of baseball was an illusion, the paper claimed. Money ran every aspect of the game. Baseball was "big business." As the *Forverts* denounced capitalism, however, it simultaneously elevated gambling to a place next to legitimate business enterprises, a quest for profit like any other. The *Forverts* classified gamblers "among the great Wall Street tycoons and men of society." "Great players in the annals of baseball became the hand-maids of the big gamblers," the paper reported, almost boastingly. Using icy logic, it concluded that "since everything is always business in America, the World Series was used for business. . . . What can be done? In America *biznez iz biznez*."[7]

This egalitarian attitude toward all forms of capital became the stance of the *Forverts* and caught on throughout the Yiddish press. That is to say, while American progressives distinguished between legitimate capitalism and Rothstein's business of hope, the Yiddish press did not. Baseball's owners packaged and sold hope. Stock brokers sold hope. If it was legitimate to play stocks and underpay players, why was it illegitimate to play craps?[8]

Soon the *Forverts* introduced a stock character to the pages of the Yiddish press: the "clever Jewish gambler." To be called a clever Jew, in the antisemitic literature of Henry Ford was no accolade, but when the *Forverts* wrote about cleverness it became a compliment. For instance, the clever Jewish gambler took prominence in an article entitled "A Sensational Trial about Irish Players and Jewish Gamblers," which obliviously conflated the terms "Irish" and "gentile." No matter. That Jews were smart and had an aptitude for business with which gentiles could not compete was the editorialist's point.[9]

Der Tog, a rather liberal Yiddish daily, later concurred with the *Forverts* when it celebrated a Jewish handicapper at Belmont racetrack who called himself "the Duke." Born in Budapest, the Duke became successful in a business where most "lose 99 percent of their hard-earned money." "The Duke is often the only one at the racetrack who can hold all of the odds in his head," the interviewer reported, "and therefore he succeeds . . . when thousands lose." The paper concluded that Jewish professional gamblers are "clever and calculating, with iron wills and steel nerves; they possess extraordinary courage and energy, and an average man must look upon them with wonder." The old Bowery gang with their marginal businesses had suddenly become Jewish-American heroes.[10]

It was thus a moment of great sadness for Eastern Jewry when, in November 1928, Rothstein was gunned down at a card game for reasons still unknown. Perhaps he had been defaulting on gambling losses. He was known to pay his debts slowly as a life insurance practice—collecting from corpses is difficult. Nevertheless, we do know that Rothstein received a message at his table at Lindy's to go to the Park Central Hotel, room 349. There, while playing cards with a minor hoodlum and hothead, George McManus, he was shot under the card table in the lower abdomen. Police found him in the stairwell at 10:47 that night. McManus hid in the apartment of beer baron Dutch Schultz for three weeks before he turned himself in. His acquittal, however, came quickly. The case was never solved.

Something had happened between the time of the Black Sox scandal and the hours in which Rothstein lay on his deathbed. The Yiddish press no longer wavered about the page on which the story should run—Arnold Rothstein made the first column for a week. Unlike for the Beansy Rosenthal murder or for the fix, the headlines now read unambiguously. *Der Tog* announced "The Tragic End for One of New York's Greatest Gamblers,"[11] while the Orthodox and traditional *Morgen Zhurnal* printed a long editorial entitled:

HOW ARNOLD ROTHSTEIN EARNED HIS REPUTATION
AS KING OF THE GAMBLERS

His First Big Win—His Power Over Millionaires and Wall Street
Gamblers—Rothstein's Magnetic Personality—Rothstein's Concern Never
to Blacken His Father's Respected Name—. . .—Rothstein as One
of the Biggest Businessmen in the Country. . . .[12]

Even the *Forverts*, still the conscience of the Eastern European Jewish community in America, came out from behind the curtain of socialism and declared openly: "Rothstein was a gentleman gambler and made his living by the old tradition of honest gaming."[13] "In Europe he would have been seen as a sportsman," declared another paper.[14] "He had the manners of an aristocrat," wrote a third, "and a rare and beautiful vocal inflection. . . . When one came across him in the street, one had absolutely no idea that this was the monarch of the underworld."[15]

Yes, he was monarch of the underworld, a point the Yiddish press never denied, and also never censured. "When his name was mixed in with the whimpers about the baseball scandal in 1919," one writer for *Der Tog* remembered, "he was totally absolved of those accusa-

tions, and rightly."[16] In fact, Rothstein's power became a source of
Jewish pride. "He has 'pull' in Tammany hall and with the police, and
is aligned with powerful politicians and mayors," the *Forverts* noted
admiringly, and it reminded readers that Rothstein had beneficently
settled the International Ladies' Garment Workers Union strike in
1925, just as his upstanding father had done for the same union in
1919.[17] The paper neglected to note, however, that unlike his father,
Arnold arbitrated by calling upon the hired gun for the garment workers, "Little Augie," and the strong-arm of the manufacturers, "Legs
Diamond," both Jewish gangsters.[18]

Whereas the Jewish community honored Abraham Rothstein for
being observant, law abiding, and a communal authority, the same
community exalted Arnold Rothstein for being a transgressive power
in New York.[19] The accolades of the Yiddish press are impossible to
exaggerate. As Arthur Goren has noted, *Der Tog* declared the consensus of the Yiddish dailies and the affections of Eastern Jewry when it
described Rothstein as he lay nearly dead in Polytechnic Hospital.
After the paper described how Mr. Lindenbaum, the owner of Lindy's
delicatessen, had provided blood for a transfusion to comfort
Rothstein in his final hours, the paper concluded: "And so it seems
that there he lies, not like one who belongs to an inferior class, but a
sort of saint."[20]

Everyone knew that Rothstein's sainthood had been complicated.
Like all saints, he had been tested. Even the Western Jewish press
had begun to excuse Jewish criminality by finding sources for the
behavior in the oppression of Jews in Eastern Europe, such as when
the *American Israelite* stated in one of its rare articles about Jewish
criminality that "in the final analysis, the Gangster Evil really belongs
to the roster of the latter day Jewish persecution. Its origin is to be
traced to the benighted policies of the late rulers of Russia, which in
turn resulted in the precipitate uprooting of thousands of families, the
disruption of a centuries-old life and institutions and the throwing of
great numbers of refugees into a strange environment and among
strange people."[21]

The *American Israelite* had blamed one historical act of uprooting
and migration in Eastern Europe, rather than the general pattern of

gentile exclusiveness, for the Jewish "Gangster Evil." Though it had excused Jewish criminality, that press still avoided the messy implication that perhaps gentile exclusiveness in America might have something to do with the problem of Jewish crime. The Yiddish press, however, had no similar qualms. One Yiddish journalist unabashedly spelled out the context of Rothstein's trial. "It is not entirely chance that Rothstein was a Jew," the writer explained. "Naturally, there are gentiles in gambling as well, but not so many as there are Jews. . . . Other careers are locked to us. One hits stumbling blocks." "It is difficult for a Jewish youth with extraordinary talents to make a place for himself," the analysis continued. "The only free outlet is to make money. Gambling permits this, and our Rothstein steps in. He doesn't want the money so much as to release the steam of his boiling blood, and to put to use his seething energy. In the last analysis, that is what comes of the abnormal Jewish life. In exile, ambitious men are wasted."[22]

global point

The explanation was as ancient as it was simple. As Jews had been in exile in Eastern Europe—outcast from the gentile economic and social order—so they were in America. Gentile society excluded Jews and forced them to enter socially tainted businesses. In short, the *goyim* had pushed Rothstein and his kind into indecent careers. It was a condition of being in exile.

"I have been victimized more than once," Rothstein had told reporters, "simply because of the business that I was in and the peculiar moral code which governs it. . . . It is not pleasant to be what some may call 'a social outcast.'"[23]

Rothstein was right. America had a "peculiar moral code" when it came to the business of gambling, and those who ran that business were considered ethically suspect, legally culpable, and socially stigmatized. By necessity, Jews had learned to subsist (and sometimes thrive) in positions along the margins of the legitimate economy as moneylenders,[24] court Jews,[25] Polish *arendators*,[26] and finally, it would seem, as professional gamblers.[27] By necessity, then, Eastern European Jewry had created legends such as the Master Thief, long in the imagination of Russian Jewry as the savvy Jew, always wheeling on the verge between legitimacy and illegitimacy, and always just one

shrewd step ahead of his Russian competition and the law. For Eastern Jewry in America, Rothstein became the Master Thief incarnate.[28]

Yet these two outlaws differed in a crucial way. Unlike the Master
Thief, Rothstein's exile had been self-imposed. New York City was not
Minsk; America was not the Russian Pale. By the late 1910s and 1920s
Jews were succeeding in mainstream American business and society.
Their justifications for entering socially tainted fields were becoming
fewer and less plausible. Certainly Jews faced stumbling blocks. Not
only were Jews excluded from certain areas presided over by the Protestant establishment, but they were excluded from businesses inhab-
ited by other immigrants and ethnics. Many groups that came during
the great wave of immigration confronted these same obstacles. If
Jews experienced stumbling blocks, Poles, Italians, and Chinese faced
them too, and often had less success overcoming them.[29]

But by the 1920s Jews were painstakingly and successfully stepping
over the barriers set before them as an immigrant group. Jews were
entering the American middle class in multitudes as they wedged
open their own worlds of law, medicine, and finance through City
College in New York. Economic historian Arcadius Kahan reminded
us that after World War I, American Jewish labor history becomes
impossible to pursue because so many Jews had left the working class
for factory ownership and other kinds of middle-class employment
during the war. Rothstein's own father enjoyed rags-to-riches success
in America and had done so legitimately. By all comparative measures
and by all empirical standards of economic well-being, Jews were
making it in America. They were flourishing as they never had in
Eastern Europe for centuries.[30]

And yet economic success in America bewildered the traditional
self-understanding of Eastern Jews as a group bound to live along
the economic margins. Judging from the language of the Yiddish
press, Jews seem to have asked themselves if it were possible to
participate in the economic institutions of a host country without
significant discrimination. To use the Jewish theological symbolism,
were the Jews still in *exile* or were they finally *home*? Despite the
obvious economic indicators of Jewish success in America, the very
notion of being home seems to have been overwhelming to Eastern

Jewish identity. Jews did not entertain the possibility for long. Instead, at precisely the moment of economic prosperity in America, Arnold Rothstein chose to live what he himself described as the life of a "social outcast" and the bulk of Eastern Jewry chose to identify with him.[31]

The baseball scandal provided a moment when the community of Eastern Jews took its stand on how the long history of Jewish economic marginality ought to be perceived in America. These Jewish Americans might have accepted their place as full participants in the American middle class and condemned the gamblers, as the rest of America did. The Jewish community might have excommunicated the criminals for breaking the American code of "fair play" and "square deals." Instead, these Jews severed themselves from most Americans and embraced the gamblers as their own—"our brothers," as one columnist put it, "sons of Israel."[32]

So as Jews commuted to their new homes in the Bronx, Harlem, New Jersey, and Long Island from their legitimate jobs in Manhattan, and as they settled down in the newspaper rooms of their new, hard won, Jewish community centers, they read about Rothstein's murder with a nostalgia for the Master Thief and a longing for a more familiar time when Jews knew precisely where they belonged. Arnold Rothstein helped these Jews maintain their worldview of exile and thereby their Jewish identity while economically, to use Deborah Dash Moore's phrase, they became "at home in America."

"A GREAT change came over Arnold Rothstein toward the end," his wife Carolyn believed. "He balanced for many years between the upper- and the under-worlds. He took lunch or dinner with men like August Belmont, or Herbert Swope, and supper with the Diamond brothers. . . . But, finally, it got to be all Diamond brothers—all underworld."[33]

After the World Series scandal, Rothstein went on to bankroll the bootlegging industry during the Prohibition years. Anyone who needed money for stills, boats, trucks, payoffs, or protection turned to him. He also helped usher heroin into America. In 1920 Rothstein closed the doors to his Manhattan casino, and by 1925 he was out of the gambling business entirely. By the time of his murder, Rothstein operated strictly as financier to the underworld.

At his pinnacle Rothstein had provided Americans with the service of gambling. In the eyes of many, that service conflicted with an ethic of hard work and rational gain, but it was something Americans wanted. More precisely, it was something Americans both wanted and would not provide for themselves for fear of social taint. As such, and in the long tradition of Jewish economic marginality, gambling became a Jewish business.

For reasons that remain enigmatic, gambling is a service Americans continue to want. I have suggested that professional gambling is the sale of hope. Rothstein's own view of its appeal recognized the fascination Americans have with making it: "People like to think they're better than other people," he told his friend Damon Runyon. "As long as they're willing to pay to prove it, I'm willing to let them."[34]

Americans paid Rothstein millions for the chance to obtain something more. For years, Arnold Rothstein stood at the door of his casino and invited Americans toward the elusive Big Win: a bought entry into an American dream in which one swaps cigars with the Real Players, at the Big Game taking place always one floor further up in the casino.

To the Jews of the Jazz Age, Rothstein offered a different American dream, one as fictive as the first, although real to the Jewish imagination. It was of a world in which a Jewish kid from the Bowery could come to pull all the strings from his reserved table at Lindy's delicatessen, not because he wanted it this way, but because in America that was what a Jew had to do to make it.

Almost incidentally, Rothstein invented the structure of modern crime to satisfy the enormous demand for the dreams that he offered, for which he employed gangsters more handy with pencils than with guns. This does not deny his menace. One need simply remember Rothstein's only religious practice, a prayer he offered for those who might fail to make their payments: "God help you if you don't."[35]

His threat wasn't empty, but neither was it usually executed. Rothstein spent his life in this marchland, where power and authority eye each other jealously and strain to see their differences. Looking through the pane window of Reuben's, or Lindy's, one could not distinguish between police and criminal, politician and netherworld power, financier and fraud. "In the grey area between the upper world and the underworld," a Yiddish journalist proudly concluded, "Rothstein was king."[36]

So it was said.

A rare photograph of Arnold Rothstein, probably in his office at the Arnold Rothstein Realty Corporation and the insurance firm of A. L. Libman, Inc., of which he was president. Both firms opened in 1919, the year of the World Series fix. (Library of Congress, LC-USZ62-116745)

One of many promotional posters and gimmicks used to help finance America's participation in the Great War. The mass marketing of Liberty Bonds introduced average Americans to equities speculation, while it taught gamblers the business of stock and bond bucketeering. (Library of Congress, LC-USZC4-2950)

"Nicholas Arnstein, alias J. W. Arnold, alias James Wilfred Adair, alias James W. Adair, alias McCormick, alias Borech and alias Brice" enjoys Atlantic City with his wife, Broadway star Fanny Brice. In sadder times, Nicky would be convicted for being the mastermind of a multimillion-dollar bond scandal. "Mastermind?" Fanny burst out when she heard the accusation. "He couldn't mastermind an electric bulb into a socket." (© Bettmann/CORBIS)

Finish of the Travers Stakes of 1921 in Saratoga Springs, where Rothstein's horse Sporting Blood trounced the filly that Harry Payne Whitney (of the Standard Oil dynasty) had primly named Prudery. Rothstein may have fixed the race. (Keenland-Cook)

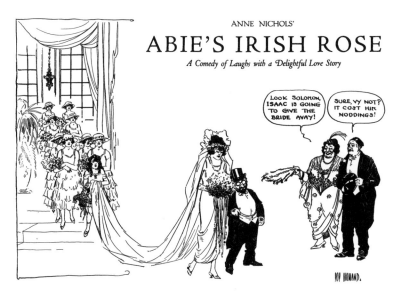

Rothstein financed several shows, including the crude, runaway hit of 1922, *Abie's Irish Rose*, about Jewish and Irish intermarriage. When pressed to explain why he also backed the African-American show *Shuffle Along*, he replied simply, "I like to hear those people talk." (Museum of the City of New York)

Four of the Chicago White Sox in 1917. Three years later the outfielders Oscar "Happy" Felsch (second from left) and "Shoeless" Joe Jackson (far right) were banned from professional baseball for their involvement in the World Series fix of 1919. (© Bettmann/CORBIS)

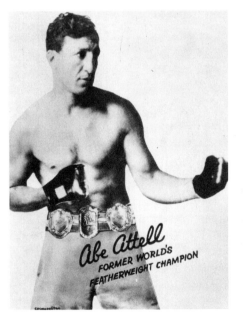

"The Little Hebrew" Abe Attell, "featherweight champion, on whose fights, win or lose, Arnold never lost a bet." Attell fixed the World Series, probably without Arnold Rothstein's approval. This did not prevent Rothstein from betting on the Series with inside knowledge. (© Bettmann/ CORBIS)

Judge Kenesaw Mountain Landis teaches the traits of skill and honesty to a young marble-shooter. After the World Series fix, Landis became baseball commissioner to revive the game's lost respectability. (© Bettmann/CORBIS)

F. Scott Fitzgerald with his wife Zelda on their honeymoon. Fitzgerald lampooned Rothstein in the character "Wolfsheim" in *The Great Gatsby*, calling him "a small flat-nosed Jew . . . with two fine growths of hair which luxuriated in either nostril." When Edith Wharton finished reading *The Great Gatsby* she dashed off a note to Fitzgerald, asserting that in Wolfsheim, Fitzgerald had created the *"perfect* Jew." (Library of Congress, LC-USZ62-111780)

At the height of the Red Scare, Galleanist anarchists exploded a bomb in front of J. P. Morgan's offices on Wall Street, killing 32 people and injuring 200. Nicola Sacco and Bartholomeo Vanzetti were both Galleanists. (Brown Brothers)

Felix Frankfurter, Jewish immigrant to New York's Lower East Side and Harvard professor of law, led the public relations effort that brought the cause of Sacco and Vanzetti to places as far from Boston as Moscow, Sydney, Paris, and Buenos Aires. (Harris & Ewing, Collection of the Supreme Court of the UnitedStates)

A. Mitchell Palmer, making a speech as U.S. Attorney General. For his unrelenting and sometimes brutal campaign to rid America of the "Red menace," he became the target of anarchist terrorism. (Library of Congress, LC-USZ62-99297)

Justices Oliver Wendell Holmes and Louis D. Brandeis, both mentors to Felix Frankfurter. Brandeis supported Frankfurter's defense of Sacco and Vanzetti, but Holmes doubted "if anyone would say that there was no evidence warranting a conviction." "It is not on the merits [of the case] that the row is made," Holmes thought, "but because it gives the extremists a chance to yell." (F. J. Collier, Collection of the Supreme Court of the United States)

Judge Julian Mack of the U.S. Circuit Court of Appeals in Chicago and president of both the American Jewish Congress and the Zionist Organization of America. "I too believe in revolution," Judge Mack pledged in support of Sacco and Vanzetti, "whether it be the American, the French, or the Russian. I too believe that there are times when the mob is fully justified in taking matters into its own hands." (Library of Congress, LC-USZ62-112324)

As a young Jewish immigrant from Russia, Ben Shahn took the Sacco-Vanzetti affair as the basis of his most influential artistic work. (Ben Shahn, *Bartolomeo Vanzetti and Nicola Sacco*, 1931–1932. Tempera on paper over composition board, 10 × 14″, The Museum of Modern Art, New York)

Al Jolson in "The Whirl of Society" (1912). In this show, Jolson played a version of his famous "scalawag servant with his surface dullness and hidden cleverness." Notice the tension in the gaze between white aristocrat and black servant. Why did Jews choose to play blacks on stage? (Museum of the City of New York)

Eddie Cantor also started his career in blackface. Here he returns to an antebellum moment and presents a nostalgic return to slavery from the perspective of the slave. Jews had long seen themselves as being enslaved in Egypt and exiled in Europe. Even in the jazz age, Jews repeated as part of their Passover service: "This year we are slaves, next year may we be free." (Museum of the City of New York)

Yip Yip Yaphank . . . a musical potpourri cooked up in 1918 by the boys at Camp Upton; with words and music by one Sergeant Irving Berlin." Berlin, born in Tumin, Russia, and raised on Cherry Street in New York City, excised "God Bless America" from the show. He felt it did not compare favorably with George M. Cohan's "Over There." (Museum of the City of New York)

The hit song of 1916 that made teenagers blush and women's benevolent societies protest. "On this island lived wild men and cannibals brimmin' / And you know where there are wild men, there must be wild women. / So where did Robinson Crusoe go with Friday on Saturday night?" The animal is unidentified. (Museum of the City of New York)

Al Jolson and other actors with President and Mrs. Coolidge. Jolson, an international star of the stage, though not yet of film, sang "Keep Cool with Coolidge" to support the presidential candidate in 1924. (Library of Congress, LC-USZ62–111396)

A crowd gathers outside of Warners' Theatre to see *The Jazz Singer* in 1927. This meditation on the Jewish fascination with jazz was not a sure-fire topic with which to premier the new and expensive technology that made the movies "talk." Before this film, the Warner Brothers had enjoyed their biggest success with *Rin Tin Tin*. (© Bettmann/CORBIS)

"Mammy, don't you know me?" Jolson cried out in the last frames of *The Jazz Singer*. "It's your little baby!" But neither a black mammy nor a yidishe mama would recognize this jazz singer as her own. He is neither from Dixie nor from the Russian Pale. He is located nowhere but in the Jewish imagination. And, of course, on movie screens worldwide. (Museum of the City of New York)

Jazz Age Politics

IN THE 1920 presidential election, "normalcy" was the most important matter. Stately Warren G. Harding, senator from Ohio, made his neologism the center of the Republican campaign against Woodrow Wilson and announced that it was time, finally, to put the war behind us. "America's present need is not heroics, but healing," he thought, "not nostrums, but normalcy; not revolution but restoration . . . not surgery but serenity."[1] Wilson, promising to keep Americans out of the mess in Europe, had thrown the country right into it. Since the war he had tolerated the importation of all sorts of foreign menaces: socialism, communism, anarchism—all Red. As a result, the country was in the middle of a "Red Scare," widely declared when an anarchist group exploded a bomb on Wall Street, killing thirty and wounding two hundred.[2]

The real culprit, Republicans contended, was Wilson's progressive strategy to create fellowship between business and labor. True, the revolution in manufacturing had created hardships for workers because labor efficiency demanded a leaner working class. It was even understandable that Red politics appealed to people who were asked to work more and receive less. But these foreign, anti-business political influences were to be quashed anyway. Anything restricting the rule of capital impeded the path to normalcy. It was time to elect a business president.

Harding won the election of 1920 and began a reign of Republicanism that lasted for twelve years. With the interest of big business seated firmly in the Oval Office, hindrances to capitalism dwindled to almost nothing. In 1920, at the moment of organized labor's peak strength before the Depression, about five million Americans were union members, just one-fifth of the nonagricultural, nonprofessional working class. Organized labor never did break into the large manu-facturing industries in the 1920s. Rather, it concentrated on mining, an important industry but not one that any longer comprised the bulk of labor. Union membership by 1929 had dropped to 3.4 million, just 7 percent of the labor force. Meanwhile, the wheels of American business churned unimpeded, and the Red Scare that had swept Wilson out of the White House became a footnote to the process of industrialization.[3]

The indelicacies of capitalists came to replace those of workers. Harding's administration became known as the Poker Cabinet, since presidential decisions were made in an upstairs study of the White House, "the air heavy with tobacco smoke," according to one shocked visitor, "trays with bottles containing every imaginable brand of whisky [standing] about, cards and poker chips ready at hand."[4] At that card table sat Albert M. Fall, secretary of the Interior, who would end up in jail for financial fraud during the Teapot Dome scandal, and Harry Daugherty, attorney general of the United States, who just barely escaped confinement himself (his assistant mysteriously com-mitted suicide). Later, the Veterans Bureau was raided for millions by yet another member of what was becoming known as Harding's "Ohio Gang." Only Mort Mortimer, White House bootlegger, sur-vived the Harding years unimpeded by the law.

Then, in 1923, President Harding suddenly died of apoplexy and was replaced by Vice President Calvin Coolidge, a virtuous and dull man compared to his predecessor. "Silent Cal" didn't say much at all except when pressed, as he was in his election campaign of 1924: "This is a business country," he summed up efficiently, "it wants a business government."[5] That political philosophy won him the elec-tion in a landslide, and his popularity was sufficient to carry the party through yet another Republican embarrassment, when it became known that President Harding had used a White House coatroom for trysts with a twenty-four-year-old family friend. When his young lover published *The President's Daughter* in 1927, revealing that President Harding had an illegitimate child by her, it became an underground bestseller. Still, the economy and the Republican philosophy were strong enough to support in 1928 the election of Herbert Hoover, who declared during his inaugural address his own premonition of business as the conduit of an American utopia:

> We in America today are nearer to the final triumph over poverty than ever before in the history of any land. The poorhouse is vanishing from among us. We have not yet reached this goal, but, given a chance to go forward with the policies of the last eight years, we shall soon, with the help of God, be in sight of the day when poverty will be banished from this nation.[6]

Those who had voted Republican from Harding to Hoover approved of the business plan for America. But while Harding had promised that the 1920s would not be a decade of heroics but of healing, some Americans could never agree. They still saw poverty, exploitation, and the need for brave political warfare. One who held this view was Eugene V. Debs, leader of the extreme Left, who sat inside a federal prison, convicted in 1918 under the Espionage Act for expressing antiwar sentiments against "the master class" and "the junkers of Wall Street." He had told his judge:

> Your Honor, years ago I recognized my kinship with all living things and I made up my mind that I was not one bit better than the meanest of the earth. I said then, I say now, that while there is a lower class I am in it; while there is a criminal element, I am of it; while there is a soul in prison, I am not free.[7]

In 1920, the Socialist Party nominated Prisoner 9653 as its presidential candidate. Debs's campaign for the oppressed brought in 915,302 votes, and proved that, despite the wheels of commerce, some Americans were not so enamored with the capitalist vision of the American way.

PART II

Frankfurter among the Anarchists: "The Case of Sacco and Vanzetti"

For it is clear enough that under certain
conditions men respond as powerfully
to fictions as they do to realities, and that in
many cases they help to create the very
fictions to which they respond.

Walter Lippmann, Public Opinion

Felix Frankfurter

ON JUNE 2, 1919, as the White Sox surged ahead in the American League, Carlo Valdinoci walked along R Street in Georgetown past the urban mansions of America's political aristocracy. He must have looked out of place, for Valdinoci had dressed himself specially for this occasion. A multicolored striped shirt and a bright blue polka-dotted bow tie complemented his best black suit, pinstriped in green. He wore brown sandals. His fedora was newly purchased from Philadelphia's Italian Market, where Valdinoci had waited between train stops from New York. On his body he packed an Italian-English dictionary, a Colt automatic, and a Smith & Wesson revolver. As he walked along the cobblestones, he struggled awkwardly with a large leather satchel, loaded down by twenty pounds of dynamite.

We know how Valdinoci dressed and what he carried because at 11:15 that night bits of his personal effects were scattered in all directions while fragments of his bone pierced windows up and down the block. Early the next morning investigators discovered Valdinoci's full torso on the roof of a building a block away on S Street. His thick black scalp lay nearby.

Carlo Valdinoci had not planned to die that night, but he had planned to kill. The attorney general of the United States, A. Mitchell Palmer, was his target, and it was on Palmer's front stoop that the bomb exploded. Although the explosion rattled the attorney general as he sat reading in his third-floor study, Palmer was not hurt. He was enraged, however, for the Valdinoci bombing was the second attempt by anarchists to take his life in six weeks.

In late April some thirty package bombs had been discovered in the central New York Post Office, addressed to A. Mitchell Palmer, Justice Oliver Wendell Holmes, John D. Rockefeller, J. P. Morgan, various senators, governors, judges, and other high-ranking government officials; even Judge Kenesaw Mountain Landis, not yet baseball commissioner, but still a famous patriot for having sentenced 101 Wobblies (members of the Industrial Workers of the World or IWW) to prison for disturbing the war effort, had been sent one of the deadly packages. All of the brown parcels found in the New York Post Office were timed to arrive at their targets for the celebration of May Day.[1]

Years later, F. Scott Fitzgerald would call May 1, 1919, the birthday of the Jazz Age. At least three thousand immigrants did not applaud the change. To those three thousand, who would defend themselves against hasty deportations at the hand of the angry attorney general, May Day, 1919, marked the beginning of the Red Scare. In four months, Palmer successfully banished eight hundred immigrants and later helped push the Act of June 5, 1920, through Congress, greatly expanding the list of dangerous aliens.[2]

Most Americans welcomed the decisive actions of their attorney general, for over the past five years newspapers had reported too many gruesome explosions at the hands of political terrorists. Anarchist dynamite had exploded a New York City tenement, July 4, 1914; a Boston police station, 1916; Preparedness Day events in San Francisco, 1916; a church in Milwaukee, 1916. Soon after came the thirty bombs of May Day, 1919, and, finally, seven bombs timed to explode simultaneously on June 2, 1919, in seven cities—Boston, Cleveland, New York, Paterson, Philadelphia, Pittsburgh, and in Washington, D.C. at the Palmer home. Because the anarchist menace was so widely recognized, the attorney general found ample support for his actions from respected legal authorities. John H. Wigmore, dean of the Law School at Northwestern, expert on criminal evidence, and famous advocate for the defense of the poor, felt that the attorney general had acted entirely within the limits of law and reason. "Prompt measures were vital," Dean Wigmore agreed. "Mr. Palmer saved the country, in my opinion."[3]

Still, not everyone concurred with the attorney general and the dean. A group of leading academics and lawyers formed a Committee of Twelve to decry the tactics of the Red Scare as rash, xenophobic, and, most damningly, lawless. Their *Report upon the Illegal Practices of the United States Department of Justice* argued that the attorney general had infringed upon civil liberties by using rampant and warrantless arrests, searches, and seizures. One member of the committee, Professor Felix Frankfurter of Harvard Law School, later called the Act of June 5 "the most extreme legislation against opinion ever enacted by Congress. It makes the Alien and Sedition Laws of 1797 seem like poor instruments of repression."[4]

Attorney General Palmer gladly would have agreed that his deportation initiative and the Act of June 5 worked against the free expression of opinion. The explosion on his doorstep had scattered some fifty copies of a thin pamphlet titled *Plain Words*, the political manifesto of Carlo Valdinoci and his cohorts. Its words indeed were plain: "There will have to be bloodshed; we will not dodge; there will have to be murder; we will kill because it is necessary; there will have to be destruction; we will destroy to rid the world of your tyrannical institutions." It was signed, simply, "The Anarchist Fighters."[5]

Nicola Sacco was an Anarchist Fighter. So was Bartolomeo Vanzetti. More specifically, they and Valdinoci were members of a group of anarchists led by Luigi Galleani, on behalf of whose dubious philosophy members were willing to impose havoc and murder. Their slogan: "No God, No Law, No Master." Other anarchist factions with slightly differing agendas competed with the Galleanists, such as L'Era Nuova of Paterson, Pro Pensa of Philadelphia, and the wandering group of Emma Goldman and Alexander Berkman. The Galleanists, however, seemed the most willing to use dynamite to propagate what they called their "beautiful idea," which to Sacco meant "no government, no police, no judges, no bosses, no authority."[6]

For the sake of the beautiful idea, in September 1917, Sacco, Vanzetti, Valdinoci, and about sixty of the most belligerent Galleanist anarchists had run off to an adobe village in Monterrey, Mexico, to protest the Great War, avoid the American draft, and dream up revolutionary ways to use dynamite. Sacco and Vanzetti returned to Boston as fast friends and became core members of the Gruppo Autonomo of East Boston, which met in the hall of the Italian Independent Naturalization Club of Maverick Square. According to Paul Avrich, scholar of anarchism, it was this group of Galleanists from New York and Massachusetts that planned the aforementioned May Day and June 2 bombings. Vanzetti, who contributed frequently to the anarchist newspaper *Cronaca Sovversiva*, was the writer of the Gruppo and may well have been the author of *Plain Words*. After Carlo Valdinoci died on that June night in Georgetown, his sister went to live with the Sacco family.[7]

Two years later, with the Red Scare well under way, Sacco and Vanzetti sat in a prison in Dedham, Massachusetts, convicted of robbery and murder on evidence that Justice Oliver Wendell Holmes considered ample. Before their death sentences were carried out in 1927, Felix Frankfurter, Jewish immigrant raised on New York's Lower East Side, would emerge as their most vocal champion. From his office at Harvard University, Frankfurter would transform the Sacco and Vanzetti case from a curious labor trial into an international cause for civil rights and justice. The campaign would result in massive demonstrations and riots throughout the world, in places as diverse as Geneva, Paris, and Buenos Aires.

In his unrelenting campaign for international public opinion, Frankfurter would garner as his closest allies such people in the Jewish establishment as Judge Julian Mack, Professor Horace Kallen, Rabbi Stephen Wise, and Justice Louis D. Brandeis, as well as the entirety of the Jewish-American press and the editorial pages of the New York *World*, then under the firm direction of two Jews, Walter Lippmann and Herbert Bayard Swope. Together, they would help end the Republican dominance of American liberalism and would herald the nascent social welfare policies of the Democrats. Frankfurter would also replace the progressive lawyering strategy of Brandeis and come to represent a new legal type: the civil rights lawyer who works to affect social policy, not by defending the humanitarian legislation of the state, but by defending the rights of individuals, particularly outsiders.

The common understanding of the Sacco and Vanzetti case has seen Frankfurter's campaign as righteous, sincere, and above all reasonable. Nevertheless, the reasons why Frankfurter and Jewish-America came categorically to support Sacco and Vanzetti (unlike any other American group, including Italian-Americans) are not at all plain. The two Italians were devoted to the annihilation of the American government; they openly espoused violence; and each was caught with a private armory on his person, one with the alleged murder weapon. Although the Commonwealth of Massachusetts tried the two and declared them guilty of murder, Felix Frankfurter and the rest of American Jewry were not satisfied. In fact, not only did the Jews not believe that the Italians had received a fair trial, but, despite the continued vows of violence on the part of Sacco and Vanzetti, the Jewish community was certain that the trial could not have been just essentially because the two were Italian anarchists in Yankee Boston. Sacco and Vanzetti were political outsiders, and thus they became a Jewish cause. At no time did a public voice of American Jewry suggest the possibility that the presiding judge of the case, the Supreme Judicial Court of Massachusetts, the governor of Massachusetts, or the Supreme Court of the United States, may have been right not to overturn the opinion of the Sacco-Vanzetti jury. To the American courts the two were convicted murders; to the Jews they were innocents, railroaded for their unpopular political beliefs. Not for the last time in Jewish-American political history, two worldviews appear to have been irreconcilably opposed.[8]

The Young Progressive

FELIX FRANKFURTER was born in a large, poor, Jewish ghetto of Vienna, Leopoldstadt, in the fall of 1882. This was not the posh Vienna of Freud but rather the city experienced by most Viennese Jews. As a typical Jewish family, the Frankfurters were rather orthoprax, and resided among recent Jewish immigrants like themselves, who as a group, "created patterns of economic and social behavior which continued to mark them as Jews both to themselves and to the outside world."[1] Frankfurter's father, Samuel Leopold, had migrated from Pressburg to earn a meager living as a peddler (or *Handelsagent*). Most Jews in both Pressburg and Leopoldstadt had come from Galicia. Thus it was in a culture of Eastern European Jewry in which Frankfurter grew up, though the direct origins of the Frankfurter family are not known. Felix would later characterize his home as a serious one. "On the whole a Jewish household is a serious household," he thought.[2]

Upon arriving in America in 1893, Samuel Leopold sold linens to finance the emigration of his wife, Emma, and children, who then arrived in New York after a steerage-class voyage on the ship *Marsala* in 1894. Once again, Felix had been planted in an Eastern European Jewish ghetto. Leopold and Emma sold their wares from the Frankfurter apartment at 78 East 4th Street. In the summertime, Leopold peddled on the streets. While the two oldest Frankfurter boys, Fred and Otto, helped their parents with the business, Felix and his younger brother, Paul, had the good fortune to attend P.S. 25 on 5th Street. Felix was twelve.[3]

Felix learned English quickly and grew comfortable in New York. He considered Manhattan "a series of villages strung together, a congeries of villages," and freely wandered from one to the next. He liked his own village, the Lower East Side, and found much in common with local boys. Young Felix, who happened to be Arnold Rothstein's exact contemporary and made the same streets his playground, shared Rothstein's interest in games of chance and skill. "There was a very intense crap shooting period," Frankfurter fondly remembered. "I also played chess. But crap shooting on the street was the thing."[4]

Unlike Rothstein, but like many of the boys at P.S. 25, Frankfurter excelled in school. Even before the great educational reform activities of the Jewish Educational Alliance under David Blaustein began in 1898 (too late for Frankfurter, who graduated that year) literacy among the Jewish children of the Lower East Side was very high. Many Jewish students chose to remain in school past the mandatory age of fourteen through to graduation. As Frankfurter grew older he discovered other educational opportunities in the neighborhood, particularly the newspaper room of Cooper Union, where he spent many hours reading. Downstairs at the People's Institute of Cooper Union, Frankfurter attended political lectures, usually about socialism, communism, unionism, and other working-class issues. Often Frankfurter followed the passions of the audiences out on to the streets and into nearby cafes. "I'd sit hours and hours and hours in East Side teashops, coffee rooms, and drink highball glasses of tea with some rum in it, or lemon, and a piece of cake, and jaw into the morning about everything under the sun."[5] The lessons in the teashops around Cooper Union must be considered his first education in politics and public policy.[6]

Frankfurter's political interests continued while he attended City College, where he matriculated and was graduated in 1902 with a class that was 75 percent Jewish.[7]

After college, Frankfurter worked in the Tenement House Department of New York City for the premeditated purpose of raising money to study law. He could not remember a time before he wanted to be a lawyer, much to the credit of the environment around 4th Street, which fostered such an estimable career goal in an immigrant. Frankfurter set his sight on Columbia Law School, as had many from his graduating class, but was encouraged by a friend whose brother had attended Harvard to apply there instead. Standards of acceptance to Harvard Law disqualified 96 percent of all American men, because Harvard insisted that applicants have a college degree at a time when most law schools thought a high school education adequate. Still, the educational opportunities of the New York ghetto had allowed Frankfurter to matriculate at Harvard, and so he packed for Cambridge. Rather, his mother packed him.[8]

Frankfurter fully exploited his opportunity at Harvard. "I went to this and that," he remembered, "went to the library, read, roamed all around, and just satisfied a gluttonous appetite for lectures, exhibitions, concerts."[9] Still, even at this irrepressible gait, Frankfurter managed to gain a position on the *Harvard Law Review* and a stellar reputation among both students and faculty. He also met several Jewish students who would become his lifelong friends. Among them was a sharp undergraduate named Walter Lippmann, a German Jew. Another was Horace Kallen, a shy but excitable graduate student in philosophy, born in Silesia (central eastern Europe), much like Frankfurter.

Perhaps the most important moment in Frankfurter's legal education was a half-hour lecture delivered by an alumnus of the law school in May 1905. Louis D. Brandeis, born to a German-Jewish family in Louisville in 1856, had graduated from Harvard Law in 1877 and would have been considered the valedictorian of his class had the circumstances of his graduation been entirely legitimate. They were not, however, for Harvard Law insisted that graduates be at least twenty-one years old, and Louis had completed his studies when he was only twenty. After a short stay in St. Louis, Brandeis had returned to Boston and became a powerful corporate lawyer. He later gained wide fame as a progressive attorney for having battled J. P. Morgan's Elevated Railway monopoly in Boston and several other powers he considered dangerous to the general welfare of the people.[10]

In his short lecture, Brandeis reprimanded the faculty for a pattern of which they were doubtless aware: In the past quarter century Harvard had become a training ground for corporate lawyers while schools such as Columbia dedicated themselves to more humanitarian legal research and problems of social organization. He warned the boys of the world they would soon enter, a thrilling world of industry and corporation, and yet one in which democracy itself was perhaps threatened. He explained that in Alexis de Tocqueville's time lawyers had served individuals, and in so doing, adversarial individuals had been equally represented. In modern times, however, in situations before both bar and legislature, corporations retained the best lawyers while individuals were left dazed, ignorant, and helpless. Who would represent the people? "We hear much of the 'corporation lawyer,'" he lamented, "and far too little of the 'people's lawyer.'"[11]

That day, Brandeis encouraged the future lawyers in his audience to practice before the legislature or city council, where public interests were involved. This, he admitted, would not pay as well as corporate law. But even a corporate lawyer might do his part. Because the corporation had sidled itself so comfortably beside the state, Brandeis thought corporate counsel had become responsible to advise its clients about the benefits of corporate benevolence. "The relations between rival railroad systems are like the relations between neighboring kingdoms," he explained to the young men. "The relations of the great trusts to the consumers or to their employees is like that of feudal lords to commoners or dependents."[12] And, like the feudal lords of old, the new corporate class had social responsibilities. Besides leading the economy, the capitalists were also the new social and political elite, and, Brandeis thought, they should behave as such.

Corporate benevolence was not only ethical, he said, but ultimately it best served the corporation. Somehow the needs of the masses would have to be met. "There will come a revolt of the people against the capitalists unless the aspirations of the people are given some adequate legal expression," he warned, "and to this end cooperation of the leaders of the bar is essential." As the crowd of students hushed, he explained further: "The next generation must witness a continuing and ever-increasing contest between those who have and those who have not," Brandeis told the future lawyers. "The people are beginning to doubt . . . whether there is a justification for the great inequalities in the distribution of wealth, [and] for the rapid creation of fortunes, more mysterious than the deeds of Aladdin's lamp. The people have begun to think; and they show evidences on all sides of a tendency to act." It would be up to the students, Brandeis thought, to determine how the will of the people would be expressed, "whether it is to be expressed wisely and temperately, or wildly and intemperately; whether it is to be expressed on lines of evolution or on lines of revolution."[13]

Brandeis favored temperance and evolution, of course, as did the larger movement for progressive reform of which he was the preeminent legal representative. As a man of his time, Brandeis did not herald the causes of individuals or civil rights. At this point in his career, he did not doubt that the needs of the people could best be served en masse and on the solid ground of capital and corporation, if only capital might behave humanely. To Brandeis, a "people's lawyer" represented the people only in their hulking, vaguely dangerous plurality, and then only indirectly through humanitarian legislation of the state and the goodwill of industry. Reform started from the top.

With this belief, Brandeis shared the spirit of Western European Jewry in America in its acts of bourgeois philanthropy, political organization, and in its own relation to the masses including the new immigrant masses of Eastern Jews. Typically, Isaiah's call to defend the fatherless and plead for the widow was the cry. Consequently, Brandeis often came to be compared with that prophet.[14]

Frankfurter absorbed Brandeis's lecture on progressive social organization, filed it next to his lessons in working-class politics from his tea-shop days, and went to practice in the world of New York corporate law where neither theory seemed at all relevant. Though at the time of Frankfurter's graduation, New York hosted several prestigious Jewish law firms, such as Guggenheimer, Untermyer, & Marshall, he decided upon the gentile firm of Hornblower, Byrne, Miller, & Potter, in which he was the only Jew. He found corporate practice discouraging, however, and soon accepted an offer from U.S. Attorney Henry L. Stimson to work in the Manhattan office.[15]

IN THE office of the U.S. Attorney, Frankfurter served his apprenticeship in public service. Stimson pursued cases that brought Frankfurter to the very frontier of progressive lawyering. Frankfurter enforced regulatory reforms concerning the corporation, prosecuted cases of political corruption by local authorities, dealt with habeas corpus cases relating to questionable detentions on Ellis Island, and worked on other timely issues. Stimson thought that because Frankfurter had himself immigrated, he was particularly suited for cases that involved immigrants, and Frankfurter agreed.[16]

Henry L. Stimson was an alumnus of Harvard Law and had deep connections in New York State and within the Republican party. In 1910, at the behest of his old friend Theodore Roosevelt, Stimson ran for governor of New York, and took Frankfurter on the campaign trail. Though Stimson lost, Frankfurter learned the many exciting details of running a modern campaign for public opinion. He also came to enjoy a rather chummy relationship with the candidate's old friend, the former president of the United States.

After Stimson's failed run for governor, President Taft asked Stimson to become his Secretary of War. Stimson took Frankfurter to Washington, D.C., and found him a post as law officer in the Bureau of Insular Affairs, a part of the War Department. Frankfurter specialized in issues surrounding waterpower. Sometimes his work took him abroad to Cuba or Panama. He argued his first case before the Supreme Court concerning land rights in Puerto Rico, and learned basic tactics of working for the public good within Washington's increasing bureaucracy. Even as the vitality of the progressive movement appeared to wane with Taft in the White House, Frankfurter and his widening circle of friends and political acquaintances maintained the spirit of benevolent reform.[17]

During these years, Felix Frankfurter met a steady stream of politicians, bureaucrats, writers, journalists, judges, and justices. Stimson spoke admiringly of Frankfurter's tremendous gift "for keeping in touch with the center of things—for knowing sympathetically men who are doing and thinking."[18] Among the most personal and intense of the relationships he fostered in these years was that with Herbert Croly, muse of the progressive movement with his seminal book *The Promise of American Life* of 1909 and future publisher of the *New Republic*. Frankfurter also became closer with his Harvard acquaintance Walter Lippmann, now a theorist of public political psychology and at work on his *Preface to Politics* and *Drift and Mastery*, both classics of the period. Frankfurter also made friends with Louis D. Brandeis, with whom he would become even more closely aligned. A letter of introduction from an old Harvard professor launched a lifelong relationship between Frankfurter and Justice Oliver Wendell Holmes, author of the greatest American contribution to legal theory,

The Common Law, a treatise on the genealogy of law and the authority behind legal change.

Although Theodore Roosevelt was no longer president when Frankfurter arrived in Washington, Frankfurter remembered the grand political influence of the Roosevelt administration even three and four years after Roosevelt had left the White House. Frankfurter also may have noted that Roosevelt had been the first president to have a Jew in his cabinet, Oscar Straus, secretary of Commerce and Labor. More importantly, Frankfurter was attracted to Roosevelt's social vision and sheer energy. "You remade society to deal with the great problems that the industrial revolution . . . had thrown up," Frankfurter remembered of the time. "Here was Teddy the Terrible himself, 'We fought at Armageddon, and we battled for the Lord.' The air was rife with intellectual enterprise and eagerness, intellectual eagerness."[19]

Elsewhere Frankfurter reminisced that under Roosevelt the "proposals of heretics and outcasts became presidential policies."[20] Under Roosevelt's influence, Frankfurter first began to express his proclivity for maverick politics, for the proposals of "heretics and outcasts." Frankfurter joined the Bull Moose campaigners who supported Roosevelt's return to the presidency in 1912 as a third-party candidate. When Roosevelt lost to Woodrow Wilson, Frankfurter was terribly disappointed. Suddenly, with the emergence of the stolid, even puritan Wilson in the executive branch, Frankfurter felt himself to be politically alone. As the decade progressed, Frankfurter's political detachment became chronic. During the election of 1916, for which Frankfurter had trouble finding a viable candidate, he complained to his mentor, Henry Stimson, "I have to be one of those who, by being outside of both camps, is going to pick and choose from election to election. . . . I don't like the situation. It is not comfortable to be politically homeless."[21]

Frankfurter would not feel welcome in Washington until another president emerged with a political vision to equal Theodore Roosevelt's. That vision came in 1932, in the incarnation of Roosevelt's cousin, Franklin D. Roosevelt. In the meantime Frankfurter searched for a place to settle until political conditions better favored his return to the political scene.

Fortunately, in 1913 a unique position presented itself. Frankfurter had made a great impression in Washington circles, particularly among members of the Supreme Court, and faculty members of Harvard Law School were eager to call him a colleague. The dean of the law school, Ezra Thayer, strongly supported the idea but conceded that there were no funds in his budget for a new position. So Brandeis successfully petitioned German-Jewish New York financier Jacob Schiff for a donation, and Stimson raised money from some of his affluent Wall Street contacts.

At the age of thirty-one, Frankfurter moved back to Cambridge to join the faculty of the Harvard School of Law. Because of his experience in Washington's bureaucracy, Frankfurter mainly taught administrative law. Occasionally he taught criminal law, based on his work in the U.S. Attorney's office as a young man. He took teaching seriously and felt "very deeply the need of organized scientific thinking in the modern state and, particularly, in a legalistic democracy like ours, the need of a definitely conceived jurisprudence coordinating sociology and economics."[22] With this as his primary teaching concern, Frankfurter spent his time at Harvard fulfilling Brandeis's call to the young men at the Harvard Ethical Society to defend the public interest from the top of the political order.

Brandeis himself had made great strides in the effort to serve the public in this way. As counsel to the National Consumers League, Brandeis had gained a reputation as the most progressive lawyer in America. In the 1900s and 1910s, when large corporations and big businesses challenged the progressive legislation of several states in the Supreme Court, Brandeis ran to the defense of the states. In a case he successfully argued for Oregon, Brandeis originated a style of argument since known as the "Brandeis brief," in which sociological principles displaced traditional arguments based on legal precedents, and thereby modern organizational theory displaced historical authority. The Brandeis brief changed the technique of arguing for progressive legislation before the Supreme Court.[23]

Brandeis also argued masterfully before another increasingly important body, the court of public approval. In cases concerning the public welfare, Brandeis always seemed willing to provide the newspapers with another comment or opinion. William Randolph Hearst's

Boston American had an outstanding offer for Brandeis to use its columns for any purpose he wished, irrespective of the editorial opinion of the paper. Irritated opponents accused Brandeis of being "more than a lawyer; he is a publicist."[24] But everyone could see that public opinion was becoming increasingly significant.[25]

Frankfurter learned these tools from the master advocate himself. At Brandeis's behest, Frankfurter served as counsel for the National Consumers League, and used the Brandeis brief technique to argue before the Oregon Supreme Court several cases concerning minimum-wage legislation as well as a case about work hours. When Brandeis was called to serve on the U.S. Supreme Court in June 1916, Frankfurter replaced him as chief counsel for the League.[26]

FRANKFURTER happily substituted for Brandeis as the country's most able defender of progressive legislation, until 1917, when the United States became a belligerent in the World War. "I had a wire from Secretary [of War] Newton D. Baker asking me to come down for the weekend, if I could," Frankfurter remembered. "I packed my suitcase, and the weekend didn't terminate until the fall of 1919."[27]

With Frankfurter's war duty came a change in his public reputation. Increasingly, he was considered not so much a progressive but a radical. This came with Frankfurter's wartime assignment as counsel to the President's Mediation Committee, a body designed to quell some of the labor troubles that had developed as the war progressed. While industrialists grew wealthier by providing the government with resources to wage modern warfare, they simultaneously appealed to their workers to accept harsh working conditions and low pay in the name of patriotism. Workers noted that the more they were called to sacrifice for the war, the greater the wealth of their employers seemed to grow. Some workers grew impatient and did not intend to be duped. "The Balkans and Germany, France and England were awfully far away from the workers in the copper mines of the southwest, or the forests of the northwest, or the oil fields of southern California," Frankfurter noted sympathetically. "The war to them was most unreal."[28]

From his work with the President's Mediation Committee, Frankfurter learned firsthand the realities of labor politics and labor extremism. He could ably distinguish between anarchists, anarchist-syndicalists, anarchist-individualists, anarchist-communists, and every other stripe of anarchist, revolutionary socialist, and communist that contested capital in the name of the worker. Although he never condoned radical or violent labor tactics, Frankfurter generally sympathized with labor and may have rationalized labor radicalism to himself by believing, as he once said, that "unsatisfactory, remediable social conditions, if unattended, give rise to radical movements far transcending the original impulse."[29]

Frankfurter investigated several political disturbances for the President's Mediation Committee, including the bombing of San Francisco's Preparedness Day in July 1916. That particular bombing killed ten, wounded fifty, landed two labor organizers (named Mooney and Billings) on trial for murder, and stirred up more labor trouble internationally than President Wilson thought tolerable for the war effort. When Mooney was convicted based upon dubious evidence, the Jewish anarchists Emma Goldman and Alexander Berkman rallied sympathizers in Russia to pressure that government to help Mooney diplomatically. The Russian government, feeling the strain of imminent revolution, appealed to President Wilson. Because Wilson wanted Russia to remain in the war, he sent Frankfurter to California to eliminate the problem, preferably quietly.[30]

After investigating the Preparedness Day bombing and the commotion surrounding it, Frankfurter wrote a passionate public report to the president that strongly suggested that Mooney had been framed by San Francisco authorities and that the IWW organizer deserved a new trial.[31] Former president Theodore Roosevelt, the man who taught Frankfurter's generation about the duty of government to protect the people, fired off a letter to the newspapers implying that Frankfurter had been far too public in his defense of the insurgents. "The 'direct action' anarchists and apologists for anarchy are never concerned for justice," Roosevelt thundered. "The guiding spirits in the movement . . . cared not a rap whether or not Mooney and Billings were guilty; probably they believed them guilty; all they were concerned with was seeing a rebuke administered to, and an evil lesson taught all public officials who might take action against crimes of violence committed by anarchists in the name of some foul and violent 'protest against social conditions.'"

Roosevelt claimed that Frankfurter had made himself an agent of radical propaganda. Moreover, Frankfurter had done this not as an independent citizen but as a representative of the U.S. government. "When you, as representing President Wilson, find yourself obliged to champion men of this stamp," Roosevelt instructed, "you ought by unequivocal affirmative action to make it evident that you are sternly against their general and habitual line of conduct."[32]

Roosevelt's concern for both American public perception of radical propaganda and its efficacy was neither hysterical nor unfounded. Alongside the war in Europe, a war raged within America about the future of democracy, and to Roosevelt and many others it was the more dangerous of the two. During and after the Russian revolution, certain factions of the American working class had raised the possibility of a similar Bolshevik uprising in America. For some, progressivism was not adequate. Revolution was needed. With such a potential threat to American democracy, Roosevelt thought the system of justice and the government of the United States needed to be given room with which to save public credibility. Frankfurter, Roosevelt thought, had entirely neglected this fundamental duty.

Frankfurter countered with a technique he would often use to upset his detractors on the issue of public impressionability and the general welfare. He minimized the question of public perception as secondary to finding the "truth, the truth painstakingly pursued, sifted and tested on the spot." Frankfurter would not relent in his pursuit of truth, even at the risk of misleading public opinion. "It is as important vigorously to promote patriotic purposes as it is to prevent ignorance or selfishness or prejudice from using the disguise of patriotism for ends alien to the national interest," he replied to Roosevelt. "It is important . . . to be sure-footed in our knowledge of facts and in our discernment of what really affects the national well-being."[33]

Throughout Frankfurter's career, the perception of his support for radicals and their causes would never faze him. After the Mooney case, the public came to know Frankfurter as a radical lawyer and a believer in radical principles. Rather than correct the misinterpretation Frankfurter seemed to relish the notoriety. He began publicly to express his dissatisfaction with corporate liberalism and progressive reform while showing renewed attachment to his Cooper Union education in working-class social theory. Perhaps Frankfurter even courted his public reputation as a radical lawyer. On Armistice Day, 1919, he presided over a meeting in Faneuil Hall to urge Americans to recognize the newly formed Soviet Union. "I dare say I shall be called a Bolsheviki," he taunted the audience. "In fact, I am sure of it."[34]

Zion and Cambridge

As a child raised on the Lower East Side and as a young adult who attended lectures at Cooper Union and informal discussion groups in tea shops along Orchard Street, Frankfurter had seen labor identity and ethnic consciousness grow. Later, as assistant U.S. attorney, he had returned to New York and revisited his immigrant experience from a more mature perspective. At the economic level, he watched as Italian and Jewish working people learned how to bargain collectively for themselves, and how to strike. At the political and cultural levels, Frankfurter saw Eastern Jewry contest the leadership of supposed mainstream Americans and uptown Western Jewry, and successfully resist their calls to homogenize and assimilate.[1]

Brandeis had no such experience. As a member of the Western Jewish establishment, he had simply assumed the position of the Reform movement and of Western Jewish philanthropic causes, and had blindly supported the project of "Americanization" of recent Eastern European immigrants. He embraced the progressive sociological model of America as a melting pot in which all immigrant cultures were transformed into something uniformly American, and he expressed misgivings about the empowerment of the working class. In 1905 he had warned students at Harvard that the working class had begun to show evidence "of a tendency to act," and that without the help of the educated classes "the people" might act "wildly and intemperately." Elsewhere in 1905 Brandeis had spoken out against the possibility of a "hyphenated American" for similar reasons. Only by completely assimilating could immigrants effectively participate in the American democracy of individuals, not groups, and in a modern society that cultivated rationalism and uniformity of mind as the most powerful means to bring the greatest good to the greatest number.[2]

88

Yet in 1910 "the people's lawyer" came face-to-face with the people for the first time and was thoroughly changed by the experience. By chance, he was called upon to mediate a labor dispute between Jewish garment workers and Jewish manufacturers in New York. Instantly he became overwhelmed by the professionalism and reasonableness of the union. He came to respect its leadership, its democratic values, and its intelligent political process. Moreover, he came to respect its cultural difference. These were ghetto Jews of Eastern origin, some with Yiddish accents and foreign mannerisms. Nevertheless, they seemed to show a heroic dedication to grassroots democracy. Perhaps, Brandeis thought, that proclivity for democracy came from their Jewish origin. Perhaps the cultural difference of Jews was an asset after all.[3]

From his experience in the strike, Brandeis began to evaluate his progressive belief in a democracy led from the top, as well as his Western Jewish insistence upon melting-pot assimilation as the means to Americanize Eastern Jewry. He also considered his attitude toward Zionism. If Brandeis had thought about modern Zionism at all since its emergence at the turn of the century, he probably followed the official opinion of the American Reform movement and agreed that Zionism was just one of the many ways in which Jews isolated themselves from Americans and subverted their American identities. Zionism emphasized Jewish difference, But after Brandeis came to see the garment strike of 1910 as an exercise in democracy of a particularly Jewish stamp, he began to speculate about the possibility of such a Jewish democracy in Palestine. In Zionism, American Jews might express the proclivity of their culture for democracy in a way that would be instructive to all Americans.[4]

Brandeis was greatly aided in his consideration of Zionism by Horace Kallen, former philosophy student at Harvard, now a young professor at the University of Wisconsin. Soon after Brandeis expressed his interest in Zionism, Kallen (an Eastern Jew) mailed Brandeis (a Western Jew) some of his own musings on the subject of Jewish-American identity and Zionism. In his correspondence, Kallen answered the Reform movement's charges that Zionism implied a dual loyalty and that Jewish cultural difference implied separatism. Kallen announced to Brandeis his own concept of "the

89

equality of the different," which he would develop and broaden to include all immigrant cultures in his seminal 1915 essay, "Democracy *Versus* the Melting Pot." Kallen proclaimed "cultural pluralism" to be the proper model with which to accept immigrant cultures, and reiterated his belief in the fundamental American "right to be different."[5] Brandeis met Kallen several times to discuss the young professor's beliefs about Zionism, Americanization, and democracy. Ultimately, Kallen was so convincing that in 1914 Brandeis accepted the leadership of the Zionist Organization of America, and proclaimed his Zionist credo in a manner understandable only from Kallen's unique perspective of cultural pluralism. "To be good Americans, we must be better Jews," Brandeis maintained, "and to be better Jews, we must become Zionists."[6]

Kallen also converted Judge Julian Mack to American Zionism. Mack's Western Jewish credentials were impeccable. He was born in San Francisco to a German-Jewish family, grew up in Cincinnati in the synagogue of the leader of the Reform movement, Isaac Mayer Wise, and was married in Chicago by Wise's successor, Emil G. Hirsch. Moreover, he had attended Harvard Law and helped found the *Harvard Law Review* with classmate John H. Wigmore, the current dean of Northwestern Law. Later, when Mack accepted a place on the U.S. Circuit Court of Appeals in Chicago and became the highest ranking Jewish member of the judiciary in American history (only to be superseded by Brandeis's nomination to the Supreme Court), Mack also accepted a seat on Harvard's Board of Overseers as its first Jew. Mack dedicated himself to Western Jewish and progressive philanthropic pursuits, such as the founding of Hull House in Chicago, the Immigrant's Protective League, and the American Jewish Committee, a Western Jewish institution dedicated to assimilating Eastern European immigrants, defending world Jewry, and decrying Zionism as separatist.[7]

While Horace Kallen taught at the University of Wisconsin in Madison, he often visited the Mack home in Chicago. The two talked of the relationship between American mores and Jewish identity. Kallen convinced Mack of the benefits of cultural pluralism and Zionism, as he had convinced Brandeis. Eventually, Mack left the American Jewish Committee in favor of the more egalitarian American Jewish Congress of which he became president. In 1918 Mack replaced Brandeis as president of the Zionist Organization of America.[8]

Before Horace Kallen, Western Jews of the American establishment shunned all inklings of cultural difference. After Kallen, some embraced their difference through Zionism. Kallen's project of redefining Western Jewish identity to include group feeling had been aided by the deep impression made upon Brandeis by the Eastern Jewish labor movement. In the lingo of the time, cultural pluralism challenged the model of "melting pot" Americanization; in today's language, multiculturalism contested assimilation. For Jews, Zionism was one battlefield of this contention, and in that particular case Eastern Jewry decidedly won. Instead of Western Jewry having assimilated the Jews from the East, the stronger influence appears to have been the other way round.[9]

At Brandeis's behest, Frankfurter also became involved with American Zionism. In 1917 Frankfurter accompanied Ambassador Henry Morgenthau to Turkey and Egypt to see what could be done for the settlements in Palestine during the World War. Frankfurter also attended the peace conference in Paris as a representative of the American Zionist movement and as a liaison for Brandeis. But while Brandeis and Mack had found a renewed sense of Jewish cultural specificity in Zionism, Frankfurter never became so inclined. He defined Zionism as "essentially a psychological force—the passionate longing by Jews for a home of their own,"[10] and did not particularly share those psychological passions. Unlike Brandeis and Mack, Frankfurter had come from the heavily bounded Jewish community in Vienna and was raised in another ghetto, the Lower East Side. Frankfurter had little need to find an institutional expression with which to remind himself of his Jewish difference. While Brandeis and Mack were just learning to embrace Kallen's "cultural pluralism," Frankfurter agreed but preferred to cultivate the ideals he frequently called "Anglo-American." This never deterred him, however, from loudly defending some decidedly un–Anglo-American causes.[11]

Although Frankfurter did not tout difference for himself, he did defend those whose civil rights or sense of citizenship he considered slighted by the American establishment. He had defended such a person in the case of the IWW organizer Mooney (some had thought too vocally for a representative of the president), and thereby gained a reputation as a Bolshevik sympathizer. The charge was certainly inaccurate, for as Frankfurter once explained to a crowd of hopeful socialists, he could not so easily "compress life into a formula." Nevertheless, in the name of equality, Frankfurter increasingly found himself publicly defending those who could.[12]

IN THE years following the war, powerful forces from within Harvard's establishment, such as alumni of the law school, attempted to silence Frankfurter. When they failed to ruffle Frankfurter himself, they targeted a younger member of the law faculty, Zechariah Chafee, whose views often emulated those of Frankfurter. Dean Roscoe Pound supported Frankfurter's politics and activities but became intimidated easily by opposing voices—particularly those of wealthy alumni. The president of Harvard, A. Lawrence Lowell, could not be accused of similar timidity. In the cases of academic freedom that surrounded Frankfurter and other members of the faculty, Lowell strongly supported his faculty. But privately, Lowell complained to Judge Julian Mack, member of Harvard's Board of Overseers, "I have sometimes felt that Professor Frankfurter was doing more outside work than was wholly wise."[13]

Justice Holmes had mixed feelings about the new directions taken by his young protégé. At one point Holmes wrote proudly to Harold J. Laski, another Jewish member of the Harvard faculty who was becoming known for his radical views: "Every once in a while, faintly and vaguely as to you, a little more distinctly as to Frankfurter, I hear that you are dangerous men. . . . What does it mean? They used to say in Boston that I was dangerous."[14] As Holmes learned the details of Frankfurter's more extreme causes, however, he wrote directly to Frankfurter. "I think you are too level-headed to be looking for martyrdom," Holmes suggested. "I believe in academic freedom but, on the other hand, it is to be remembered that a professor's conduct may affect the good will of the institution to which he belongs."[15]

The attention from detractors seemed to invigorate Frankfurter. He began to defend immigrants from being deported at the hands of Attorney General Palmer, and published along with eleven other lawyers the *Report upon the Illegal Practices of the United States Department of Justice*. Riled by the tactics of the Red Scare, Frankfurter agreed to sit on the National Advisory Committee of the newly formed American Civil Liberties Union. He also became lead counsel for the Amalgamated Clothing Workers of America, and represented them in a labor dispute in Rochester, New York, which he lost. Although Frankfurter was moving well beyond progressive lawyering and toward the direct defense of civil rights and union representation, as a favor to Brandeis he continued to appear as counsel for the progressive National Consumers League. All the while, Frankfurter wrote increasingly sharp pieces in the *New Republic*, some of which flirted with socialism. His activities in the early and mid-1920s culminated in what one noted biographer has called "the period of his most militantly outspoken utterances."[16]

Frankfurter's most vocal crusade on behalf of his own people, however, was decidedly different from Brandeis's campaign for the "right to be different" through Zionism. Frankfurter's Jewish cause in 1922 was for the right of all who were meritable to enter the highest institutions of the American establishment. It was provoked when he learned that Harvard intended to institute a quota on Jewish admissions. To Frankfurter, merit came regardless of either cultural conformity or difference. Therefore, he felt, quotas were fundamentally antidemocratic.

A survey by the Bureau of Jewish Social Research published in the *American Jewish Year Book* in 1920–21 revealed that 10 percent of Harvard's total student population was Jewish, while Jews constituted only 3 percent of the American population. Harvard did not face the situation alone. The University of Pennsylvania was 14.5 percent Jewish, Johns Hopkins 16.2 percent, the University of Chicago 18.5 percent, and Columbia University 21.2 percent. Although the trend of increasing Jewish enrollment, particularly in urban schools, had been consistent for at least twenty years, it was not until 1922 that President Lowell decided that Harvard had a Jewish problem. Instead of pursuing a silent policy of admissions discrimination as did Princeton and Yale, Lowell wished to institute an official Jewish quota. He appointed a special committee to investigate the matter, and suggested

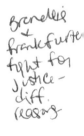

93

that the group look into several allegations of Jewish disruption of campus life, including disproportionate incidents of Jewish dishonesty and sexual offense, in part because of unduly "strong race feelings on the part of the Jews themselves."[17]

From his seat on the Harvard Board of Overseers, Julian Mack rallied forces to oppose President Lowell. When he suggested to Lowell that Frankfurter be made a member of the special committee, Lowell replied frankly, "I do not myself feel—and I find that the vast majority of the people with whom I have spoken do not feel—that Professor Frankfurter has the quality of solid judgment that would make him a good member of the Committee."[18]

Frankfurter did not wait for Mack to defend him. "I am told that you regard my views on a policy of limiting the proportion of Jewish students at Harvard as 'violent' and 'extreme,'" he wrote Lowell.[19] Lowell replied that he did not pretend to know Frankfurter's opinion on the subject of Jewish students. He only wished to "select a committee that would not advocate anyone's views, but approach the question in a large and open-minded spirit."[20]

The volleys continued—Frankfurter insinuating that the committee had been selected to find a preordained conclusion, Lowell responding that he wanted nothing more than objective discussion.[21] Finally, Frankfurter lost his temper. He insulted the Jewish members selected to be on the committee as inept. Specifically Frankfurter attacked Harry A. Wolfson, assistant professor of Semitic literature and philosophy, founder of the academic discipline of Jewish Studies in America, and born in Lithuania. "Prof. Wolfsohn [sic], whatever his views may be, is a naive bookish man, without talent or training which would enable him to share effectively the direction of such an inquiry as is called for by the Overseers' vote," Frankfurter roared. "Doubtless your own estimate of this aspect of Dr. Wolfshohn [sic] is not very different."[22] Lowell ended their correspondence. Wolfson, it should be noted, performed remarkably on the committee.

Frankfurter began a campaign for public opinion that included his friend Walter Lippmann, recently made an editor at the New York *World*. Lippmann testified before the committee, but to no avail. He may not have been terribly convincing because, it seems, he tended to agree with President Lowell. Lippmann believed there was in fact a serious Jewish problem. Wherever existed Jewish group feeling, he thought, it became manifest as flamboyance. Lippmann suggested that if Jews wished to enjoy the right to participate in mainstream American institutions, they would have to shake off their cultural bias to "huddle together in a steam-heated slum." He warned his fellow Jews in the *American Hebrew*, that "the rich and vulgar and pretentious Jews of our big American cities are perhaps the greatest misfortune that has ever befallen the Jewish people. They are the real fountain of antisemitism. They are everywhere in sight, and though their vices may be no greater than those of other jazzy elements in the population, they are a thousand times more conspicuous."[23] It was a curious thing for a Jew to say publicly, even in a Jewish forum, and yet it reveals Lippmann's rather coarse Western Jewish desire to eliminate Jewish cultural difference. These harsh words seem to have been the only contribution to the campaign for Jewish equality that Lippmann was capable of making. If Jews wanted social equality, he argued, then their culture must be brought in line with the establishment. Later, in the editorial pages of the *World*, Lippmann found he could express with much greater clarity and eloquence his appreciation of cultural difference in the defense of Sacco and Vanzetti. Through the two Italians, Lippmann, and perhaps many like him, could better express displeasure with perceived hegemony.[24]

Lippmann's analysis of the Jewish Question and its solution may not have helped Frankfurter's campaign to derail Harvard's Jewish quota, although the more sensible advocacy of Julian Mack and Harry Wolfson eventually did. After a prolonged battle among the Overseers and in the press, the committee decided against the recommendation of President Lowell. Lowell hastily admitted defeat and began to emulate the tacit quotas already established at Princeton and Yale.

The next time Frankfurter would rally his Jewish allies in a battle for public opinion was for two Italian anarchists.

CHAPTER 10

Sacco and Vanzetti

ON APRIL 15, 1920, just as the Black Sox scandal became public
and in the middle of the Red Scare, a $15,000 heist of a shoe company
payroll in the Boston suburb of South Braintree left the dead bodies
of the company paymaster and his guard on the factory's curb. After
a short investigation, Nicola Sacco and Bartolomeo Vanzetti, two well-
known members of the Galleanist Anarchist movement in Massachusetts, were charged with the crimes of robbery and murder for the
incident. The evidence against the two anarchists was substantial.
Multiple eyewitnesses to the crime testified to the guilt of the accused. Furthermore, at the time of their arrests Sacco and Vanzetti
were found, in the words of one reviewing judge, "armed to the
teeth," Sacco with a .32 Colt automatic (the alleged murder weapon),
Vanzetti with a .38 Harrington Richardson revolver. Initially, the case
received some small attention for two reasons. Fred Moore, a colorful
lawyer well known for his radical clients and his drinking, had been
hired to defend Sacco and Vanzetti by the anarchist Carlo Tresca,
while Sacco and Vanzetti's Galleanist cohorts exploded a bomb on
Wall Street to protest their trials and convictions, killing thirty people
and injuring two hundred.[1]

   The Sacco-Vanzetti case may have begun, as one reporter thought,
with "just a couple of wops in a jam."[2] Initially, the Italian and Jewish
needle trade unions, centered in New York, Philadelphia, and Chicago, were the only ones paying any attention to the case. But by
1927, after seven years of motions, appeals, denials, and earth-shaking
rallies in both Europe and the Americas, the case of Sacco and Vanzetti would come to represent internationally what Brandeis prophe-
sied in 1905 as the "continuing and ever-increasing contest between
those who have and those who have not."[3] This would be Frankfurter's doing.

Frankfurter maintained that he first heard of Sacco and Vanzetti in 1923, two years after their trial and convictions, when he learned that a Boston attorney of some prominence had involved himself in the case. William G. Thompson had presented a motion for retrial based on the affidavit of an expert witness for the prosecution that he had been coached to mislead the jury. Captain Proctor, ballistics expert, admitted he had testified for the district attorney that the bullet found in the murder victim was "consistent with being fired" by Sacco's .32 Colt because he refused to testify that the bullet actually *had* been fired by Sacco's pistol. The district attorney later agreed with the substance of the Proctor affidavit.[4]

Webster Thayer, presiding judge for the Sacco-Vanzetti trial and every post-trial motion, did not consider Proctor's affidavit about the behavior of the district attorney grounds enough to grant a retrial. Legal opinion remains divided as to whether Judge Thayer acted properly. For an expert witness to testify that a piece of evidence is "consistent with" certain attributes can be misleading, sometimes intentionally so. Nevertheless, testimony of this kind was standard legal procedure in the 1920s and remains so today.[5]

Nevertheless, Frankfurter thought that the meaning of the Proctor affidavit was clear and absolute. "When I read about that motion something happened to my insides," Frankfurter remembered three decades later. "If what Proctor said was true, it was reprehensible beyond words, and it undermined any confidence in the conduct of the case, that a district attorney should try to get an expert to swear to something that he repeatedly said that he couldn't swear to."[6]

Despite his memory, Frankfurter probably knew of Sacco and Vanzetti sometime before the Proctor affidavit through Mrs. Elizabeth Glendower Evans, a woman of Boston society and close friend of the Brandeis family, who had taken a strong interest in Sacco and Vanzetti soon after their convictions. Auntie B., as she was known to Frankfurter and Brandeis, would head and finance the Sacco-Vanzetti Defense Committee through their executions. In 1923 she pressured Brandeis to find the men decent counsel to bring the case to the Supreme Judicial Court of Massachusetts, and Brandeis pressured Frankfurter. In December 1924, Frankfurter enlisted W. G. Thompson who, Brandeis felt, took a remarkably high fee of $25,000.[7]

From then on, Thompson and Frankfurter worked two sides of the case as a team. Thompson handled courtroom advocacy, while Frankfurter organized public opinion. Frankfurter enlisted the services of anyone who was willing to write a letter, send a donation, or simply make a casual remark across the right dinner table. He sent out hundreds of letters about the case, often including points of great detail, sometimes writing with tremendous passion. Often Frankfurter convinced his listeners. "What a triumph it will be," Rabbi Stephen Wise encouraged Frankfurter, "if it can be fairly established that these men have been foully rather than fairly dealt with." Wise, a leading rabbi of the Jewish Reform movement, came to ennoble Sacco and Vanzetti in the press.[8]

Frankfurter's campaign for public opinion achieved its first great success when it conquered the conservative *Boston Herald*, which on October 26, 1926, carried an editorial entitled "We Submit." This column, which won the Pulitzer prize the following April, suggested that Sacco and Vanzetti deserved a retrial after W. G. Thompson produced an affidavit from a convicted criminal that he and his gang were responsible for the South Braintree murders. "We Submit" may be considered the turning point for the campaign to save Sacco and Vanzetti. After it appeared, respectable members of Boston society could permit themselves to join the Sacco-Vanzetti cause. Brandeis, ever watching Frankfurter's development, recognized as much when he sent off a note of congratulations just days after the editorial came out. "You have done an extraordinary thing in educating the Herald to its stand on S.V.; the World also."[9]

The *World* had been easier to convince. Its editor, Herbert Bayard Swope, best man at Arnold Rothstein's wedding in 1909, had hired Frankfurter's close friend Walter Lippmann away from the *New Republic* in 1922 to run his editorial page. Among the causes that Lippmann had adopted in the 1920s at the *World* were the debunking of spiritualism, for which he enlisted Harry Houdini in May 1924,[10] and support for the presidency of Al Smith, the Irish Catholic governor of New York, whom Lippmann backed expressly because he felt Smith represented the American immigrant classes against an older, stodgier, American order. "Here are the new people, clamoring to be admitted to America," Lippmann wrote of the Smith campaign, "and there are the older people defending their household gods. The rise of Al Smith has made the conflict plain."[11] Frankfurter agreed with Lippmann about Smith and convinced Lippmann that Sacco and Vanzetti were just two more examples of the same conflict. From 1926 Frankfurter remained in continual contact with Lippmann, advising the newspaper man about legal details of the case and discussing strategies of rhetoric. Frankfurter also wrote unsigned editorials for the *World* and the *New Republic*, for which he affected a remarkably Runyonesque tone.[12]

Frankfurter also enlisted Judge Julian Mack into the fight. After Mack and Brandeis lost the bid to continue leading the American Zionist movement at the Cleveland Convention of 1921, Mack still found himself inclined to champion the cause of cultural pluralism, this time for the two Italians. As an Overseer of Harvard University, Mack was thoroughly connected to Boston's establishment. Mack told Frankfurter about the negative opinions he heard circulating in the Back Bay and among members of the Union Club and Boston bar, and Frankfurter instructed Mack about the best ways to develop counter opinions.

Mack also introduced the plight of the Italian anarchists to the man who had introduced him to Zionism, Horace Kallen. Kallen came to support Sacco and Vanzetti with such vigor that he was arrested for blasphemy in Boston after he compared the two anarchists to Socrates and Jesus.[13]

Besides inducing his influential friends to work for the Sacco-Vanzetti cause, Frankfurter also tacitly guided the actions of Elizabeth Glendower Evans's Sacco-Vanzetti Defense Committee. By the summer of 1927, as Sacco and Vanzetti came closer to the electric chair, the Defense Committee collected an eclectic group of participants, many of whom were upper-class, establishment women, many of whom were also radicals and communists. Ellen Hayes, retired professor of astronomy and mathematics at Wellesley, participated, as did Jeannette Marks, Mount Holyoke professor of literature, and Lola Ridge and Paula Halliday, a poet and a Greenwich Village restaurant proprietor, respectively. There was also Ella Reeve Bloor, an older woman everyone enjoyed calling "mother," Dorothy Parker, from the Algonquin table writers' group, and Edna St. Vincent Millay. The men included Powers Hapgood, who later became a Congress of Industrial Organizations (CIO) leader, Michael Gold and Bertram D. Wolfe, both communist intellectuals, and Isaac Don Levine, a radical journalist. Michael A. Musmanno, a Pittsburgh lawyer who ran legal errands for the Defense Committee, was eventually appointed to the Pennsylvania Supreme Court. John Dos Passos also became involved.[14] And from New York came Arthur Garfield Hays, an attorney with such a proclivity for publicity that he had managed to get himself a seat next to Clarence Darrow at the defense table of the Scopes "monkey" trial in the summer of 1925.

Arthur Garfield Hays, whose parents had but for a vowel managed to squeeze the names of three successive presidents into their son's name, was born in Rochester, New York, in 1881. His family were Jews from Frankfurt am Main. His father and both of his grandfathers were clothing manufacturers. In the year that Frankfurter went to City College, Hays went to Columbia. When Frankfurter went to Harvard, Hays attended Columbia Law. When Frankfurter moved to Washington, D.C., Hays moved to New Rochelle. Like Frankfurter, Hays was drawn to progressive Republican politics. When Theodore Roosevelt made his run for the presidency in 1912, Hays "became an ardent Bull Mooser, . . . ran the Progressive party in New Rochelle and was recognized as the local 'boss' of the small but vociferous group that ran the Roosevelt campaign." In New York City, Hays gained notoriety as a libertarian lawyer, willing to take most any case he considered a challenge to civil liberties. Like Frankfurter, he distinguished between defending the political views of his clients and defending their rights. Yet Hays claimed less righteousness for his causes than did Frankfurter: "To press for some cause bigger than oneself, however hopeless it may seem, is not necessarily noble," he thought. "It's just about the best fun there is in life for people of my disposition." He would take any case in the name of liberty, whether it was "the liberty of a businessman to conduct his business without undue governmental interference or the liberty of a despised radical to speak his mind about the way business is conducted in this country." One of the businessmen whose liberties he defended from undue interference during the bucket shop investigations in 1922 was Arnold Rothstein. Among the despised radicals were Sacco and Vanzetti, whose defense provided for Hays the greatest thrill of all. "The stirring emotional reactions derived from fighting for the underdog demanded expression," he recalled of the time. "The Sacco-Vanzetti story—my Sacco-Vanzetti story—must out!"[15]

Frankfurter participated in detailed conversations about practical tactics of defense with W. G. Thompson. Their relationship, however, remained quiet. Frankfurter was exceedingly careful to claim "no relation to the case other than as a disinterested student of the administration of criminal justice."[16] Once again, as he had in the wake of the Mooney investigation in 1918, Frankfurter stood behind a shield of claimed objectivity. He grew "furious," he remembered, when he heard of people taking the side of Sacco and Vanzetti, not from their own reasoning, but simply because he had taken on their cause.[17] He harangued a supportive colleague at Harvard who had not, to Frankfurter's satisfaction, subjected the case to "those tests of reason which you would apply to it were it a parchment discovered in some Egyptian catacomb."[18]

Yet on rare occasion, and in secret, Frankfurter would admit how desperately and unsuccessfully he searched to find the facts that would justify his position. "The incidents in the record aren't very good," he admitted in a telephone conversation tapped by Massachusetts authorities. "He [Judge Thayer] certainly was very careful. That cuss is cunning you know and he constantly was doing stuff which in itself is all right."[19]

Meanwhile, W. G. Thompson pored over the court record, looking for reasons to appeal the findings of the jury. The Proctor affidavit concerning the testimony of the ballistics expert for the state had been only one point of appeal. Others included the claim that the jury foreman had brought his own bullet cartridges into the jury room to aid discussion of the ballistics evidence. Thompson also made a motion for a new trial based on the confession of Celestino F. Medeiros, prisoner of the Commonwealth found guilty of a different murder, who said that he and a group of professional bandits known as the Morelli gang of Providence, Rhode Island, had committed the crimes for which Sacco and Vanzetti were convicted. Thompson made several other motions for a retrial, most of which were reasonable and might have been accepted by some judges, although none of which was altogether persuasive. Judge Thayer received each motion individually and then found due reason to dismiss each. When Thompson appealed to the Supreme Judicial Court of Massachusetts, it ruled that Thayer's decisions and conduct fell within the realm of his jurisdiction and adequately fulfilled his judicial duty.

While Thompson worked unsuccessfully within the Massachusetts judicial system, Frankfurter continued to spin these failures to the press and to the other vessels of public opinion he had been cultivating all the while. Finally, in the spring of 1927, three years after he had arranged for W. G. Thompson to take the case and after an immense and utterly successful campaign for public opinion of which he was the undisputed leader, Felix Frankfurter finally emerged, ex cathedra, with his objective opinion of the case—proclaimed not as counsel for the defendants but as professor of criminal law at Harvard University.

"The Case of Sacco and Vanzetti" appeared in the *Atlantic Monthly* in March 1927. In it, Frankfurter first argued the facts of the case. He went over W. G. Thompson's several appeals and motions for retrial, and opined that any of these motions should have moved a reasonable judge to grant a retrial. He carefully attempted to discount the reports of eyewitnesses, and tried to discredit the fact that Sacco and Vanzetti had been caught heavily armed by claiming that the "extensive carrying of guns by people who are not 'gunmen' is a matter of common knowledge." All of his points on evidence and procedure had been made by W. G. Thompson in various motions and appeals. Most had already been ruled upon and denied by the Supreme Judicial Court of Massachusetts. Eventually that court would deny them all.[20]

Frankfurter's core argument, however, did not address the evidence itself. Rather, it questioned the very possibility of justice for two Italian anarchists. He admitted the following: "Sacco and Vanzetti were notorious Reds. They were associates of leading radicals; they had for some time been on the list of suspects of the Department of Justice; and they were especially obnoxious because they were draft-dodgers."[21] Having stated those ugly facts, Frankfurter turned them to his advantage. Because Sacco and Vanzetti were radicals, they were not granted a fair trial by the Commonwealth of Massachusetts. "By systematic exploitation of the defendants' alien blood, their imperfect knowledge of English, their unpopular social views, and their opposition to the war," Frankfurter claimed, "the District Attorney invoked against them a riot of political passion and patriotic sentiment; and the trial judge connived at—one had almost written, cooperated in— the process." This could happen because of the fallacious and irrational sentiment aroused by Attorney General Palmer and his Red Scare. "Outside the courtroom the Red hysteria was rampant," Frankfurter concluded, "it was allowed to dominate within."[22]

An unusual circumstance of the Sacco-Vanzetti trial had revealed to the jury the political beliefs of the defendants. In the proceedings of a typical trial, the political belief of a defendant is considered immaterial and inadmissible. For this reason the prosecution in the Sacco-Vanzetti trial had not mentioned that the two men were known to be anarchists. The district attorney simply presented the facts of the murder case. One of those facts, however, was particularly problematic for the defense. When arrested, both Sacco and Vanzetti had been deliberately evasive and untruthful when answering questions and had acted suspiciously. In legal parlance, they displayed what is known as "consciousness of guilt." The defense wished to argue that indeed the men had displayed consciousness of guilt, although not for the murders, but for the fact that they were both anarchists. Such an argument was perfectly lucid and persuasive, yet it snared the defense in a terrible catch: To make their argument before the jury, Sacco and Vanzetti would have to reveal their political beliefs and activities. This, the defense rightly thought, might prejudice the jury. Nevertheless, after studying the situation thoroughly, the defense decided that it had to discredit the prosecution's strong evidence of consciousness of guilt, even if the politics of the accused men were revealed in the process. After the defense lawyers informed Judge Thayer that this was their intention, the judge gave them an extra day to consider their options, and noted the risk of using this tactic. Still, the defense decided to open Pandora's box of anarchy in the courtroom.

Whether Sacco and Vanzetti were convicted based upon the weight of the evidence linking them to the murders or from prejudice against their political beliefs, we can never know. After the conviction, however, the snag that had tripped the defense now tripped the prosecution. How could Sacco and Vanzetti have had a fair trial if the jury knew they were anarchists?

This is the essence of the argument Frankfurter pled. In "The Case of Sacco and Vanzetti," Frankfurter's reasoning managed to turn what had been considered defects in the characters of Sacco and Vanzetti into assets. The more one pointed to Sacco and Vanzetti's open espousal of anarchist politics, the more they became the innocent victims of Red hysteria. Frankfurter argued not about the innocence or guilt of the two men but about the unfairness of their trial. It was a profoundly more penetrating argument. By suggesting the possibility of systemic judicial bias, Frankfurter had shifted discussion from the crime of the defendants to the lawlessness of the state, both in Judge Thayer's courtroom and in Attorney General Palmer's America. The Massachusetts judicial system had itself become an enemy of the law.

Judge Thayer well understood the depth of the accusation. In one opinion during the case he had even classified the defense's position as yet another kind of "hysteria . . . called 'lego-psychic neurosis'. . . which means: 'a belief in the existence of something which in fact and truth has no such existence.' . . . This disease would seem to have reached a very dangerous condition," Thayer surmised, when the defense charged "Mr. Sargent, Attorney General of the United States and his subordinates, and subordinates of the Former-Attorney General of the United States Mr. Palmer and . . . the District Attorney of Norfolk County, with being in a conspiracy to send these two defendants to the electric chair, not because they are murderers but because they are radicals."[23]

Frankfurter had never sought to enlighten Judge Thayer. From the beginning his cause had been to expose to the general public the impossibility of finding a fair verdict for two anarchists within the Massachusetts system of justice. For this reason Frankfurter had not joined the defense team or addressed officials of the Massachusetts courts. Rather, he had courted public opinion and had pled his case in that realm.

Frankfurter was familiar with what he once recognized as "the limited appeal that relevance has for a discussion."[24] Therefore, besides arguing over the specific evidence of the case, Frankfurter attempted to show the public that his opinion of the decrepit state of Massachusetts justice was not his alone but was also held by the majority of reasonable and respected members of Massachusetts society. To do this he appealed to several seemingly independent sources. He noted how much respectability the Sacco-Vanzetti cause had gained when the Boston attorney W. G. Thompson replaced the radical lawyer Fred Moore as lead counsel. "The espousal of the Sacco-Vanzetti cause by a man of Mr. Thompson's professional prestige at once gave it a new complexion and has been its mainstay ever since." Frankfurter also noted that distinguished journals of opinion now called for a retrial. "A study of [Thayer's] opinion in the light of the record led the conservative *Boston Herald*, which long held the view that the sentence against these men should be carried out, to a frank reversal of its position."[25] In his book-length exposition of the affair, also called *The Case of Sacco and Vanzetti*, Frankfurter recited the names and esteemed social positions of a drove of supporters from Massachusetts.[26] He also reminded readers of the general popularity of his cause, implying that world opinion was on his side. "A long succession of disclosures has aroused interest far beyond the boundaries of Massachusetts and even the United States, until the case has become one of those rare *causes célèbres* which are of international concern."[27] In this way Frankfurter meant to demonstrate how eminently reasonable, neutral, and global perspectives had come to agree with the narrative he suggested, seemingly by the simple force of the facts.

Frankfurter neglected to note, of course, that it was he who was most responsible for creating this wave of public opinion. If W. G. Thompson had brought respectability to the case, which he surely had, Frankfurter had arranged for Thompson to become lead counsel and had seen to his salary. If the *Boston Herald* and the New York *World* had come to defend Sacco and Vanzetti, it was through Frankfurter's direct campaign to achieve this end. Frankfurter had cultivated the opinions of the clan of Massachusetts Brahmins with equal vigor, both directly—through a campaign of letters to most everyone he knew of importance in Massachusetts—and indirectly—through his close friends on the Harvard Board of Overseers and similar institutions, most notably and consistently through Judge Julian Mack. With the help of W. G. Thompson's steady work in the courtroom,

Frankfurter had managed to carry the Sacco-Vanzetti cause beyond the labor journals in 1924 and into worldwide consciousness by 1927.

In no small part Felix Frankfurter had created the cause célèbre. Frankfurter had managed to represent Boston as "the establishment" to people in Sydney, Moscow, Paris, and Buenos Aires. He accomplished this by what may be regarded as an early example of political "spin," what Walter Lippmann understood as the cultivation of press contacts to manipulate the shape of public discussion. Frankfurter pitted two anarchists and the Boston establishment against one another, and then guided the public to the more just. The world round, people who imagined themselves as disenfranchised came to identify with Sacco and Vanzetti. It was a performance in the organization of public opinion equal to anything Walter Lippmann had in mind when he had popularized the concept in *Public Opinion* in 1922.[28]

Judge Thayer realized he needed help to counter this master of propaganda. He hurriedly informed the *New York Times*, "In reference to the articles published by Professor Frankenstein (sic) of Harvard in the *Atlantic Monthly*, I would say that these will be answered by one of the best authorities in the United States at the proper time."[29]

JOHN HENRY WIGMORE, Harvard Law classmate of Julian Mack, founding member of the *Harvard Law Review*, dean of the Northwestern School of Law, famous advocate of justice for the destitute, and author of the four-volume and definitive *Treatise on Evidence*, appeared in the pages of the *Boston Evening Transcript* to address the charges posed by Frankfurter. On April 25, 1927, and then again on May 10, Wigmore "offered a few words of refutation of a gross libel that is now being circulated." A "prominent pundit in a leading law school" had brought into question the fairness of the Sacco and Vanzetti trial, and had brought into question the justice of its verdict. The "dangerous plausibility" of the pundit's charge "naturally calls for some exposure of its errors."

The respected authority on criminal evidence, however, did not expose those errors very thoroughly. He blundered terribly when he accused Frankfurter of intentionally misquoting the record when Frankfurter had made no such mistake. Furthermore, Wigmore's tone was alarmist and injudicious. As he threw the politics of Sacco and Vanzetti in with "the thugs of India, the Camorra of Naples, the Black Hand of Sicily, the anarchists of czardom," Wigmore backed into Frankfurter's trap.[30] With such accusations, he demonstrated, more persuasively than Frankfurter could have hoped, that Sacco and Vanzetti could not have had a fair trial in such an atmosphere of bias. Yet Frankfurter did not even mention this in his rebuttal. He simply addressed Wigmore's technical arguments, carefully and gracefully disarmed every one of them, and declared "without fear of contradiction that Dean Wigmore could not have read the record." The considered opinion of America's foremost expert on criminal evidence had been based entirely on hateful passion.[31]

The rebuttal of Dean Wigmore marked Frankfurter's complete mastery of public opinion. The opposition had leveled its heaviest guns and thoroughly missed the target. From then on, Felix Frankfurter was the only public intellectual in the fracas; no one rose again to challenge him. Buried in Dean Wigmore's attack, however, beneath the indiscriminate accusations and name calling, rested a genuine and penetrating question that Frankfurter would never adequately address. "If any honorable member of the bar believed that he ought to help to secure a fair trial even for a bandit or a thug," Wigmore asked, "why should he not, as William G. Thompson here did, add his name gratuitously as of counsel, and assist in preparing and arguing the case up through the regular channels of justice? Why should he choose to appeal in the press to the general public outside the Court? Why should he abuse the Court itself in that appeal?"[32]

Frankfurter, after all, was a famous and respected figure of authority in American law. If he had joined the defense team, Wigmore thought, Frankfurter might have worked from within the judicial system of Massachusetts to ensure proper legal procedure. That participation would have both served the defendants and publicly affirmed Frankfurter's confidence in the judicial system. Instead, Frankfurter had trumpeted aloud from outside the system that two anarchists had not received a fair trial in Massachusetts. Thus Frankfurter had pitted the legitimacy of the Massachusetts judicial system squarely against two known anarchists, and had deliberately done so in public for all to see and interpret.

Frankfurter had never intended to support anarchism. He always distinguished carefully between the political beliefs of the defendants, with which he did not agree, and the importance of unbiased legal procedure. Yet by handling the Sacco and Vanzetti affair the way he had—by developing a public interest and then making his argument there—Frankfurter had created a situation easily misunderstood by the public to which he appealed. The public might take a retrial as evidence that capitalist courts were inherently unjust, as Sacco believed; it might equate a retrial with a legitimation of anarchist politics and criminality. Was it not incumbent on Frankfurter—professor of law at Harvard, respected member of the American legal system, figure of authority—to preclude this potential misreading by the public?

This was precisely what Theodore Roosevelt had claimed almost ten years earlier after the Mooney affair. Roosevelt had reminded Frankfurter that the guiding spirits of the anarchist movement were interested only in seeing "an evil lesson taught all public officials who might take action against crimes of violence committed by anarchists in the name of some foul and violent 'protest against social conditions.'" As a factor concerning the Sacco and Vanzetti affair, was this not as relevant as the right of the two men to a fair trial? As Roosevelt had argued (and as Wigmore had, in a less elegant way), when Frankfurter found himself "obliged to champion men of this stamp," he was responsible "by unequivocal affirmative action to make it evident that you are sternly against their general habitual line of conduct."[33] Roosevelt and Wigmore appealed to Frankfurter that if he felt it his duty to protect procedure in a case concerning violent radicals, it was equally his duty to maintain in the public mind the legitimacy of the courts and the government. As a figure of authority, if he could not so persuade and control the public mind, he had no business appealing to it on behalf of anarchists in the first place.

Indeed, that Frankfurter had made his appeal to the public was the most troubling part of his stand, even to those he considered his allies. One friend wrote, "I was very much disturbed by your book on the Sacco-Vanzetti case—not by the arguments, but by the fact that you wrote them."[34] When a bomb exploded at the home of a member of the Sacco-Vanzetti jury, Walter Lippmann suggested that Frankfurter might ask Vanzetti to appeal publicly to his anarchist comrades for nonviolence. Frankfurter replied coolly that "every kind of explosion in Massachusetts during the last years has been shrieked as 'Sacco bombs'—yet again and again later the charge has been denied."[35] Frankfurter would not recognize his own responsibility for having helped foster an excuse for the spree of anarchist violence becoming rampant as the media hype developed. To him there was only one issue, from which he would not be deterred. "I have consistently refused to make defense or otherwise divert attention from the central issue, and the only issue, namely, were the processes of criminal justice fairly and rightly applied in the sentences of death which now hang over these two Italians."[36] Frankfurter simply would not address the question of whether his manner of appeal to the public might have been irresponsible for a person of his stature in the legal community. Perhaps he did not recognize the danger, or perhaps he was uncomfortable with the special responsibilities coincident with the position of authority he occupied in America.

On June 1, 1927, at the behest of a sizable group of Massachusetts patricians and clergy, Governor Alvan T. Fuller created a special advisory committee to investigate the Sacco-Vanzetti trial so he might make an informed decision about executive clemency. On the three-person committee sat the president of MIT, Samuel Stratton; a retired judge, Robert Grant; and the president of Harvard University, A. Lawrence Lowell.

That the committee would be led by the force behind Harvard's Jewish quota concerned both Frankfurter and Harold Laski. Laski had been watching the events from the London School of Economics where he had moved after experiencing his own difficulties with the faculty and Overseers at Harvard over his radical politics.[37] Although distraught over the composition of the governor's committee, Laski wrote his friend Justice Holmes of his hope that "a reading of Felix's book ought to lead them to the salient points and result in a full pardon. It would be terrible to have an unsatisfactory ending with the Mooney case so recently before the attention of Europe."[38]

Instead, on August 3 the Lowell committee issued a short report that there was ample evidence with which to convict Sacco and Vanzetti. Lowell later explained that when Frankfurter's article first came out he had been "very much impressed," but when he read the evidence himself he felt forced to conclude that "the whole matter had been grossly misrepresented to the public."[39]

The next day Judge Julian Mack wrote a frantic note to Frankfurter. "I was up until the news came last night. It is terribly crushing. I just cannot understand it, and if Lowell's report is no better than Fuller's decision, it will be a complete evasion of all of the questions that you raised. . . . It is too crushing to think about."[40]

At the New York *World*, Walter Lippmann also envisioned the end. After the Lowell report, he felt that the *World* should make a simple and direct plea for mercy to the governor. He thought that any criticism of the report would only ensure the executions of the men. Frankfurter insisted, however, that the report be discredited. He would not have the affair end ambiguously with a merciful reprieve granted from the governor without the courts' having admitted wrongdoing. Frankfurter desired nothing less than either an admission from the executive office that the judiciary had acted injudiciously or a retrial, which would be tantamount to an admission. Frankfurter took a train to New York City. After a long meeting with Lippmann and his editorial staff, Frankfurter convinced the *World* to publish a criticism of the Lowell report.[41]

Meanwhile, Arthur Garfield Hays drove to Ludlow, Vermont, to find Attorney General Sargent at his summer home. Hays believed that if Sacco and Vanzetti had been under government surveillance for their anarchist activities, official records might contain alibis for the two men on the day of the murder. The attorney general greeted Hays in his bathrobe, listened genteelly but casually to Hays's request, and then diverted the New York lawyer to Assistant Attorney General Farnum in Washington, D.C. On his way to Washington, Hays dashed off a telegram to Calvin Coolidge asking, as counsel to Sacco and Vanzetti, to meet with the president. "It seems to us that the honor of our country would be irretrievably sullied if these men were put to death when millions of people sincerely believe that important evidence is kept secret by the Government."[42] Hays did not get his meeting with Coolidge, and the assistant attorney general did not permit Hays to see the classified records. Hays returned to the Massachusetts State House, where, on August 22, the day before the executions, Governor Fuller listened to appeals from most anyone who cared to come in. When Hays got his chance he asked the governor to postpone the executions until the secret government records could be subpoenaed and checked. After some polite questions the governor finally asked, "Don't you think I know more about this case than you do?"[43]

Others made appeals to Justice Holmes for a writ of habeas corpus based on his dissent in the Leo Frank case of 1914 when the justice had argued that violent, antisemitic mobs outside the courthouse where Frank was tried had unduly affected the decision of the jury. For Sacco and Vanzetti, however, Holmes held that no such violent threat had existed, and that "a line must be drawn between external force, and prejudice—which could be alleged in every case."[44]

Harold Laski had been needling Holmes about Frankfurter and the Sacco-Vanzetti case for months. Once he wrote to Holmes how Frankfurter's response to Wigmore had given him much pleasure. At another point he compared Sacco and Vanzetti to Leo Frank and Alfred Dreyfus. He confidently pontificated to the justice of the U.S. Supreme Court that "the whole thing is an injustice characteristic of the American courts."[45]

Holmes did not respond. He waited until Sacco and Vanzetti were dead and thereby unquestionably out of his jurisdiction. The day after their executions he fired a note off to Laski: "Your last letter shows you stiffed up like the rest of the world on the Sacco Vanzetti case. . . . [M]y prejudices are against the convictions," he announced, "but they are still stronger against the run of the shriekers." Then, Justice Holmes—author of the historic dissent to the Abrams case concerning wartime censorship and thereby one of the greatest champions of free speech ever to sit on the Court—explained to Harold Laski what Theodore Roosevelt had explained to Felix Frankfurter. No responsible person in a position of authority could ignore the danger of giving stage to the political views of anarchists, views that were decidedly not about justice: "The lovers of justice," he thundered, "have emphasized their love by blowing up a building or two and there are guards in all sorts of places, including one for this house."[46] A week later Holmes repeated his lesson. "I think the row that has been made idiotical, if considered on its merits, but of course it is not on the merits that the row is made, but because it gives the extremists a chance to yell." As to the merits of the Sacco-Vanzetti defense, he concluded definitively, "I doubt if anyone would say that there was no evidence warranting a conviction."[47] Laski said no more about it.

Holmes had not quite finished his lesson, however, which the eighty-nine-year-old justice delivered more gently three years after the affair. "I think that the wisest men from Confucius and Aristotle to Lincoln (if he is entitled to the superlative) have believed in the *via media*," Holmes wrote Laski. "I say it because little things once in a while make me wonder if your sympathies are taking a more extreme turn as time goes on. I always am uncertain how far Frankfurter goes. But I notice that he and you are a good deal more stirred by Sacco and Vanzetti, who were turned into a text by the reds, than by a thousand worse things among the blacks."[48]

Sacco and Vanzetti had been turned into a "text by the reds," and Frankfurter, by choosing two anarchists as his test case for Massachusetts justice, had served that violent cause. There had been enough injustices in the courts against wholly innocent African Americans with which Frankfurter might have made his point. Holmes himself had been wounded three times in the Civil War for that cause. Civil rights for African Americans, Holmes noted, lay along the via media. Yet instead of taking up their cause and heralding justice from along the via media, always a more persuasive and responsible position from which to speak, Professor Frankfurter had chosen to flirt with political extremists.

JUSTICE BRANDEIS had no such lesson for Frankfurter. Brandeis had been as partisan and active for Sacco and Vanzetti as a justice of the Supreme Court could be. Perhaps his actions went beyond the ethical limits for a judge who might have had to hear the case. At the behest of his close friend Elizabeth Glendower Evans (Auntie B.), Brandeis had enlisted Frankfurter to find a lawyer and maintain a watchful eye on the case. Frankfurter did much more than this, of course, but entirely with the justice's blessing. Brandeis had encouraged Frankfurter's courting of the press and waited impatiently to read Frankfurter's book on Sacco and Vanzetti. He hoped the book would "prove an event of importance with bench & bar; perhaps a turning point."[49] In April 1927, after the Supreme Judicial Court of Massachusetts denied yet another appeal, Brandeis comforted Frankfurter by suggesting their action would help "the holy cause. . . . Another instance of 'the Blood of the Martyrs becoming the seed of the Church.'"[50]

The night before the execution, however, when lawyers for Sacco and Vanzetti approached Brandeis on his front porch in Chatham, Massachusetts, for a writ of habeas corpus, just as they had approached Holmes, Brandeis refused even to listen. He had become too close to the case, he admitted. He had shown too much sympathy. Auntie B., his friend, had been a basic force in the defense of Sacco and Vanzetti, and his wife and daughter had become active as well. And there was his relationship with Frankfurter himself. Furthermore, he knew there were no grounds on which the Supreme Court might reverse the decision of the Supreme Judicial Court of Massachusetts. By the time the matter had reached him, the cause was already lost.

The public did not understand Brandeis's or Holmes's decision. "These two Justices are the symbols of liberalism in the Federal Supreme Court," Vanzetti wrote in one of his last letters, "and they turned us their shoulders [sic]."[51] Horace Kallen absolutely agreed. He wrote Frankfurter expressing utter disbelief of what had happened. "What was a slap in the face to me," he said, "was not so much Holmes as L.D.B. How could he have evaded the issue like that?"[52] Later, Kallen further explained himself to Judge Mack. No legal rationale should have prevented Brandeis from stepping in, he thought. "It was not merely the lives of the two men that were at stake," Kallen wrote, "but a whole complex of ideals and perspectives so tangled and so profound that nothing but arbitrary action could have saved them from the arbitrary action which has destroyed them. There is more to say than I can write."[53] For Kallen, Sacco and Vanzetti had come to represent the "whole complex of ideals" of cultural pluralism and the right to be different. In the case against the two anarchists, Kallen thought, American legal procedure had become arbitrary— not progressive or scientific—and it was, therefore, an obstacle to true American ideals. If the American system of justice could not see to adequate justice for "hyphenated Americans" no matter their extreme or violent political beliefs, then Justice Brandeis should have stepped out of his office as upholder of that law and defied the American system of justice.

Judge Mack responded passionately to Kallen's suggestion, himself swept away by the revolutionary spirit the Sacco and Vanzetti case had aroused. "I too believe in revolution," Judge Mack pledged to Kallen, "whether it be the American, the French, or the Russian. I too believe that there are times when the mob is fully justified in taking matters into its own hands. But I can never believe that a judge, *pretending* to exercise the judicial function, would deliberately evade the law and exert his own unrestricted judgment as to what is best for the community."[54] Though Mack ultimately backed Brandeis's decision, he had applied incredible language in doing so: revolution, mob rule, vigilantism. That was how much Frankfurter's Sacco and Vanzetti campaign had damaged even Judge Mack's beliefs in America, its judicial system, and its democratic process. And yet he and Frankfurter shared a more balanced view than Kallen with respect to judicial authority. After Mack informed Frankfurter about Kallen's plea for "arbitrary action," Frankfurter wrote Kallen that he was "shocked beyond expression." "Your ethic seems to me as vicious, as its tactics seem to be self-defeating," Frankfurter lectured. "You are just like the anarchist Tories—because S and V don't believe in law, we must be lawless! says Harry Kallen—since the other side throw[s] overboard what we pitifully are seeking to build up, we must throw our whole case overboard and surrender the essential ethical claims we made and make in this case. Really, Harry, I am more disturbed that such an outlook seriously guides you than I dare put in words."[55] To Frankfurter, Sacco and Vanzetti had represented a singular battle to uphold the tradition of Anglo-American justice, represented in this instance by the right to a fair trial for all. Frankfurter understood that as a judge, Brandeis could not overtly transgress the legal process, even to uphold that right.

If the Jewish press agreed with either camp, it was decidedly that of Horace Kallen. The various voices of the Jewish press concluded, categorically, that Brandeis had failed them, although their reasons differed. Support for Sacco and Vanzetti from Jewish labor had come early in the case. As early as 1923, the Sacco-Vanzetti Defense Committee published a twenty-page autobiography of Vanzetti called "The Story of a Proletarian Life," which the committee had translated into Yiddish. Excepting this early interest from the more radical portions of the Jewish needle trades, most Jews followed the rest of America and paid little attention to the curious trial in Boston until Frankfurter published his article in the March 1927 edition of the *Atlantic Monthly*. The article, combined with Frankfurter's covert campaign for public support, brought world attention to the Sacco-Vanzetti case, including that of Albert Einstein, which the Yiddish press duly noted in the headlines of its first coverage of the case.[56]

The *Forverts*, a socialist newspaper, maintained one unswerving stand that paralleled the campaign of other American communists and socialists: Sacco and Vanzetti were simply "two sacrifices for class justice." The *Forverts* saw the entire episode from within this predictable perspective of class struggle, and accused Brandeis of participating, albeit unwittingly, in the capitalist conspiracy.[57]

The *Yidishes Tageblat* was a daily that considered itself socially conservative, which meant it supported the American government and what it thought to be mainstream American mores. Nevertheless, after the Lowell Report was released and Governor Fuller proclaimed his intention to see the death sentences through, the *Yidishes Tageblat* respectfully suggested that the governor was responsible to persuade the millions throughout the world who still had doubts about Massachusetts justice.[58] "One should forget all of the awful propaganda and pay attention only to the details of the case itself," the paper advised the governor, itself disgusted by the radical rhetoric.[59] The higher meaning of the case, the paper thought, was not class conflict but rather "justice forlorn," for in fact the two men were innocent. The details of the case would prove the innocence of Sacco and Vanzetti, just as they would bring justice back to Massachusetts. When the two men were executed, the paper predicted that "the feeling of justice will long remain unsatisfied and doubting." "We can only sincerely wish," the paper offered, "that this feeling of doubt will not be transformed into a feeling of bitterness and an accusation against the entire system of American justice."[60]

Der Tog, a liberal newspaper, agreed with the *Yidishes Tageblat* that the issue was not class. Nevertheless, *Der Tog* thought that Sacco and Vanzetti represented something other than the unfortunate but honest mistake of Massachusetts justice. *Der Tog* thought the issue was injustice for those who were not part of the ruling group. The paper proclaimed the inherent injustice of a system in which "a 'Yankee' from Yankeeland"—by which it meant Governor Fuller— "decides the fate of two poor, foreign, condemned men." The paper recognized that Sacco and Vanzetti were not Jews, and that Jews as a group had no obvious connection to the two Italians. To those readers who asked "What have Sacco and Vanzetti got to do with us?" *Der Tog* cried out: "Jews!—because Dreyfus was a Jew!"[61] Thus *Der Tog* compared the antisemitic injustice the French military courts administered Alfred Dreyfus, a Jewish captain in the French army, to the behavior of the Commonwealth of Massachusetts. Jews and Italians around the world, the paper thought, were equally vulnerable outsiders.

The theme of injustice for groups outside of the political establishment was continued by *Der Amerikaner un Froyen Magazin*, which supposed "if the prisoners had been American citizens and not foreigners, the jury would have found sympathy," and Sacco and Vanzetti "would not have been 'railroaded.'" But the two were "underdogs" and therefore the jury could not see its way through to the truth of Sacco and Vanzetti's innocence. As had the other moderate Jewish papers, *Der Amerikaner* publicly disagreed with the radical interpretation of the events. "This was not about class hate, as the communists would like to believe," the paper claimed. Rather the Sacco and Vanzetti trial turned on "a race conflict of Nordics against non-Nordics." "And that," the paper confidently told its readers, "is the source of the protest from liberals in America and from all parts of Europe."[62]

The reasons suggested by the Yiddish press differed, but their support for Sacco and Vanzetti as outsiders was unqualified. Everywhere, the Yiddish press scolded Justice Brandeis for refusing to grant a writ of habeas corpus for the two convicted men. Everyone proclaimed surprise when even the *Morgen Zhurnal*, usually the voice of religious orthodoxy and cultural isolationism, joined in the lambasting. "The Jewish Justice of the United States Supreme Court had an excellent opportunity to stay the execution of Sacco and Vanzetti," the *Morgen Zhurnal* wrote, "and millions of Jews will regret that he did not find it proper to make use of it." The paper had no patience for legalistic arguments that defended Brandeis's position. "He was the right man on the Supreme Court to break through the wall of 'technicalities' which have prevented the sentenced from obtaining a new trial. . . . A doubt of 1 percent against 99 should have been sufficient to forget what is proper [legally] and what is not proper." The paper then noted with ethnic pride unusual to its columns that "more people among us [Jews] than among other men and women were against the execution of the sentence" and further thought that "it would have made a marvelous impression upon the entire world if a Jew would give the word for which tens of millions waited with the greatest suspense. Even such persons who believe that under normal circumstances it is better for the Jew not to attract too much attention would admit that this case is an exception."[63]

Unlike the Yiddish press, the English-language Jewish press tended not to take explicit positions on the Sacco and Vanzetti case at the time of the executions, although several carefully worded treatises on the themes of justice, the death penalty, and even circumstantial evidence seemed to cluster in the August and September 1927 issues of those magazines. Also, the *Menorah Journal* printed a qualified accolade of leftist Jewish political activity in its considered opinion of "The Jew as a Radical" in those months, and the Chicago *Sentinel* dared to ask "Is Justice Brandeis Guilty?"—and to answer in the affirmative. Two years after the execution, the *American Hebrew* safely declared its postmortem partisanship for "the lives of a poor shoemaker and fish peddler who were executed by the state of Massachusetts for a crime of which the whole intelligent world believed them innocent."[64]

It remains the irony of the episode that in the shoring up of unanimous support among American Jewry for the two Italians, Brandeis, who had originally suggested the cause to his protégé Frankfurter, became the traitor to Jewish ideals. Brandeis stood by his decision, however, and ignored the accusations of the Jewish press. Although ultimately Brandeis could do nothing for the two Italians, he greatly admired Frankfurter's actions. Brandeis realized that Frankfurter had superseded him as "the people's lawyer" by taking a case that Brandeis himself would never have considered in his days of argument before the bench. Brandeis had lawyered in the classic progressive mode, aiding the government to protect the worker and the poor, though neglecting civil rights. Frankfurter had advanced the technique of the liberal lawyer by directly representing persons of extreme political views and suspected criminal activity. Thus Frankfurter had combined his tea-shop social education from the Lower East Side with Brandeis's style of progressive lawyering—West and East—to create a new Jewish ideal: the lawyer bent on administering justice by defending the civil rights of everyone, including—perhaps especially—outsiders. Brandeis came to call Frankfurter "the most useful lawyer in the United States."[65] After the executions of Sacco and Vanzetti, Brandeis sent Frankfurter his condolences with the hopeful prophecy: "To the end, you have done all that was possible for you, and that all was more than would have [been] possible for any other person I know. But the end of S.V. is only the beginning. 'They know not what they do.'"[66]

Aftermath

NOT MANY THINGS left Felix Frankfurter speechless. Yet when he was called to accept an award from the National Institute for Immigrant Welfare he stumbled with his words. "I can express with very limited adequacy," he said, "the passionate devotion to this land that possesses millions of our people, born, like myself, under other skies, for the privilege that this country has bestowed in allowing them to partake of its fellowship."[1] Frankfurter believed passionately in American democracy; he dedicated his life to the administration of that democracy. As a young man he had left the world and the money of corporate law to serve what he considered a higher calling, first in the office of the U.S. attorney in New York and then in Washington. When Frankfurter thought that his effectiveness in Washington was waning he returned to Harvard to teach administrative law and hoped to affect the execution of democracy from behind the lectern.

Ultimately, Frankfurter believed that the great American experiment relied upon properly informed citizens. He explained in 1928: "In a democracy, politics is a process of popular education—the task of adjusting the conflicting interests of diverse groups in the community, and bending the hostility and suspicion and ignorance engendered by group interest to the reconciliation of a common interest and a common understanding."[2] To Frankfurter, his work for Sacco and Vanzetti was a calculated exercise in public education and the realignment of group interest. He had a lesson to teach America. What was it?

At the time of the affair, many thought Frankfurter's defense of Sacco and Vanzetti tantamount to a defense of their anarchist politics. Of course Frankfurter was no anarchist. Today the public often hears of an attorney who represents a known criminal or a violent political cause, not in the name of the crime or the cause, but to maintain the legal rights of the accused. But in 1928 if this position existed at all, it was only nascent. With Scopes and with Leopold and Loeb, for instance, Clarence Darrow appealed to no particular legal right of the accused. He simply disagreed with the law as written. If anyone had progressed to the position we find today, of the lawyer who defends the known criminal in the name of the law, it was Arthur Garfield Hays, willing to take most any case "that involved liberty in some form or another. . . . Would I defend the individual Nazi in this country if his civil rights were violated?" he asked himself in 1942. "Probably I would."[3]

This was not Frankfurter's position. In the case of Sacco and Vanzetti, he did not advocate civil rights and liberties for their own sake. He did, however, believe in the right to unprejudiced, proper criminal procedure, and he took the letter of this law, and all democratically authorized law, "very seriously, deeply seriously," he said, "because fragile as reason is and limited as law is as the expression of the institutionalized medium of reason, that's all we have standing between us and the tyranny of mere will and the cruelty of unbridled, undisciplined feeling."[4]

Frankfurter believed to his core that unbridled, undisciplined feeling, embodied by the Massachusetts courts, had convicted Sacco and Vanzetti, and that nothing short of an appeal to the public could save others who might find themselves in such a position. If only he could educate establishment Boston that they were mistaken, that he, Felix Frankfurter, Jew from Leopoldstadt, was the true voice of Anglo-American law. To a Back Bay lawyer he complained of the "anarchists among the so called respectables," and of the "blissful ignorance of some of the leaders of our own profession in Boston who said that the men ought to die, guilty or not." When the Boston lawyer suggested that Frankfurter repeat that he did not share the political views of anarchism, and that he affirm the rightness of government and law, Frankfurter exploded into a blaze of rage and despair.

Have you ever seen a line I have written, or ever heard me utter a word that expressed or indicated a disbelief in government or law? . . . What have you—or some of my other critics—ever done for law and order compared with my five years work as a prosecutor, or my work on the Cleveland survey of criminal justice, and my present work on the Boston Crime Survey, to make the criminal machinery more effective? My whole life has been given to Law—and wouldn't it look silly for me to write a letter saying "I believe in law." You'll next be asking me to deny that I believe in free love and make public avowal of my love for my wife!

"But I suggest that you consider what law really means," Frankfurter continued, and answered the charge that he had tried to "frighten" upper-class Boston into action by heralding the rights of two vocally violent anarchists. Here, Frankfurter finally answered the accusations of Theodore Roosevelt, John H. Wigmore, and his hero Oliver Wendell Holmes, and proclaimed his most frank utterance about what he deeply believed to be his vocation: "Anybody can give law to his friends," he said: *it's the essence of law to give it to our enemies!*"[5]

Although Anglo-American jurisprudence is structured to hear the arguments of adversaries, Frankfurter meant something more than just this. In the case of Sacco and Vanzetti, Frankfurter intentionally had not joined the defense table. To repeat the accusation of Wigmore, Frankfurter had chosen to "abuse the Court." He had done this because he needed to teach Boston what it could never learn for itself from within: that the very complex of the Massachusetts legal system was in fact the enemy of law, that the entirety of establishment Boston was in fact the enemy of Anglo-American justice. As professor of law at Harvard, and not as private counsel to Sacco and Vanzetti, Frankfurter thought it his duty to deliver this lesson to Boston. He had to instruct the enemies of law and Anglo-American justice who sat in the Union Club, in the Back Bay, in the president's chair at Harvard, and in the governor's mansion. To Frankfurter, establishment Boston was not simply of a different, legitimate, legal opinion about Sacco and Vanzetti. It was not just wrong about the crime in South Braintree. Its entire worldview was systemically corrupt. Frankfurter had to teach Boston what he *knew*.

Yet Boston would not listen. For Frankfurter, a casual comment made by John F. Moors, Boston Brahmin and yet a supporter of Sacco and Vanzetti, summed the entire affair by personifying establishment Massachusetts in the form of the president of Harvard. "Lawrence

Lowell was incapable of seeing that two wops could be right and the Yankee judiciary could be wrong." "That posed a dilemma for Lowell which his mind couldn't overreach," Frankfurter thought. "His crowd, the Yankees, were right, and the alien immigrants were what they were—pacifists and draft dodgers. He was incapable of doing what men have done, namely, say their crowd was wrong."[6]

For Frankfurter the case had revolved around "crowds." There were those who could see the simple truth that Sacco and Vanzetti were innocent, and those who were inhibited by the worldview of their group that would not allow political outsiders to be innocent. When A. Lawrence Lowell had submitted the Lowell Report to the governor, he was not being dishonest or unscrupulous, Frankfurter thought. His Yankee perspective could not perceive the truth. The two Italians had managed to blind Lowell's crowd—"the Yankees"— to the basic principles of law and justice. For this reason Frankfurter thought the Sacco-Vanzetti affair possessed "almost every important, really sizable issue that cuts deeply into the feelings and judgments and conduct of the community, implicates factors that transcend the immediate individuals who, in the main, are instruments of forces that affect many, many beyond the immediate actors in the affair."[7]

What were these group forces that blinded men to law and truth? "I can give myself some answers," Frankfurter said.

People want to avoid unpleasantness. Life is hard enough even if you've got a bank account. Life is hard enough as it is. Why take on something extra? "Why go out on a limb?" as the phrase runs. "Why stick your neck out?" that other lovable invitation to do nothing! Even people who are economically independent are not socially independent. They may have money in the bank, but that isn't all they want. They want to be asked to dinners at certain houses. They want to run for office. They want to become Grand Masters of the Masonic Order. They want to get a degree from some college or university. They don't want to make trouble for their wives. They have silly wives with social interests or ambitions. Or if they get into public controversies their boy in prep school will be a marked character, "Oh, it's your Dad who says this." There are a thousand and one considerations beyond the immediate enslavement of economic dependence which I know make people hesitant, timid, cowardly.[8]

Frankfurter intended to write a second work on the case of Sacco and Vanzetti that would expose the insipid worldview of the enemies of law in Massachusetts and throughout America that excluded outsiders because of timidity, cowardice, and misplaced group feeling. This book would be less passionate than the thin, devastating one he had dropped into calm Boston Bay in spring 1927. He intended to write a careful, scientific study in which he would gently demonstrate the "psychological forces whereby the most influential citizens of Boston, with rare exception, failed to see that the great way to vindicate the greatness of the Puritan tradition was to show that 'a good shoemaker and a poor fish-peddler' were not real threats to the security of the Commonwealth."[9] Someday, after the tension had eased, after Harvard and Boston had returned to the pace of New England life, Frankfurter would explain to the establishment of Massachusetts the essence of its Puritan tradition of law and justice for all, and how it became forsaken one summer in the execution of two innocent outsiders.

He had wished acutely to say something while the men were still alive. "Every instinct of my nature impelled me to speak out," he wrote W. G. Thompson, "but I found . . . that I was the center of irritation and hostility (to put it mildly) and any peep from me would harden still more the stern purpose to kill Sacco and Vanzetti. . . . When I tell you that Wiggin [counsel to the governor] . . . still circulates the statement that one of 'the gravest features of the whole business' is that I should for years have been on 'the secret payroll of the Sacco-Vanzetti Defense Committee' and have gotten big money for stirring up the whole matter, and that I'm at the bottom of it all, etc., etc., etc."[10]

His thought trailed off. That he had accepted "big money" had been an antisemitic accusation that appeared the moment Frankfurter had entered the case. Furthermore, Frankfurter felt it was no coincidence that he, personally, along with the two Italians, had become in the mind of Boston "the center of irritation and hostility." "Criticism of me," Frankfurter wrote Julian Mack, "in the conservative circles in Boston . . . is compounded of the fact that I am supposed to be a 'radical,' at all events that my views run counter to their opinions and that it so happens I am not only an outsider in this community, but also a Jew."[11] Because of his outsider status in Boston, Frankfurter felt, he had understood the position of the two Italians. As an outsider and as a Jew, he could see what Lawrence Lowell and his crowd of Yankees could never see. "I have read a little history," he reflected as fall turned to winter in 1927, "and had some personal contact with the forces of fear and hate operating against outcast people and outcast opinion." Accordingly, Frankfurter had seen Sacco and Vanzetti as two of his own. When they died for being outsiders, as Frankfurter believed they had, his dream of America died a little, too. Still, he tried to understand his deep emotional response to their executions abstractly, philosophically, and with detachment. "I think I can honestly say that the sadness of it all is very impersonal."[12]

SACCO AND VANZETTI remained in the popular Jewish imagination for some time. Yiddish plays about the affair were written. Annual memorials were held. A young Jewish artist and immigrant from Russia by the name of Ben Shahn took on the depiction of the Sacco-Vanzetti affair as the basis of his life's work. Arthur Garfield Hays became a hero to the English-language Jewish press.[13]

The political implications of the Sacco and Vanzetti affair for the rest of America were enormous. Politically, Frankfurter had helped to quash the dying progressivism of the Republican Party among upper-class liberals, and introduced them to the nascent civil rights and social welfare policy of the Democrats. At the level of working-class politics, labor historian David Montgomery has said that the massive demonstrations for Sacco and Vanzetti deserve much credit for emulsifying the political organization of the labor movement, thereby linking labor to the Democratic left and forming the voting block that would elect Franklin D. Roosevelt and his New Deal.[14]

Frankfurter might have been proud to think so. Nevertheless, he had taken the case to accomplish the more modest task of saving the two Italians from being railroaded by a worldview of intolerance bigger than the two of them or Frankfurter or the very ideal of Anglo-American law. The truth was very simple. "The two men were innocent," Frankfurter explained to one inquirer after the ordeal was over, "as innocent as you and I."[15]

Two years after the affair, after Frankfurter's wife, Marion, had collected and published the letters of Sacco and Vanzetti, Walter Lippmann wrote a kind note to Marion. "If Vanzetti was a professional bandit," Lippmann assured her, "then historians and biographers who attempt to deduce character from personal documents might as well shut up shop. By every test that I know of for judging character these letters are overwhelming proof of innocence."

"These two sentences," Felix Frankfurter wrote back to Lippmann, "(you will, of course, include Sacco) seem to me powerfully telling and I hope you will permit their use."[16] Frankfurter must have intended to use Lippmann's observation in the book he would never write, in which he would explain how the Yankees had been blind to a truth obvious to everyone not of their crowd.

Alas, perhaps it was Frankfurter's confidence in his eye, trained as he thought it was as an outcast of Boston—perhaps it was this outcast's eye that had failed him and thereby helped create the fiction that became the international fury. For in 1983 a team of impartial ballistics experts, under the supervision of Dr. Henry Lee (now known for his work during the O. J. Simpson trial) examined the bullet that killed the paymaster of the Slater Morill Shoe Company that April afternoon, 1920, and determined definitively that it came from the Colt automatic of Nicola Sacco.[17]

Jazz Age Culture

GILBERT SELDES knew something about high art. After all, he was a writer and critic by trade, well connected to the major cultural currents of the 1920s through his position as managing editor of *The Dial* literary magazine. He had reviewed James Joyce's *Ulysses* favorably when it was first published, and oversaw the November 1922 issue of *The Dial* featuring T. S. Eliot's poem "The Wasteland." Seldes also shared a longtime literary relationship with F. Scott Fitzgerald, particularly after he reviewed *The Great Gatsby*, calling it a masterpiece and hailing Fitzgerald as "leaving even farther behind all the men of his own generation."[1] That review grated on Ernest Hemingway, who lampooned it tartly in his first novel, *The Sun Also Rises*. Seldes became a lifelong focus of Hemingway's anxiety, and was derided even from the grave, as it were, when he was mocked in *A Moveable Feast*, published posthumously in 1964. But Hemingway's obsession seldom bothered Seldes. When it did, he could take comfort in the company of other such celebrated friends as Pablo Picasso, who sometimes drew silly portraits for him.

Though he lived among great artists, Seldes also enjoyed the popular, or "lively" arts. In 1923 he drew up an outline for a book he called *The 7 Lively Arts*, in which he intended to discuss these popular forms:

Slapstick Moving Pictures
Comic Strips
Revues
Musical Comedy
Colyums [*newspaper columns*]
Slang Humour

Popular Songs
Vaudeville[2]

That he had listed eight mattered little. It was the treatment of popular material by an established critic that was so surprising. In his book, Seldes went on for pages about such seemingly inane subjects as the "Krazy Kat" comic strip and the Tin Pan Alley songs of Irving Berlin and Jerome Kern. He loved Charlie Chaplin's character "the Little Tramp," and wasn't the least embarrassed to praise Ziegfeld's raunchy and fun revue, the *Follies*.

Traveling shows, popular songs, burlesque, minstrel acts, and circuses were all longtime American traditions. Advances in media technology, however, suddenly introduced local and popular talent to a national audience. Vaudeville stars could perform in the family room on the radio, and Broadway headliners were seen in movies along every Main Street. Even the improving highway system helped live entertainers put "the show on the road." Some thought that with the new technology, popular arts might someday replace the high arts. In 1923 movie director D. W. Griffith was asked to foresee American life in the twenty-first century. "The great publishing industry will be the publishing of motion pictures instead of print," he thought. "Motion picture libraries will be as common as private libraries to-day—more so."[3]

As prescient as that prediction may now seem, in the 1920s after scarcely a decade of the studio system, the movies were still experienced primarily in public. At the local American movie theater, of which there were about twelve thousand in 1921, audiences gathered to see one of the seven hundred films produced by domestic studios each year. In the big cities that supported such regal theaters as Loew's, the Paramount, the Fox, the Keith, the Orpheum, or the Majestic, patrons were greeted at the curb by uniformed attendants, had their Saturday-night overcoats checked, were guided to assigned seats by flashlight, enjoyed a vaudeville style show before the feature, and ran off to loll in the palatial rest rooms over which these theaters competed for their luxury. Only then, after a mood of fantasy and import had been established, did the lights go down for the silent Hollywood feature.[4]

The three popular artists who Gilbert Seldes most admired were Charlie Chaplin, Fanny Brice, and Al Jolson, all of whom started on the stage but migrated to the screen when film came to dominate the popular arts. All three were Jewish (as was Seldes himself), but only Brice and Jolson identified themselves as Jewish on stage and in film and included Jewish mannerisms and jokes as part of their acts. Seldes enjoyed this immensely, and thought he understood why many other Americans did, as well. Seldes wrote, "These two stars bring something to America which America lacks and loves—they are, I suppose, two of our most popular entertainers—and . . . both are racially out of the dominant caste. Possibly this accounts for their fine carelessness about our superstitions of politeness and gentility."[5] Whatever the reason, Brice and Jolson were indeed two of America's favorite performers in the 1920s. They were so popular that in 1928, Walt Disney, then a young cartoonist, may have dressed a new mouse character (later named Mickey) in white gloves to look like Al Jolson—in blackface.

PART III

"Mammy, Don't You Know Me?": Al Jolson and the Jews

Let me sing of Dixie's charms,
Of cotton fields and Mammy's arms,
And if my song can make you homesick,
I'm happy.

*Irving Berlin, "Let Me Sing
And I'm Happy"*

Al Jolson

HE COULD play the innocent. With a simple purse of his lips, Al Jolson could break your heart. Yet his eyes always seemed to suggest the way to the bedroom, particularly to the pretty faces in the front row. Above those eyes switched thick eyebrows that could arch to recount the tale of Jewish suffering that endlessly entertained his audiences. His features were proudly Jewish. His shtick was proudly Jewish. And every night, often three hundred nights a year, he smeared burnt cork all over that Jewish face and pretended he was black.

For his minstrel act, everyone called Jolson the World's Greatest Entertainer. "He was a no-good son-of-a-bitch," George Jessel remembered more than twenty years after Jolson's death, "but he was the greatest entertainer I've ever seen."[1]

Though the transformation from Jew to black required thick coats of theater makeup, it wasn't such a messy affair. A *New York Times* critic once noted "the dexterity with which Mr. Jolson outlines his mouth . . . as he smears his face with black."[2] First came a light roll of the burnt cork between the palms and fingers. When the cork was sufficiently warmed by his hands, Jolson would swipe across his upper lip and chin and then his jowls, left and right. Caught somewhere between black and white, his famous Mammy's boy mouth now formed, Jolson liked to pause.

The details came next: nose, chin, brow, ears, neck, and the job was all but done. Only a woolen skullcap remained. Finally, with the wig snugly on his head and a grin flashing white slices of teeth, Asa Yoelson came to embody his own imagination of American blackness. Throughout the 1910s and 1920s, sometimes with an overall strap falling from his shoulder and a straw hat on his head, sometimes in his plantation suit of black, but always painted and bewigged, Jolson took center stage and performed hundreds of blackface routines, all of which were entirely invented visions of African-American culture, most of which would now be considered terribly offensive.

The strongest intimations of the offense have been captured in filmed re-creations and expansions of Jolson's stage shows. Take, for instance, the centerpiece of Jolson's 1934 film *Wonder Bar*, a skit called "Goin' to Heaven on a Mule," whose choreography rivaled the very best of the elaborate dance fantasies of Depression-era Hollywood. In fact, "Goin' to Heaven on a Mule" was an Al Jolson–Busby Berkeley collaboration. Although this particular routine had not appeared in the stage version of *Wonder Bar*, it was well within the tradition of minstrel skits in which Jolson had participated since childhood. Of course, the choreography for a film could be more fantastic than that of a stage production, yet Berkeley's production is true to the stage form in that it is a grand cinematic tribute to Jolson's career and lifelong fascination with blackness. An attempt to imagine black without white, "Goin' to Heaven on a Mule" is nothing less than Jolson's final vision of "coon heaven."[3]

In the shade of a slave's cabin, with a burnt-corked baby bouncing on his knee, the blackfaced and overalled Al Jolson imagines an entirely black hereafter, and further imagines that it is approached on the back of "an old Missouri mule" named Zeke. Standing next to a blackfaced St. Peter, "Mammy waits at those pearly gates." Old Black Joe is there. Uncle Tom is there. The Emperor Jones is there too. In heaven's barbershop, blackfaced customers read a Yiddish newspaper called *Der Gan Eden Stern* (The Garden of Eden Star) and appear to understand it. Complete with watermelons that dance, pork chops that grow from the trees, and roast chickens that fly, "Goin' to Heaven on a Mule" was Al Jolson's self-recognized masterpiece. He had outdone himself and he knew it. Jolson was so taken with the number that he considered it the greatest film production to date.

He may not have been wrong to think so. This was Busby Berkeley's first mature choreography, and the heaven scenes would later be taken, practically frame-for-frame, and incorporated into the Emerald City scenes of *The Wizard of Oz* (1939). Today when *Wonder Bar* is shown on television, usually late at night, "Goin' to Heaven on a Mule" is discretely edited out because of scheduling constraints.

Jews performed this kind of minstrelsy in the 1910s and 1920s better and more often than any other group in America. Jewish faces covered in cork were ubiquitous. After Jolson successfully embraced blackface, other Jewish entertainers were forced to try. At one time or another Sophie Tucker, George Burns, Eddie Cantor, little Georgie Jessel, Ed Wynn, and bandleader Ted Lewis, all made their livings in blackface. Except for Jolson, however, none considered minstrelsy a vocation. George Burns explained how he came to wear burnt cork: "I had seen Jolson and I figured if he was a hit with a big wide mouth, I'd be a riot with a bigger one."[4]

Al Jolson was neither the first nor the last to perform in blackface, though he was the best. When Jolson first happened upon minstrelsy in 1908, it was a dying troupe art, considered lowbrow, somewhere between the freak show common to dime museums where Harry Houdini got his start and the raunchy burlesque circuit where Fanny Brice got hers. Single-handedly, Al Jolson transplanted blackface from the minstrel tent and vaudeville stage to Broadway. At the Winter Garden Theater, owned by Jake and Lee Shubert, he catered to Manhattan's most sophisticated audiences. From the Winter Garden stage, Jolson led a one-man American revolution—he brought a prestige to minstrelsy that it had not enjoyed before and made for it a place in what was then known as the legitimate theater. Moreover, Jolson's minstrelsy had a peculiarly Jewish twist that had been absent in earlier American blackface performance. In the tradition of Exodus 14:11–12 and 16:2–3, and Numbers 14:1–3, in which the unshackled Israelites proclaim their preference for bondage, Jewish minstrelsy envisioned a nostalgic return to slavery from the imagined perspective of the slave.

The two types of songs that Jolson used most often in his blackface repertoire exemplify the nostalgia for slavery and exile inherent in Jewish minstrelsy: Mammy and Back-to-Dixie. In both types, Jewish songwriters of the 1910s and 1920s imagined that African-American identity was founded on being strangers and in dreaming of home. Jews revived this theme of homecoming from a tradition of minstrelsy that hadn't existed since before the Civil War, when slavery was a fact. (Minstrel performance after the Civil War had created images of African Americans that emphasized worn racial stereotypes, and had

had plots that helped symbolically circumscribe and control the new black presence in the North.)[5]

Back-to-Dixie was the older of the two homecoming song types. Stephen Foster established the theme with his minstrel song "Old Folks at Home" (1851), while Dan Emmett's "Dixie Land" (1860), also a minstrel tune, hardened it even more. The popularity of antebellum Back-to-Dixie songs waned after the Civil War while minstrelsy deteriorated, until a Jewish immigrant named Irving Berlin (born Israel Baline in Russia) suddenly revived the theme in 1912 with "When the Midnight Choo-Choo Leaves for Alabam'." With the help of Izzy Baline, the South once again became America's honorary homeland, so much so that apple-pie performers like Judy Garland found themselves shouting "Swanee" well into the 1960s.[6]

Unlike the Back-to-Dixie song, the Mammy song was not so antique, although Al Jolson made colossal revisionist efforts. "People have been making fun of Mammy songs," Jolson once griped, "and I don't really think that it's right that they should, for after all Mammy songs are the fundamental songs of our country."[7] Ten years after this public assertion of their legitimacy, Jolson had the confidence, in his last feature film, to rhyme Mammy with Uncle Sammy. In that same picture, Jolson could even pass off a joke about the antiquity of the Mammy song when he sang bittersweetly "my Mammy may be ham today, she made me what I am today!" Perhaps Jolson had forgotten that he had only introduced his Mammy eighteen years before, in 1918, in the show *Sinbad*. Mammy songs, along with the vocation "Mammy singer," were inventions of the Jewish Jazz Age.[8]

By the 1910s and 1920s, Al Jolson and other Eastern Jews in America had taken over the American project of depicting African-Americans, and had done so in their own unique way and for their own ends. Unlike the post-bellum minstrel tradition of hegemony and circumscription, Jewish minstrelsy in the 1910s and 1920s commonly represented "the scalawag servant with his surface dullness and hidden cleverness," as Gilbert Seldes noted in 1924.[9] The Jewish minstrel was always one smart step ahead of the master. This more closely resembled the forms of minstrelsy of the antebellum period, which Eric Lott has understood as a means by which a white working class could have identified with enslaved African Americans. But Lott notes that whites could only identify with blacks in a period when there existed an institutional and hardfast division between black and white in the form of slavery.[10] By Al Jolson's time, however, the racial barrier was growing ever more porous[11] and to suppose that Jolson or his kind were trying to revive a barrier through blackface does not meet the basic facts of Jewish minstrelsy, including the liberatory themes of Jewish minstrel songs and performances. Rather, Jolson's acts were exercises in cultural fluidity and mutual longings for freedom. To Jolson, the greatest barrier between himself and African Americans was the color of his skin. Even this he tried to overcome—cosmetically and with an imagined black diction that he took with him everywhere offstage and systematically interspersed with Yiddish.

Of course, Jolson's depictions of African Americans were exceedingly stereotypical. The phrase "imagined blackness," used herein, is a scholarly, detached euphemism for what was once known as "playing the coon." No matter what Jews imagined about African Americans or believed about minstrelsy, they were participating in an extremely problematic American tradition that no branch of scholarship can yet claim to fully comprehend, and about which this analysis provides only one discrete perspective. Moreover, it merits emphasizing that Jewish imaginings of blackness were indeed imagined, not actual mimesis of African-American cultural forms. Over and again readers will learn how places such as Swanee and people like Mammy, long dead in the American minstrel tradition, once again became standard bearers of the representation of blackness through the tireless advocacy of Jewish Americans. By reviving and injecting the themes of Swanee and Mammy with a tale of final return to more familiar times of being a separate, marginal culture, Eastern Jews in America maneuvered to see in African-American life their own story of exile and slavery. Jewish depictions of blackness were explicitly and unambiguously understood by Jews as a form of identification. Jews believed they saw their own history reenacted before them in the form of African-American culture, and longed to participate in that culture.

Jolson's project has become a part of the Jewish imagination of the twentieth century. Including *The Jazz Singer* and its remakes, there have been no fewer than five Hollywood films that claim Jolson for biographical inspiration, while fans the world over have come to know him simply as "Jolie." Lately, his story has been played on British, Canadian, and American stages. Asa Yoelson, immigrant from Lithuania, made it in America. But Jolson shared a complaint common to most successful entertainers: His overnight success had taken fifteen years. "I've had my heartaches, too," he said in 1928 as the elder statesman of his profession. "There were the months and months of the bitterest disappointments while I was in vaudeville, but only I can remember them now."[12] This unhappy story, of how Asa Yoelson became Al Jolson, star of the first talking film, cannot be divided from how Jolson came to blackface with the support of a sector of the entertainment business and its accompanying culture, both of which were largely Jewish.

CHAPTER 13

Asa Yoelson Discovers
the Theater

SOMETIME in March 1894, Hirsh Yoelson nudged his little brother Asa onto the back of a hay wagon and jumped up after him. Mother Naomi and daughters Rose and Etta were already on board. The family was on the first leg of a cross-Atlantic trip to America. After a four-year job search in the United States, family patriarch Rabbi Moshe Reuben Yoelson had finally sent for his family. He had found a position as the rabbi of the Talmud Torah Congregation in Washington, D.C.

The hay wagon was the most familiar in a string of vehicles increasingly modern and monstrous to the eyes of young Asa, a wide-eyed boy of eight who had not ventured much beyond the dirt road along which he was born in Seredzius, Lithuania. The hay wagon brought the family to a locomotive, which in turn brought it to a steamship in the port of Memel, from which the next stop was Liverpool, England. In Liverpool, Asa first spotted the ocean liner *Umbria*, which would bring his family to America.[1]

Five years later, Asa was performing on the American stage. In 1899 Israel Zangwill, an English-Jewish writer of socially conscious novels, turned his popular book, *The Children of the Ghetto*, into a play and toured the stage production throughout the United States. When the show reached Washington, D.C., Zangwill trolled the slums for realistic urchins whom he would pay twenty-five cents per show to appear as extras in *Children*. There he found little Asa playing in the streets. Asa was seventy-five cents richer before Rabbi Yoelson discovered and stopped his son's clandestine stage career. Perhaps Asa's older brother Hirsh, who had recently run away to New York to try his luck in the theater, had turned the rabbi against show business.

Perhaps the ungodly theme of the play, which questioned the relevance of Jewish sacred law, bothered Rabbi Yoelson. Either way, the theater was no place for the rabbi's boys.[2]

But then neither was the pulpit. Everything about Rabbi Yoelson was traditional, including his tendency as a rabbi to be unemployed, and he had no desire to pass that tradition to his children. In Eastern Europe the rabbinate and its supportive Jewish communal structure, the *kahal*, had been deteriorating ever since the reign of Tsar Nicholas I (1825–1855). Because Eastern European rabbis had followed the hope of finding gilded synagogues in America, the rabbinate had been significantly represented in the great migrations of the 1880s and 1890s. Nevertheless, the nineteenth-century Eastern European custom of unemployment followed that rabbinate to America. Even after Rabbi Yoelson found a congregation in Washington, D.C., he had to supplement his income by finding rabbinical odd jobs. Having learned the hard way, Rabbi Yoelson wanted the advantages of regular, legitimate work for his sons. To the rabbi, even artistic endeavor was more realistic than any clerical ambition: "My father was a Rabbi, but he didn't want me to be a Cantor, as the story tells you," Jolson remembered. "He wanted me to play the violin."[3] More precisely, Rabbi Yoelson dreamed that Asa would someday play Steinway Hall in New York City. So had Asa's mother, Naomi, before she died in 1894. To the rabbi, however, show business was neither legitimate nor cultured.[4]

Whether Rabbi Yoelson considered the theater cultured, professional entertainment had become a more marked cultural influence than it had been ever before. Wild West shows, minstrel troupes, circuses, carnivals, vaudeville, and burlesque circuits—these spectacles crisscrossed the continent with performers who were as homeless as sailors and just as crass. In the springtime of American modernity, when newspapers turned yellow in the reader's hands as if embarrassed by their own fictions and when wars resembled Buffalo Bill Cody's Wild West Revue, the *show* was real. Entertainment was truly a counter culture and counter discipline to the talmudic and cantorial, as a young Jewish playwright, Samson Raphaelson, would later understand and construct as a central conflict of his play, *The*

Jazz Singer. The difference between these two vocations, of course, was that the talmudic culture of Jolson's father was founded upon interdicts that circumscribed right behavior (known to Jews as commandments), while the discipline of theater loudly announced behavioral *possibility*.[5]

The very range of a performer's unique roadside experiences gave audiences both at the homespun Grand Opera House of Keokuk, Iowa (where Jolson played), and in disenchanted New York City the impression that show people were somehow in the know—carriers of a privileged cultural knowledge, usually sinful in nature. Both male and female performers took most of their meals in restaurants, usually well after midnight. They played cards until dawn. And when they eventually did retire to sleep, it was in some downtown hotel. That is to say, entertainers were worldly, and much of their art was to make an audience believe it was worldly as well. By "getting" a joke or by recognizing a reference in a lyric, an audience decoded privileged knowledge, and revelation occurred. Those codes might be delivered subtly, as in W. C. Fields's wry references to alcohol, or in jargon, as when Fanny Brice used nonsense Yiddish to seduce her man, or in an earthy manner, as when Jolson reminded his cosmopolitan audiences about the girls in "O-Hi-O (O!-My!-O!)": "A country girl, you know, is just like a Ford. / They're not so stylish but the service, oh Lord!"[6]

Armed with a knowledge known to mediating elites of culture since the biblical prophets, that coding a message can intensify the power of delivery (known to Jewish performers as shtick), performers became mediating elites of their own culture of fluid possibility, and proclaimed their lessons from the stage. If audiences liked the content and delivery of those lessons, they bought tickets and made stars.

Next to the segments of the touring entertainment culture stood the nightclub scene, still new, but beginning to make itself felt in America's major cities at the century's turn. Nightclubs, which emerged from restaurants with singing waiters, had their own special wisdom to convey: ethnic knowledge. Advanced lessons were learned inside such academies as Carey Walsh's Saloon in Coney Island where, in the early years of their careers, Eddie Cantor and Jimmy Durante provided the syllabus of songs and laughs. Or one might go down to old Chinatown to the Pelham Cafe, referred to by everyone in the know as Nigger Mike's (the nickname of the kinky-haired Jewish proprietor, Mike Salter), then considered New York's premier slumming palace.

Just before the Jazz Age, before Harlem was in vogue and while "the melting pot" was still the slogan of the socially astute, street knowledge meant *ethnic* knowledge. Since 1904, midtown Manhattanites flocked to the Pelham Cafe to view the gallery of Chinese opium addicts, Jewish prostitutes, and Irish Tammany politicians surrounded by their minions of Jewish and Italian gangsters. Sophisticated people came to Mike's to taste ethnicity in-the-raw. The singing waiters, expert in randy lyrics if not with a piano keyboard, captured the grand scene in song.[7]

As a young man, still going by the name Izzy Baline, Irving Berlin apprenticed in the Pelham Cafe, and the catalog of Berlin's earliest work reflects this. Most have German, Irish, Italian, and Jewish themes. Later, as Berlin moved farther from his singing waiter days, he wrote less about the different ethnicities he had seen constructed at the Pelham Cafe and increased the number of songs he wrote about blackness. If Americanization meant the display of various ethnicities to the Jewish songwriters of the turn of the century, songs about imagined African Americans would become the dominant song type in the 1910s and 1920s. Likewise, the socialite nightclub would move uptown.[8]

It was still the turn of the century, however, in the ethnic worlds of singing waiters, street corners, and vaudeville, when the Yoelson boys first entered the world of the theater. Little Asa, whose elementary lessons in urban sociology he had learned from Zangwill as an urchin in *The Children of the Ghetto*, quickly turned to lessons in history taken in front of the Hotel Raleigh in Washington, D.C. There Asa would serenade the national powers who came and went at all discreet and indiscreet hours of the day and night. "We knew all the popular songs," Jolson's brother Harry remembered thirty years later: "Sweet Marie, The Sidewalks of New York, Maggie Murphy's Home, Daisy Bell, Say Au Revoir but Not Good-By—but we found that some of the songs which the gray-haired statesmen and jurists liked best were old ones that carried them dreaming back into the past—Suwanee River, Old Kentucky Home, and When You and I Were Young, Maggie."[9]

With such formidable history lessons well learned at the knee of Stephen Foster and his canon, and with an entertainment culture that was as wide open with possibility as America itself, Asa ran away with a tiny carnival called Rich & Hoppe's Big Company of Fun Makers. He was eleven years old.

Jewish Minstrelsy Emerges

ASA YOELSON moved from carnival show to burlesque house to dime museum, up and down the Eastern seaboard. Usually his job was to "plug" songs to the audience to induce a sing-along for established acts. Occasionally he took the stage himself. At fourteen he was established enough in show business for his face to grace the cover of a piece of sheet music, and was billed as Al Joelson. Still, Al often turned up at his father's home penniless and unwashed.

Al needed an act. He searched for a specialty with which to cover up his average voice. Eventually Jolson found his voice in blackface. Although he claimed that his lifelong use of burnt cork was born of a happy accident, Jolson was never one to be taken at his word.

Happy accident was the general method of entertainment innovation. At least this was the claim of the typical show-business autobiography, entertainment press article, and other pieces of historical pseudoepigrapha. For a performer to admit that any thought at all had gone into creating a successful stage incarnation, particularly one with which the performer became permanently identified, was considered contrived and counterfeit. To concede that a stage gimmick had any meaning or purpose except as raw entertainment was anathema. This is not to say that successful entertainers modestly thought they had just been lucky. Each considered himself or herself the hardest worker on the circuit, willing to do most anything to move an audience. Nevertheless, while most considered sweat before stage lights to be part of the vocation, hard thought about the innovation of stage material was deemed somehow unnatural.

Fanny Brice, wife of the "bond Fagin" Nicky Arnstein, claimed that her career started serendipitously.[1] This is her version of a typical evening in 1910, and what turned out to be the performance of her life.

Irving [Berlin] took me in the back room and he played "Sadie Salome" . . . a Jewish comedy song. . . . So, of course, Irving sang "Sadie Salome" with a Jewish accent. I didn't even understand Jewish, couldn't speak a word of it. But I thought, if that's the way Irving sings, that's the way I'll sing it. Well, I came out and did "Sadie Salome" for the first time ever doing a Jewish accent. And that starched sailor suit is killing me. And it's gathering you know where, and I'm trying to squirm it away, and singing and smiling, and the audience is loving it. They think it's an act I'm doing, so as long as they're laughing I keep it up.[2]

Brice recognized this routine as the birth of her career. "I put my soul into Sadie Salome," Brice explained, "and she rewarded me."[3] Although she claimed to know no Yiddish, her learned Jewish accent and her persona as a hapless but hysterical seductress became the two props with which she found fame and kept it for the better part of her career. Brice traced these crucial aspects of her act to two accidents: a split-second, backstage decision to sing with an ethnic accent with which she claimed (improbably) to be utterly unfamiliar, and the zealousness of the laundry attendant who starched her costume.[4] Had Irving Berlin suggested "an Irish song and done it with a brogue," Brice supposed, she "would have been an Irish comedienne forever."[5] One suspects that some planning helped Brice forge her act, and that her being Jewish had something to do with her choice of ethnic material, if only for reasons of politeness. As Brice well understood, "It is okay for one Irishman to call another Irishman anything, any kind of name. But if you are not an Irishman, keep the mouth shut. The same with all people."[6]

Personal identification between player and character was the usual source of ethnic humor, especially as 1890s' vaudeville characters entered the more ethnically sensitive 1910s and 1920s. More often than not, Irish performers played "Pat," and Jews, "Izzy." The mockery of an ethnic group by one of its own was commonplace. Even those, like Brice, who claimed they had little experience with the people they represented on stage, felt that they were somehow in the know. "In anything Jewish I ever did, I wasn't standing apart, making fun of the race," Brice maintained. "I *was* the race, and what happened to me on the stage is what could happen to them. . . . They identified with me, and then it was all right to get a laugh, because they were laughing at me as much as at themselves."[7]

Not all Jews applauded Fanny Brice's kind of act. The Anti-Defamation League of B'nai Brith and the Associated Rabbis of America objected vigorously and officially to the Jewish caricature commonly known as "the stage Jew."[8] the *Jewish Tribune* contained a representative statement of disapproval, albeit a rather scathing one, as it recounted the typical stage Jew character, seemingly always named Izzy. He is the "vile figure which once dominated the cheap music halls." The article commented on his depicted profession: "Izzy on the stage, not infrequently, was made a criminal"; on his physiognomy: "Izzy had the roguish eye and the lascivious lip of a libertine"; on his vocabulary: "Izzy was speaking of 'fires' and 'failures' and 'shickses' when he opened his hair-overgrown mouth"; on his essence: "Izzy secreted the cunning of the serpent under his scalp"; on his origins: "in the case of Izzy the malice and the accumulated prejudice of centuries had added their considerable mite"; and on his demise: "His quiet and unheralded death marks the unregretted end of a noisy and vulgar era." The article was about the passing of Ben Welch, whom the magazine considered the last of the "Hebrew Comedians," if a beard was necessary to that type. Of course, George Jessel, Ben Rubin, Lew Holtz, George Price, and Fanny Brice continued beardless in this tradition well into the 1930s, although theirs was a friendlier stage Jew.[9]

But if the newer caricatures were friendly, they were not always so obviously Jewish, which was a source of terrible confusion in the Jewish periodicals. For a stage character to make sense to the Jewish audience, that character's ethnicity had to be located somewhere, most typically in the genealogical background of the character's player. When compared to his competitors, Buster Keaton and Harold Lloyd, Charlie Chaplin became the "Eternal Jewish 'Shlemiehl.'" A film critic for the *Jewish Tribune* wondered about Chaplin: "How did I ever fail to recognize the awkward Yeshiva Bocher [Talmud student] in the world famous comedian?" The critic thought Buster Keaton was "the typical English comedian" because "Keaton never suffers. He is surprised, stupefied, but untouched, cold, within." Harold Lloyd was "the Yankee par excellence. Cool, with perfect sang

froid. It is his capacity for rapid thinking, his American resourceful-
ness that makes him surmount all obstacles." According to "a typical
jewish mother, shedding bitter tears" sitting next to the film critic in
the theater, however, the Little Tramp was positively Yiddish. "'What
they want from him, the goyim?'" the yidishe mama cried. "'Why
they pick on him? What he done to them?'" The critic thoroughly
agreed. "Charlie Chaplin is essentially the victim. He provokes merri-
ment when he is down, defeated, tragically helpless. He never really
wins. He only escapes. He smiles wanly, because life is too sad an
affair to cry about. If you would forget that Charlie is there to make
you laugh, you would be inclined to cry yourself." The Jewish people,
it would seem, were laughable only in their essential victimization,
defeat, and sadness. Because the Little Tramp shared these character-
istics, and because Chaplin was in fact a Jew, his act became Jewish.[10]

Given the ethnic connection between character and player that
seemed so natural to Jewish audiences, many Jews began to notice
the increasing Jewish fascination with blackface, and were puzzled.
"It is a curious thing that there are so many points of resemblance
between Jews and Negroes," the *Morgen Zhurnal* pondered. "It is a
notable thing that at least three of the most popular makers of music
on the American stage should be jewish boys, two of whom blacken
their faces and sing Negro 'Mammy' songs while the third has written
many songs in the Negro dialect."[11] The three were Al Jolson, Eddie
Cantor, and Irving Berlin, and they were a curious trio indeed. Berlin's story must come later, but this is how Cantor and Jolson first
came to depict Jewish versions of blackness.

With happy accident serving as the pat showbiz explanation of how
an entertainer came to his character, Eddie Cantor too resorted to
serendipity to answer the question of African-American identification.
While young, undiscovered, and playing the third wheel to the vaudeville team of Bedini and Arthur, Cantor found himself, he claimed,
experimenting one night with burnt cork. While trying to emphasize
certain wrinkles on his boyish face, the cork smeared out of control.
The more he tried to fix his makeup, the more it colored him black.
Wearing a dandyish suit and white eyeglasses (which shielded the
eyes from cork dust, Cantor claimed), he had found his career-long
blackface incarnation: the feeble Negro, a man too genteel for his

race. In the first skit in which he tried his new look and displayed the African-American plight, someone chased Cantor about the stage swinging a hammer. The two sprinted through the aisles, and just when his pursuer was winded Cantor paused dramatically to announce, "He means to do me bodily harm!" Cantor's haughty inflection, along with the white spectacles, removed his blackface character from any previous attempt to depict blackness. Even Zip Coon, the nineteenth-century minstrel dandy, had used a recognizably black accent. It was precisely the surprise of blue-blooded effeteness under a black face that made Cantor's poor slapstick routine about racial violence somewhat amusing. The blackface skit proved so popular that the old vaudeville team put a new name on its marquee: "Bedini and Arthur, Assisted by Eddie Cantor."[12]

Jolson's story is also filled with supposed moments of serendipity, the most outrageous of which is his claim to have first fallen to one knee because of an ingrown toenail. Unlike Cantor's account, Jolson's serendipitous introduction to blackface was very much in the spirit of playing a minstrel part. In the fall of 1904, while still billing themselves under the name Joelson & Joelson, Al and Harry met an established burlesque performer, Joe Palmer. Recently confined to a wheelchair, Palmer had many friends in show business circles, one of whom was "Professor" Ren Shields, a song and skit writer. Saddened over his friend's new handicap, the Professor wrote a skit for Palmer and the Joelson boys, "A Little of Everything," about a doctor (Harry Joelson), his patient (Palmer), and a comic orderly (Al). The trio was booked to play its uncharacteristically competent skit in Keeney's Theatre in Brooklyn for a week, which was a nice job for the struggling Joelsons and a morale boost for Palmer. The story goes that although Al usually played the straight man, the Professor mistakenly wrote him a comic part. When the boys discovered the mistake and appealed to the Professor, he refused to rewrite the script. Since Al was too young to play a doctor and too nervous to play the comic orderly, a minstrel comedian named James Francis Dooley (apparently an Irish-American), booked in a different act at the same theater, suggested that Al perform the part of orderly in blackface.

This version of Al's first brush with burnt cork comes from his biographer, Herbert G. Goldman, and it would be convenient to believe the story of happy accident that led Jolson to his career incarnation as it conveniently encompasses the minstrel transition from Irish to Jewish. But it is far more likely that the part of the hospital orderly was written specifically for blackface. Service positions were typical minstrel parts, as they later became typical parts for black actors in Hollywood films. Al probably tried to act the part as written and found he was particularly adept at playing in blackface. Incidentally or not, it was for this act that Joelson changed his stage name to Jolson (again, according to lore).[13]

Jolson worked exclusively in blackface for the next five years. He traveled from carnival gig to burlesque house, sometimes with his older brother Harry, sometimes without, while he developed his vision of blackness and honed his comic timing. In 1908 Jolson played Portland, Oregon, where Lew Dockstader and his Minstrels were also playing. Dockstader caught Jolson's show and was so impressed, he offered Jolson a job. Because Dockstader's troupe was considered one of the best in the land, Jolson immediately accepted Dockstader's offer to join his troupe for seventy-five dollars a week. By February 1909, after Dockstader's Minstrels played a week at Springer's Grand Opera House in New York, Jolson was blessed by *Variety*, already the premier magazine of the theater: "As it stands now, Jolson's offering is capable of holding down a place in any vaudeville show."[14]

One cannot deny the common wisdom of the vaudeville audience that ethnic groups tended to represent themselves on stage because they felt most familiar with those self-representative characters. And yet Jews had a particular proclivity for playing African Americans. In the case of Jewish minstrelsy, as in all other recollections of stage gimmicks, serendipity was a cover that legitimated an act by implying that the performance was naturally inspired. In the case of Jewish minstrelsy, serendipity implied that Jews had been called to play a part seemingly very different from their own imagined selves. Given the ethnic identification made between character and actor that was assumed by performers and audiences alike, the Jewish depiction of blackness became a conundrum. Why had Eastern Jews, some born in the Russian Pale, taken upon themselves the depiction of African Americans?

Blackface Arrives on Broadway

WHILE JOLSON traveled with Lew Dockstader's minstrels, that troupe rose above its stiffest competition, the minstrel acts of George Primrose, Billy West, George Thatcher, and George Wilson. Much interest in Dockstader came from his unique practice of making a minstrel show more than a rapid succession of skit-length travesties. Also, before Dockstader's 1908–1909 season the main joke of minstrelsy was to present famous white situations in blackface. This included Dockstader's own skit "A Dull Day at the White House," which portrayed Teddy Roosevelt and all his staff as black (no small comment on progressivism, surely). Dockstader's 1908–1909 show innovated in two ways. First, it played an entire "musical comedy in blackface" in which "Seventy Real Minstrels" developed a unified plot. Second, it introduced an imagined world of blacks without whites.

Lew Dockstader's minstrel show of 1908–1909, in which Jolson participated, parodied the current fad of the rich to make expeditions to the North Pole. Its second act began in "Boo Hoo Land," a black jungle paradise into which stumbled the provincial explorers Professor Hightower (Lew Dockstader) and his scrawny assistant Acie (Al Jolson). These explorers—inexplicably, both in blackface—soon find themselves in the tribal soup pot.[1]

Dockstader's innovation portrayed blacks in their "natural" environments, safe spaces secluded from white machinations. This technique later became a staple of Jewish minstrelsy, as in Jolson's aforementioned "Goin' to Heaven on a Mule" routine. It was not until the Jews took over blackface, however, that the portrayals of black without white looked once again toward antebellum minstrel depictions of Dixie, Swanee, and Mammy for inspiration.

Meanwhile, Jolson stole scene after scene in Dockstader's traveling show. Critics and fans soon learned Jolson's name, while several talent agents took interest in his stage presence. But it was twenty-four-year-old Arthur Klein, long established in the business from his days as a child performer, who finally impressed Jolson with his ability to book profitable performances. He became Jolson's agent.

When Dockstader's show closed for the summer in 1909, Arthur Klein immediately put Jolson on the vaudeville circuit. The step from minstrel troupe to vaudeville was immense, for even vaudeville was considered high-brow compared to troupe minstrelsy. Yet Klein had enough power in the United Booking Office to arrange it without much trouble. Then it was up to Jolson to perform well on the circuit and to gain a vaudeville reputation, which he did easily. His crowning vaudeville appearance took place at Hammerstein's Victoria for a Monday matinee on December 27, 1909. Long famous as the premier vaudeville theater, the Victoria on Monday afternoons housed mainly a show-business audience. Fellow performers, producers, and managers went there to scout the very best vaudeville talent. To have arrived on Oscar Hammerstein's stage for a Monday show after only a few months on the vaudeville circuit was a testament to both Jolson's comic gift and his ambition.

While Arnold Rothstein ran his crap game in the theater's prop room, Jolson began his routine that afternoon with a story about his own craps mania. Rothstein's friend, Florenz Ziegfeld, was so impressed by Jolson's appearance that he reportedly offered an instant audition. Jolson's reported reply was that he didn't do auditions.[2]

All of this impressed Jake and Lee Shubert, and Jolson eventually landed his breakthrough Broadway role in their musical comedy *La Belle Paree*. Jolson took the stage as Erastus Sparkler, "a colored aristocrat from San Juan Hill, cutting a wide swath in Paris." This made Jolson the first performer to perform minstrel comedy in what was then called the legitimate theater.[3]

The Shubert brothers intended for this show to open their new Winter Garden Theater in the Broadway district of Manhattan. The

Winter Garden itself was the realized dream of Lew Fields. Fields had started his career in 1881 as part of the "Dutch" team of Weber & Fields, which premiered at the Lower East Side's Turn Hall. In the succeeding three decades, Fields established enough of a mainstream reputation to begin the construction of a grand Broadway theater on the site of the old American Horse Exchange. When Fields fell ill, his friends and business associates the Shuberts completed the theater and planned to open it on March 11.

Because of added rehearsals, Monday night, March 20, became the actual opening day. Still, none of the last minute adjustments helped. Written by Frank Tours and Jerome Kern (the latter would go on to write *Show Boat*, the groundbreaking musical about miscegenation), *La Belle Paree* starred such top talent as Melville Ellis, Mitzi Hages, Harry Fisher, Dorothy Jordon, George White, and Stella Mayhew as the mulatto maid who performed the following duet with Jolson:

> JOLSON: Never going back again to Yankee land.
> MAYHEW: Got a lot of customs there that I can't stand.
> JOLSON: Like hanging a coon.
> MAYHEW: Working in June.
> BOTH: Hunting chicken thieves night and noon.
> JOLSON: Don't know how to treat us colored gentlemen.
> MAYHEW: Call us colored ladies "wenches" now and then.
> BOTH: There's one place for the race—

"Paris is a Paradise for Coons" announced Jolson's presence on Broadway, although the New York *World* announced him separately, and erroneously, as Al Johnson. Jerome Kern had noted, correctly, that Paris was more hospitable to blacks than America, and he borrowed heavily from Lew Dockstader's minstrel innovation of imagining a safe black space. Thereby, through Jolson, Kern brought "Paris is a Paradise for Coons" and minstrelsy to Broadway.[4]

Though the Mayhew-Jolson duet received praise from critics, the show was generally panned. Four hours long and with a plot loose even by vaudeville standards, let alone for fancy Broadway, audiences expected more from the Shuberts and their greatly anticipated Winter Garden Theater. Even with extensive revisions, the second night was no better. On the third night Jolson took extraordinary measures. He addressed the audience directly and without a script, in vaudeville fashion.

> Lot of brave folks out there. Either that, or you can't read. Come to think of it, after the reviews we got, there's a lot of brave folks up here on the stage. Hey, I know you. You was in the audience the last time I played Brighton Beach. You used to like my act. What's the matter, you come into this classy joint you think you shouldn't have a good time? C'mon, this place ain't so much. I remember when it was the Horse Exchange. That's better—now I got a few songs to sing—if you'll listen.[5]

Apparently, they did. According to all reports and biographies, the third night at the Winter Garden made Jolson's career. He then went on to two full decades in theater without a single flop. Later, Jolson credited the resuscitation of *La Belle Paree*, and the initiative of bringing minstrelsy to Broadway, entirely to himself.

> I'll never forget the first real opportunity I had. It was with Shubert. I had worked for weeks, and then, on the opening night, my number was a flop. The second night I died too—now I can admit it. But on the third night I got a new idea. A cat may have nine lives, but I know very well that when a man dies for the third time he's finished. So I went to the manager and asked him if I could paint my face black and change my scene a little. At first he swore a bit to me, but I was used to that. The main thing was that he let me do what I wanted, and the third night my act revived. After that, it was all right.[6]

As usual, Jolson's memory changed the past as he recounted it. The performance certainly did not happen this way because after the first show of *La Belle Paree*, the *New York Herald* lauded Jolson's "genuine Negro unction."[7] Moreover, Jerome Kern's conception of "a colored aristocrat from San Juan Hill" had been written for blackface.

Yet, once again, Jolson's version of the story provides a perspective on the truth. The presence of blackface in mainstream entertainment had been a target of many critics and had been resisted by the legitimate theater since minstrelsy first appeared in the nineteenth century. The phenomena that enabled Jolson to become the first performer to play comic blackface on Broadway were unique and not entirely celebrated. "Al Jolson is coming to your town," warned *American Magazine*, "Jolson and all his kind."[8] By now, Jolson's "kind" should be evident: it included Arthur Klein, Oscar Hammerstein, Florenz Ziegfeld, Jerome Kern, the Shubert brothers, Lew Fields and his thirty-yearlong vision of building a Broadway theater, and countless other Jews who constituted a nearly self-sufficient portion of the entertainment business.[9]

To summarize, the emergence of blackface on the Broadway stage came because of a Jewish performer, represented by a Jewish agent, performing songs written by a Jew, in a theater company produced by Jews, which played in a theater built by Jews. Entertainment certainly was not strictly a Jewish business. Nevertheless, as in other businesses and with other peoples, the Jews in entertainment kept close. At least in part, the theater had become a Jewish-American institution, much like the fashion industry, the department store, and the casino. And the Jewish part of the theater had taken a decided interest in the depiction of blackness.

The Jews on Tin Pan Alley

EIGHT YEARS after *La Belle Paree*, at the height of his stage career, Jolson took out the following ad in the 1919 New Year's issue of *Variety*: "Everybody likes me. Those who don't are jealous! Anyhow, here's wishing those that do and those that don't a Merry Christmas and a Happy New Year—Al Jolson."[1] Detractors often cite this sort of conduct as evidence of Jolson's egomania. In fact, no mania is evident. In the same year that Jolson took out his ad there were two big musical-comedy productions in America, Ziegfeld's *Follies* and the Shuberts' *Sinbad*. For Florenz Ziegfeld's *Follies* of 1919, which theater critics have since dubbed its classic year, Ziegfeld had enlisted a legion of talent including Eddie Cantor, Will Rogers, Bert Williams, Fanny Brice, Van and Schenck, Marilyn Miller, Anne Pennington, and the mordantly brilliant W. C. Fields. The Shuberts had only one star—Al Jolson. Alone, Jolson stood fast and favorably against the entire cast of the *Follies*, as he had for each year in the preceding decade for every musical comedy in which he appeared. Much of Jolson's appeal can be traced to his stage presence and comic timing, which by all accounts were flawless. Yet critics also recognize that it was Jolson's ability to deliver a song that made him a star. Among the numbers Jolson introduced in *Sinbad* were "Swanee," "Rock-a-Bye Your Baby with a Dixie Melody," and the melody by which he has been known since, "My Mammy."

Though Jolson often claimed authorship of his biggest hits so he could bilk royalties, he never did write a song. That art he left to those on Tin Pan Alley. "It is a clever group of scoundrels that monopolize the lyric-writing game at present," the *Jewish Tribune* noted proudly, "—all Jews."[2] There was Gus Kahn, for instance, author of many a Jolson standard. Kahn was probably born in Eastern Europe in 1886 and arrived in America six years later. After spending his adolescence pushing clothes carts up the avenues of Chicago's garment district, he pushed his first hit song, "Gee, I Wish I Had a Girl." It sold one million, seven hundred thousand copies. Before Kahn's career was through he had added "Yes, Sir, That's My Baby," "Toot, Toot, Toot-sie, Goodbye," "Carolina in the Morning," and the entire score of Eddie Cantor's musical *Whoopee* to the vocabulary of the Jazz Age. When asked by the *Jewish Tribune* what themes made for good songs, Kahn unreflectively answered: "Oh, that's a cinch. 'Mother,' 'Sweetheart,' 'Home,' and 'Yearning For You.' All these simple heart tugs have infinite variations."[3] F. Scott Fitzgerald saw Kahn's wisdom when he canonized one of the songwriter's lyrics in the fifth chapter of *The Great Gatsby*. "In the morning, in the evening, ain't we got fun?"—Fitzgerald chose to pair this question with comments about his title character, regarding "the colossal vitality of his illusion."[4]

Gus Kahn and the rest of Tin Pan Alley made their livings by presenting the American illusion with easily hummed melodies. Jews were adept at this task for a variety of reasons. For one, the abundant presence of Jewish songwriters in the American industries of theater and song was much influenced by social and economic factors. In the days of the great Eastern European Jewish migration, Tin Pan Alley could be entered upon more quickly than most paths open to Eastern Jewish immigrants. Tin Pan Alley was far less forbidding than what would come to be called Fashion Avenue, mostly because Western Jews who were established in the music business actively cultivated the songwriting talents of recently arrived immigrants, while Western Jews in the clothing industries tended to let Eastern Jewish industry go less rewarded. Moreover, Jews in Eastern Europe had demonstrated a proclivity for the theatrical and musical arts. On the other hand, Carolina in the morning, noon, or nighttime, had had very little to do with Jewish visions of the world while they were in Europe. Still, the South became a subject of the Eastern Jewish songwriting imagination, and thereby took footing once again in the American imagination. Here's how that happened.[5]

By the time Gus Kahn arrived in Chicago at the age of six, Charles K. Harris, a German Jew raised in East Saginaw, Michigan, and comfortable using such Yiddishisms (tempered by their equivalent Anglicisms) as "*mshugga* (crazy)" in his 1926 autobiography, had already founded a firm in Milwaukee to publish his own songs.[6] "It was the days of dancing before the great god Jazz had cracked his whip," Harris wrote in that autobiography. Before the fox trot, and even its ancestor the turkey trot, "couples then glided about the floor gracefully, executing the waltz, minuet, quadrille, and schottische."[7]

In 1892, when Gus Kahn came to Chicago as a young boy, Harris sold two million copies of sheet music of a song he wrote himself, "After the Ball." Before "After the Ball" had run its course, five million copies had been grabbed up in a period when a successful hit rarely sold more than a million. Harris was one of the first music writers to become a self-publisher. Irving Berlin would later use this business technique to maintain artistic control, and to much financial advantage. It was also on the sheet music of Harris's "For Old Time's Sake" that Al Jolson's fourteen-year-old face had first appeared.

Harry Von Tilzer, another Jewish song writer of the Gay Nineties and the early twentieth century, learned Harris's lesson in self-publishing and then went a step farther. Having apprenticed with Maurice Shapiro in the late 1890s, Von Tilzer (born Harry Gumm in Detroit) opened the Harry Von Tilzer Music Publishing Company in 1902 on 28th Street along New York's Tin Pan Alley, where several years before, M. Witmark and Sons (also Jewish) had led the music business in a mass migration from the 14th Street theater district. Von Tilzer dominated music publishing throughout the first decade of the century, mostly by publishing his own work.

But as prolific and talented as Von Tilzer was at writing and publishing, what he really loved to do was "plug"—that is, sell. Von Tilzer could spend hours bragging of his best techniques. Typically, between the first and second act of a vaudeville show, he remembered, he would stand up in his box seat and begin singing. "The audience is startled. Ushers run through the aisles. A policeman comes in and walks toward the box. About the time the policeman is where he can be seen by all the audience, I step out on to the stage in front of the curtain and begin the chorus, with the orchestra playing and the audience, that is now onto the game, clapping so hard it almost blisters its hands."[8]

Von Tilzer apprenticed Irving Berlin in the song publishing business, and Berlin's first job in the industry was plugging Harry Von Tilzer Music Publishing Company songs.

Von Tilzer also initiated the Jewish tradition of fascination with the "coon" song. Such tunes of his as "Down Where the Cotton Blossoms Grow" (1901) and "Alexander (Don't You Love Your Baby No More?)" (1904) paced the later standards "Down Where the Swanee River Flows" (1916, written in part by brother Albert Von Tilzer) and, of course, Irving Berlin's "Alexander's Ragtime Band" (1911). Harry Von Tilzer found the most success, however, with "What You Goin' To Do When the Rent Comes Round?" (1905) supposedly inspired by Von Tilzer's overhearing a black woman publicly berate her humbled spouse, one Rufus Rastus Johnson Brown.[9]

"Coon" songs used the rhythms and stories on which Jolson had been raised as a child performer and professional plugger, and these were the songs that Jolson liked to use in his Broadway repertoire. One that thoroughly captured Jolson's attention and the Jewish imagining of the South was "Waitin' on the Robert E. Lee," whose lyrics were written by L. Wolfe Gilbert in 1912. "Waitin' on the Robert E. Lee" was about a spot "way down on the levee, in old Alabammy" where a black banjo-playing crowd—with the biblical names Ethan, Hammy, Noah, and Sammy—gathered to load a cotton steamer. Born in Odessa in 1886, Wolfie Gilbert had never seen Alabammy. If African-American/Israelite joy along the banks of the Alabama was located anywhere, it was in the South of the Jewish imagination.[10]

When it came to capturing the larger American imagination, Jewish and other, Irving Berlin was among the best that American songwriting has produced. The Norman Rockwell of melody, Berlin captured the quintessence of American life using only the piano's black keys. "I write what the people want, what they understand, what hits them and hits me," he declared. "I'm attempting to get over an idea in the simplest, most effective way."[11] An example of his simple, effective way with lyrics comes from one of his many World War I tunes. "They Were All Out of Step but Jim" is a mother's song, sung as she watches her son march off to Europe. In that taut title Berlin managed to capture the hapless but earnest courage of a teenage soldier, all the delight of a parade, the pride of Mama, and a proper dose of laughter. That is, he caught the very spirit of American patriotism in 1917.

"They Were All Out of Step but Jim" was one of his least remembered songs. Berlin captured America with song after song, hundreds of times in a career that spanned five full decades. "I don't mind what people say about my songs," he said to a burgeoning army of critics. "I realize perfectly well that they are not art. I know my lyrics are atrocious in their rhymes and their meter, but I'm not writing for the few. I'm writing for the masses, for the crowd."[12]

This was precisely what the most alert critics of popular song resented. A typical criticism rejected Berlin's songs as untutored and shallow. "Popular music is a matter of the feet rather than the soul," one detractor maintained. Moreover, popular songwriters "are born to this function as certain bees are born to fulfil certain functions in a hive." High-brow critics considered songwriters an uncultured lot, many of whom "do not even take the trouble to learn harmony, and others cannot even write down a melody, being content to whistle or sing a tune of their own composition, or 'pick it out' with one finger on the piano, leaving others to write it down and put chords to it."[13]

Concerning this latter point, the critics happen to have been correct. To address the burning question of Charles K. Harris fans who "naturally wonder how it was possible for me to write music to a song when even to this day I cannot distinguish one note from another" Harris explained in his autobiography the work of his "arranger."[14] Alexander Wollcott, Irving Berlin's first biographer and the man who covered the 1912 Beansy Rosenthal murder for the *New York Times*, well understood that "Berlin can neither read music nor transcribe it. He can only give birth to it."[15]

Some who criticized Berlin's sort of music were rather sharp. Mrs. Anna Faulkener Oberndorfer of the General Federation of Women's Clubs felt that popular music had a rather pungent influence upon the young. "When one knows that in one of Chicago's biggest and best high schools the students bought two thousand popular songs in two weeks," Oberndorfer noted, "and that the committee of students appointed by the school found only forty which they considered fit for boys and girls to sing together, don't you really think something

should happen to awaken American parents to their responsibilities?"
In her travels to eliminate the threat of popular music, Oberndorfer
encountered a music-shop manager who confided that "seventy-
five percent of her customers were high school boys and girls who
bought nothing but trash, and she said that they blushed when they
asked for it."[16]

What teenager would not blush to ask for the sheet music to the
Jolson hit of July 1916, "Where Did Robinson Crusoe Go with Friday
on Saturday Night?"

> One fine Saturday night they had nothing to do,
> So they started counting all the girlies they knew.
> Friday counted to thirteen, and Crusoe said "Brother,
> You know thirteen's unlucky. Let's go get another."
>
> Every Saturday night they went starting to roam,
> And on Sunday morning they'd come staggering home.
> On this island lived wild men and cannibals brimmin',
> And you know where there are wild men, there must be wild women.
>
> So where did Robinson Crusoe go with Friday on Saturday night?[17]

Other critics, though they remained critical, were less damning.
The music of the "cultured man" may differ from the popular song in
that it is "more refined," wrote a music columnist. But the same columnist would not conclude that popular music had a "deteriorating
effect" upon "the people." "Such a claim is absurd in view of the fact
that it is not the music which makes the people, but the people who
make the music to suit them. Popular music is not forced upon the
people; it is created out of their own spirit."[18] The *American Israelite*
added a note of patriotism to that spirit: "Irving Berlin is a good
example of that vague something or other we call 'Americanization.'
And his songs, too, he likes to describe as 'typically American,'
the product of that same force which molded him into manhood."[19]
The Jewish songwriters tended to agree, and often spoke of tapping
into the American consciousness. Irving Berlin wanted it known
that "the public is the final and supreme judge of song merit," and,
further, predicted that "the time will come when this indirect censor-

ship will produce song[s] that will express real human emotion in the way such emotion should be expressed."[20] Exceedingly aware of the realm of public opinion, Berlin thought of himself as its conduit, a real American.

If indeed Berlin and his ilk perpetuated a sentiment of folkish nationalism in their understanding of the creative process, it was a peculiarly American version. Which other nation could take the composite nature of popular music as a point of national pride? "It's a distinctive form of music, typically 'melting pot'" Berlin thought, "for it's derived from the music of many countries."[21] Despite the movement for "100-percent Americanism" that came with the Great War, the immigrant songwriters asserted that they were mediating a counter-sentiment for a nation of nations, one that sprang directly from "the people," and moreover, that this vision of a multicultural America was the legitimate one. This was a significantly more generous vision of "the people" than had been expressed even by the "people's lawyer" himself, progressive Western Jew Louis Brandeis.[22]

Berlin most strongly expressed how one might love an adopted country in "God Bless America," a song written for his show *Yip, Yip Yaphank*, so named for the army base in Yaphank, Long Island, where Berlin was stationed for the First World War. The army commissioned Sgt. Berlin to write a musical featuring military personnel, including Berlin himself, who took the stage alone to sing "Oh, How I Hate to Get Up in the Morning." Both Al Jolson and Fanny Brice attended opening night at the Century Theatre, August 19, 1918. A month later, *Yaphank* concluded its Broadway run with a final act in which the boys literally marched off the stage, down the aisles, and out to the troop carriers that would bring them to the trenches. Remarkably, Berlin excised "God Bless America" from the repertoire before the show even began—he felt it did not compare to George M. Cohan's "Over There." But "God Bless America" is a prayer with lyrical precision to rival even the Psalms:

> God bless America, land that I love.
> Stand beside her and guide her
> To the right with the light from above.

From the mountains to the prairies
To the oceans white with foam,
God bless America, my home sweet home.[23]

The song is all the more impressive because it is the prayer of an immigrant from Mohilev, Russia, a man raised in an American slum who spoke Yiddish with his mother. "And there is not a Friday night when he is in New York," the Jewish press gushed, "that does not find him at his mother's for the regulation Sabbath meal."[24]

Years before the Great War, in 1911, this boy from the Lower East Side announced himself as the principal muse of "the people" by producing a "coon" song. "Alexander's Ragtime Band" was an unsyncopated attempt to convey to America the spirit of ragtime, then a music of African Americans. By contemporary accounts and by critical cultural histories since, "Alexander's Ragtime Band" definitively bridged black ragtime and white America and paved the way for white acceptance of jazz, blues, rock 'n' roll, and rap musics.[25]

Irving Berlin had intimations of his prophetic function. For "Alexander's Ragtime Band" he used every songwriting technique in his vast archive to announce ragtime widely, popularly, and, above all, loudly. "Let me lead you by the hand," the lyrics offered, and according to Berlin's own crisp analysis, that was not all. The song's "opening words, emphasized by immediate repetition—'Come on and hear! Come on and hear!'—were an *invitation* to 'come,' to join in, and 'hear' the singer and his song," Berlin explained. Moreover, "the idea of *inviting* every receptive auditor within shouting distance became a part of the happy ruction—an idea pounded in again and again throughout the song in various ways—was the secret of the song's tremendous success."[26]

The "ruction" since has been less than happy. From the moment of its publication, lines were drawn over whether Berlin or his kind were capable of writing "Alexander." Once it was well established that Berlin had, the big question became whether "Alexander" was actually ragtime at all, although it was apparently ragtime enough for Scott Joplin who accused Berlin of plagiarism. The ignobility of the accusations against Berlin far exceeded any imaginable transgression, whether he had handled the genre less than dogmatically, or whether he was simply a Jew from Cherry Street. Most of the slurs appealed to the well-established traditions of antisemitism that had bedeviled both Rothstein and Frankfurter, such as huckstering, cultural disloyalty, and impurity. That Berlin had "paid a Negro ten dollars" to write "Alexander" was the preferred libel.[27]

Admittedly, one of the musical techniques Berlin left out of his ragtime masterpiece was syncopation, which by all accounts *defines* African-American ragtime. As Berlin acknowledged years later, "Alexander's Ragtime Band," syncopated in only a single verse, is a peppy funeral march. Berlin conceded that at the time he wrote the song, which was to sell one million copies of sheet music within three months and would change the pace and race of popular music, he did not quite understand what ragtime was. The ragtime in "Alexander"— like Wolfie Gilbert's Alabammy—had been an invention of the Jewish imagination. Nevertheless, despite his sometime ignorance about rhythm, Berlin would later maintain that "syncopation is the soul of every American."[28]

For a while, Berlin and his colleagues tried to pair syncopation with lyrics not expressly about African Americans but about other imagined groups as well. "The Yiddisha Rag" of 1909 was a typical attempt, both with respect to subject matter and inelegance: "Have you ever heard that clever Yiddisha rag, it's a daisy, / It's so spoony, nothing cooney, still it will set you half crazy."[29] That gem happened to be the handiwork of gentiles. Berlin himself toyed with the syncopation of "Jewish" themes in such pieces as "Yiddle on Your Fiddle, Play Some Ragtime." As often as songwriters tried to apply syncopation to groups other than blacks (usually to Jews or Italians, sometimes to Germans or the Irish), the songs never worked very well, and eventually such songs deteriorated into sheer travesty. If a ragtime protagonist was not black, then "the point of the song becomes the attempted appropriation of black music and dance by another of America's 'alien' groups, to comic effect," thinks music historian Charles Hamm. "Ragtime remained the music of America's marginalized population."[30] Rather, one might suggest, ragtime was the music that Jews *imagined* and therefore *constructed* to be

163

the music of all marginalized peoples, including themselves. More-over, Jews saw in their own experiences and in the experiences of African Americans something "typically American," namely, romantic marginality.

Berlin thought that "Russian Jewish boys who have grown up on the East Side" were able agents of ragtime and other "typically Ameri-can" musics because "they too are the products of that melting pot we call 'Americanization.'"[31] Berlin's vision of "Americanization" and the "melting pot," however, did not agree with the call to assimilate the immigrants into the mainstream social order. If Berlin believed that his aptitude for writing ragtime was the result of "Americaniza-tion," and that he was the real voice of "the people," then American-ization for Berlin was the call of the people to participate in African-American culture. George and Ira Gershwin, both born in Wil-liamsburg, Brooklyn—an area of second settlement for Eastern Jewry—made their definitive statement on true Americanism in their first collaboration, "The real American folk song—IS A RAG!"[32] Eight years later, when Jews helped jazz replace ragtime as the vogue music, the Jewish team of Rodgers and Hart expressed a similar belief that Americanization meant identification with imagined African-American culture. Note the particular attention that "Bugle Blow" (1926) pays to Jewish Americanization through jazz while heterogene-ity remains.

> We've a race that's het'rogeneous
> With folks from all the earth.
> A moving picture Metro genius
> Can come from foreign birth.
> And the race that used to be gypped
> By the Pharaohs down in Egypt
> By the gross appear,
> And we're mighty glad they're here.
> All were diff'rent when they came,
> But jazz has made them all the same!
>
> They take their places upon the dance floor,
> And then races all blend somehow!

We all are jazz relations!
We're all good Americans now![33]

"[T]he race that used to be gypped / By Pharaohs down in Egypt" become "good Americans," not by assimilation with a dominant Protestant culture but by blending on the dance floor, all to the rhythm of African-American musics. In the vision of the melting pot constructed by Eastern Jewry, Americanization is cultural incorporation, primarily from African Americans, and thereby America *is* "het'rogeneous."

Why "Russian Jewish boys" took what they considered African-American music and simultaneously imagined it to be "melting pot" music, "the people's" music, even "typically American," is the complicated but explicit point of Jolson's *The Jazz Singer*. Analysis of that central point is postponed, then, along with analysis of the parallel phenomenon of Jewish blackface, to the discussion of the film in the next chapter. Ultimately, Irving Berlin could only explain his attraction to the cacophony of the motifs of blackness with which he believed he wrapped himself by appealing to the American spirit of "het'rogeneity" he had come to represent: "If a Negro could write 'Alexander,'" he wanted to know, "why couldn't I?"[34]

Moreover, Berlin did not consider writing "Alexander" his own choice. "You write in the morning," he said, "you write at night. You write in a taxi, in the bathtub, or in an elevator. And after the song is all finished it may turn out to be very bad, but you sharpen your pencil and try again. A professional songwriter has his mind on his job all the time."[35] "Sometimes I turn out four or five songs a night," he claimed, tinkering at his piano until dawn. More often he averaged "from four to five songs a week."[36] Still, at this frenetic pace one does not write ragtime music for any reason but hypnotic fascination with the genre. The Jewish songwriters did not sit alone at their pianos for twelve hours a day for any such sly purpose as huckstering or theft. Rather, those Russian Jewish boys were in love with ragtime, and later they fell in love with jazz. Any love of the music so strong as that of Irving Berlin, as well as the dozens of other Russian Jewish boys who were Tin Pan Alley, can hardly be divorced from their genuine,

albeit confounded, fascination and identification with what they imagined—and simultaneously constructed—to be blackness.

Let us recall how Russian Jewish boys took Stephen Foster's "Old
Folks at Home" and reinstated the Swanee River into the American
vocabulary after seventy years of near amnesia. Remember that in
1919 Al Jolson was invigorated by the tremendous success of *Sinbad*,
so much so that he wished a happy New Year to fans and rivals alike.
Typically, he liked to take a public drink or two after a show, both to
vent the energy of his performance and to continue to clown into the
night for a select crowd of New York sophisticates. Not the sort of
man who would arrive anywhere alone, Jolson often called Buddy de
Sylva to join him in his rounds of hotel bars and private parties. One
night de Sylva brought along his young friend, George Gershwin.
At that midnight soiree, Gershwin quickly surrounded a piano with
admirers as he played rag after rag. Jolson sang along on some. Gershwin decided to plug his "Swanee," with words by Irving Caesar, yet
another Jew in their circles. Jolson liked it. Though "Swanee" had
already been introduced at the Capitol Theater with several dozen
chorus girls and a big band, it had not sold any sheet music. Jolson
sang it at his next opportunity, his famous Sunday night concerts at
the Winter Garden Theater. Before 1919 was through, "Swanee" had
sold more than two million records and a million copies of sheet
music. It was Gershwin's first hit, and it would be his biggest.[37]

Al Jolson eventually came to realize just how complicated the Jewish imagination of blackness was, but only after years of singing about
his beloved "Swanee" as if it were home. On most nights in the 1920s
an audience somewhere across America could hear Jolson proclaim
he would "give the world to be among the folks in Dixie." But Jolson
became gravely disappointed while on tour through southeast Geor-
gia when he finally arrived as a pilgrim at the banks of that river.
There Jolson discovered that the Swanee, like its mythical ancestor
the mighty Jordan, is nothing more than a pathetic trickle.

The Jazz Singer

CONFUSION abounded about the Jewish depiction of blackness until Samson Raphaelson finally decided to try to clear the muddle. A clean-cut undergraduate at the University of Illinois, Raphaelson went to see Al Jolson star in "Robinson Crusoe, Jr." in 1917. Sometime in the course of the show, Raphaelson claimed he finally understood the phenomenon which his coreligionists had only vaguely intimated: "My God, this isn't a jazz singer," he realized. "This is a cantor!"[1] Someone had finally made the connection explicit. Jews had become the group most responsible for the construction of blackness—not mimics, but creators—and their project was deeply indebted to something in their Jewish faith.

The image of the blackfaced cantor remained in Raphaelson's mind for five years before he wrote "The Day of Atonement," his fictionalized account of Al Jolson's life. Shortly after its publication, Jolson read the short story and decided that a comedic version of it, starring himself, would look good on the screen. D. W. Griffith, director of *Birth of a Nation*, agreed that the stage's most celebrated talent should work in film, and for a while Griffith considered directing the picture himself. Ultimately, he dropped that idea because even he considered the story "too racial," by which he meant its subject was too Jewish.[2] As Jolson worked his Hollywood connections looking for a studio and director to film his biography, he found that most of Hollywood agreed with Griffith. For modern movie audiences "The Day of Atonement" was too Jewish.

Meanwhile, Raphaelson turned his short story into a dramatic play, which he called *The Jazz Singer*, and brought it to Broadway on September 15, 1925. For the next two years it performed successfully to mostly Jewish audiences.[3] For a poll conducted by the *Jewish Tribune* to determine the best Jewish plays of the 1920s, Miss Rose Leby of

Richmond, Virginia, solemnly wrote to cast her vote for *The Jazz Singer* as the play that had "best analyzed the Jewish Question." She paid particular attention to the righteous behavior of the Al Jolson character, Jakie Rabinowitz. For Miss Leby, Jakie embodied "the struggle that was older than the oldest of them—the struggle between the old and the new." "The new generation of Jews is no different from that of other races," she felt. "Their cry is liberty, liberty in life, in work, in everything. And yet, Jakie was not a bad son." Despite the timeless and universal struggle for liberty, a struggle that Miss Leby did not consider particular to America, Jewish parents had nothing to fear. "The most profound belief gained from this play," Miss Leby claimed, "is the thought that a child reared in the atmosphere of Judaism cannot forget it. Let each mother and father take heed; and when their children seem to be breaking away from their faith, let them have patience and remember Jakie." Taken as a comment on the Jewish Question, *The Jazz Singer* proved for Miss Leby that neither Americanization nor any other generational divide threatened Jewish group life.[4]

Miss Leby might have been delighted to know that the founder of Jewish Studies in America, Professor Harry Austryn Wolfson of Harvard University, partisan against that school's Jewish quota and born in Lithuania, also believed that Americanization did not essentially conflict with Judaism, despite the presence in America of a "perennial type of Jewish *déraciné*" found throughout Jewish history. He suggested a certain inevitability to Jewish survival as well, and saw as the foundation of Jewish group life "a religion of sacrifice, of self-sacrifice." He proposed that Jewish-American life, like life in Eastern Europe, would have to surrender certain gentile advantages. "Some are born blind, some deaf, some lame," he thought, "and some are born Jews. To be isolated, to be deprived of many social goods and advantages, is our common lot as Jews. Are we willing to submit to Fate, or shall we foolishly struggle against it?" As with Miss Leby, escape from Judaism was not a realistic danger. To Wolfson, whether Jews would come to accept their inevitable identity and accompanying marginalization was the question.[5]

Neither Miss Leby nor Professor Wolfson could know how well applauded Jakie's righteous and inevitable return to his people was destined to become, for while *The Jazz Singer* lingered on Broadway, a small motion-picture company named Warner Brothers looked for a vehicle to premiere a modern miracle—the talking picture. Three Jewish brothers, Sam, Harry, and Jack Warner, had successfully premiered Vitaphone technology to an audience of industry elites in 1926 with a film short called *Don Juan*. But the new technology was not yet proven before paying audiences. Because the Warners made two Vitaphone feature films that flopped after the premiere of *Don Juan*, they knew that the new and expensive technology required the perfect vehicle. The Warners also knew that their studio would be financially threatened by another failed Vitaphone film. A breakthrough had to come soon or never.

In 1927 the Warners resolved to base their Vitaphone production upon the script that no other studio had ever seriously considered. For many reasons, *The Jazz Singer* was not a sure hit. For one, Warner Brothers originally signed the virtually unknown lead of the Broadway production, George Jessel, to star. Even Sam Warner's later hiring of Jolson did not ensure the film's success. Jolson's experience was entirely in stage comedy, while *The Jazz Singer* was a drama. Further, Jolson's name had never sold a single movie ticket. Moreover, D. W. Griffith had been right—the subject matter of *The Jazz Singer* was indeed "racial." Some film companies enjoyed moderate success with ethnic themes targeted at ethnic audiences, although this practice was less popular in the 1920s than it had been earlier. Warner Brothers, however, had achieved most of its previous successes by producing movies with universal appeal; *Rin Tin Tin* was by far its largest grossing picture before 1927.

The racialism of *The Jazz Singer*, however, is hardly limited to its conspicuous attempt to appeal to a particular ethnic audience. Additionally, the explicit theme of the film is the conflict of competing "racial" musics. Specifically, *The Jazz Singer* compares the liturgical music of Jews and the imagined music of African-Americans. Prayer and jazz become metaphors for Jews and blacks.

The opening scene of Raphaelson's play set the tone for the film. It introduces Samson Raphaelson's conception of Jewish liturgical music. In it, Cantor Rabinowitz, Al Jolson's fictive father, instructs a young Torah student in the ways of the Jewish liturgy.

CANTOR: [Stops student]. No, no, no! Didn't I tell you how you should sing it? Sing it with a sigh. Do you understand, my child? With a sigh![6]

Thus the first line of Raphaelson's play establishes the essence of Jewish liturgical music and therefore the imagined essence of the Jews: the interdictory "No." That fundamental law established, the cantor then instructs his student with the sad commentary of diaspora: "Sing it with a sigh." Throughout, the film depicts Jewish music as solemn, sad, painful, practiced, and above all interdictory—circumscribing right behavior—at least for those like Cantor Rabinowitz, who, according to an intertitle, "stubbornly held to the ancient traditions of his race."

Jazz music is quite different. In the film it is first heard while the jazz singer Jack Robin (born Jakie Rabinowitz), played by Jolson, sits in an American nightclub before a plate of down-home ham and eggs. With the music of a jazz band in the background, the camera catches Jolson as he dances a forkfull of the illicit meal into his mouth in syncopated time to the music. Saxophones, violin, drum kit, and dancing flappers—in contradistinction to the liturgical sigh of the Jews, American transgression is accompanied by untutored and irrepressible musical joy.

Throughout the film, jazz music is portrayed as light, gleeful, spontaneous, liberatory, and natural. As Jack the jazz singer explains to Cantor Rabinowitz, "Tradition is all right, but this is another day!" The Cantor responds with the strongest expletive in his vocabulary, "I never want to see you again—you *jazz singer*." The central musical symbols of the film (liturgy and jazz), the two worlds represented by them (Jewish and black), and the controlling matrices of those worlds (authority and release therefrom), have been established as utterly adverse, as either/or.[7]

After constructing prayer and jazz—imagined Judaism and imagined blackness—as irreconcilable, the film proposes a paradox: the jazz singer is Jewish. And we know, as did viewers of the film in 1927, that the paradox extends beyond the frames of the film: Al Jolson, the real jazz singer on which the fictive one is based, is Jewish; the author of nearly every song in the film, both liturgical and jazz, is Jewish;

the parts of the music, film, and stage industries that have brought popular jazz to America are Jewish.[8]

Thus the paradox constructed in the film reflects one constructed by the culture and industry of Jewish jazz more generally. Jews are the primary authors, performers, and disseminators of a music that their own imaginations will not allow them to write, perform, or disseminate *as Jews*.

The Jewish imagination had bullied itself into a corner. Because Jews had constructed Judaism and blackness, prayer and jazz, as opposites, how might Jews participate in jazz culture?

They wore blackface. Jews simply acted as though they were black. As fantastic a solution as it may seem, that is what they did. They studied ragtime and jazz, wore plantation clothing, brushed burnt cork on their faces, took on an imagined black diction, and played the "coon." That is, Jews constructed an elaborate vision of American blackness, nearly irrespective of actual African Americans or African-American culture, and then attempted to embody that vision. As a blackfaced cantor/jazz-singer, Jolson became the paradox incarnate, and thus became the incarnation of the Jewish imagination.

Playing the "coon" was real in the same sense that Johan Huizinga felt representational rituals are real. "Representation is really *identification*," Huizinga thought. "The rite produces the effect which is then not so much *shown figuratively* as *actually reproduced* in the action."[9] Like all symbols, blackface *is* what it represents, and is also *a wish to be* what it represents. When the Jews wore burnt cork and sang "Swanee," ritualistically, thousands upon thousands of times to audiences worldwide, the symbolized thing that they wished to be was unequivocally black. Jews *identified* with their own constructions of blackness.

Michael Rogin offers a different perspective on Jewish blackface. He understands blackface as a Jewish attempt to become assimilated, white Americans. In his view, minstrelsy separated the performer from both Jewish and black identities. Rogin claims, "Blackface emancipated the jazz singer from Jews and blacks by linking him to the groups he was leaving behind." Elsewhere he says, "By giving Jack his own voice, blackface propels him above both his father and African

Americans into the American melting pot." He continues, "Jack Robin plays a person of color instead of being confused for one. By painting himself black, he washes himself white."[10] One might suggest, however, that there are more straightforward ways for someone to demonstrate he is white than by acting black.

Rogin also relies on the mistaken assumption that this community of Eastern Jews was so desirous to "leave behind" other Jews, to wash themselves "white," and to be propelled into "the American melting pot," if that melting pot implied a loss of Jewish ethnicity and group feeling. That attitude is more typical of Western European Jewry.[11] Only with deep qualification can one propose that the community of Eastern Jews who produced and performed minstrelsy shared a similar drive to assimilate. Overwhelmingly, Eastern Jews voluntarily remained in Jewish communities and congregations throughout the 1920s and after,[12] while Jewish gangsters made delicatessens their offices. Nevertheless, Rogin insists that blackface is about escape from group life, and therefore he posits a reason for this driving desire to escape. Like many others, he turns to antisemitism as the stimulus. "Anti-Semitism is *The Jazz Singer*'s structuring absence."[13] But antisemitism is simply absent. Moreover, the relative absence of debilitative antisemitism in the period was a unique experience for Eastern Jews, and, as has been suggested in the Introduction, this void was in fact a source of confusion for Eastern Jewish identity.

Scholars in the field of whiteness studies have incorporated Rogin's view. Matthew Jacobson, for instance, has posited an "*E Pluribus Duo*," a "binary system" of racial categorization in America that forced such immigrants as Jews to choose between black and white in their quest to become American. The minstrelsy in *The Jazz Singer*, then, "appropriates blackness to constitute Jews' whiteness." "Paradoxically," Jacobson offers, "by donning blackface the Hebrew becomes Caucasian. . . . In playing black, the Jew becomes white."[14] Unfortunately, these have become now axioms. They may fit theories that see America in black and white but not the basic facts of Jewish group identity—or the facts of Jewish minstrelsy. Scholarship errs, I think, when it disregards how Jews viewed their relationship to their own group. It is also mistaken to ignore what Jews themselves said they were doing in writing ragtime, performing minstrelsy, and making

The Jazz Singer. By excluding Jewish voices, scholars have returned to Sartre's notorious view of Jewish identity, where antisemitism is its foundation and Jews only kowtow and conform, anxious to be included in the mainstream.[15]

But the sources speak differently. In Jewish-American descriptions of ragtime and minstrelsy, becoming "Caucasian" does not appear as a need, desire, or even a question. (We shall soon see what Jews believed by reading what they actually said.) Despite recent scholarship, Jews will not fit easily into a larger American tradition of whitening and Americanization based on racism. For most Jews in America, the deepest and most direct traditions from which their behaviors concerning assimilation derived were, of course, Jewish. Scholars have been too willing to throw these Eastern European Jews into an American "melting pot" as if their identities, culture, and behaviors had been created in the United States, ex nihilo. If Jewish identity and culture were formed in opposition to anyone, it had happened in the mutual practices of exclusiveness and tolerance in Eastern Europe in which Jews had lived en masse from shortly after their first charter in Lithuania in the thirteenth century.[16]

The culture and society of Eastern Jewry must be considered for the sources of Jewish behavior in America, particularly in a generation so heavily populated by immigrants. Moreover, scholarship might respect the rather pronounced longings among the descendents of Eastern European Jewry for ethnic identity and group feeling in America, rather than impose assimilation, acculturation, whiteness, or any other model that suggests that Jews decided to change into something other than themselves because in America they could. As a matter of historical fact, in the 1920s when some Jews wished to divorce themselves from their Jewish identities, they assimilated rather freely. As matters of biographical fact, Eddie Cantor was extraordinarily involved with the Jewish community, and both he and Jolson requested and received Jewish funerals. Blackface is a symptom of *confusion* about Jewish identity in America. Confusion is not tantamount to abandonment.[17]

That being said, Jewish identification with imagined African-American culture was profoundly confusing. The central conflict of the plot of *The Jazz Singer* underscores the torment of living in two imagined worlds, untenably in both. Jolson's character, Jack Robin, must choose. His father, Cantor Rabinowitz, is dying. The cantor's last wish is for his son to replace him at services for Yom Kippur, the Day of Atonement, and to lead the Kol Nidre prayer, which welcomes each wayward Jew back into the Jewish community no matter the transgressions. But this opportunity for Jack Robin finally to reconcile the ways of a jazz singer with the ways of his father and his people cannot happen, for on the evening of the Day of Atonement, Jack Robin must perform his blackface routine on Broadway. The show's producer has made plain that if Jack abandons opening night, his career is over. The sexton of Cantor Rabinowitz's synagogue appeals to Jack in the name of tradition: "Would you be the *first* Rabinowitz in five generations to fail your God?" Jakie's mother can only plead to her son that, even now, as he stands in blackface, it is not yet too late: "In two hours the sun will be out of the sky. Atonement begins— come home, Jakie."

Backstage, covered in burnt cork, Jack Robin begins to question to which race he belongs. "But there's something, after all, in my heart," he sobs, "maybe it's the call of the ages—the cry of my race." Both the racial ambiguity and the angst of that line are accurate. Asa Yoelson, the son of a rabbi, born along a dirt road in Seredzius, Lithuania—for forty years he sang ragtime and jazz, wore plantation clothing, brushed burnt cork on his face, took on an imagined African-American diction, and pretended he was black. When Jack Robin calls out about the cry of his race, about which race he speaks is deeply ambiguous. Jack moves to his dressing-room mirror and sees himself as black, then the mirror fades into a vision of Cantor Rabinowitz praying *kol nidre*, and then the black face reappears. The mirror reflects the central paradox of the phenomenon of Jewish minstrelsy and jazz performance: What is Jack Robin, cantor or jazz singer? What is Irving Berlin, Gus Kahn, or Jerome Kern? What is Rodgers or Hammerstein or Hart? What is Eddie Cantor or Sophie Tucker? What is George Gershwin? And what is Al Jolson, Jew or black?

SAMSON RAPHAELSON was not at all happy with how his fiction had turned out. "Something happened between my original conception of the theme and the actual completion of the play," he said. "I don't know what. I felt like the young man who starts out with the noble intention of going to synagogue and somehow or other ends up in a burlesque show."[18] Indeed, the Jewish fascination with blackness had made a travesty of both Jewish and jazz music, and of both Jewish and African-American cultures. But why the Jewish fascination with African-American music in the first place? What had been so alluring about the curious comparison of cantors and jazz singers that caused Jews to risk their secure places in American society at a time when large parts of the American middle class were defining their identities *against* the new presence of African Americans in the North? Why had Jews identified so strongly with another group that they wondered whether their own Jewish identity might be in jeopardy?[19]

The answer may be as simple as the hackneyed comparisons of Jews and blacks suggest. In its review of *The Jazz Singer*, the *Morgen Zhurnal* spoke characteristically for all the Jewish papers. "Is there any incongruity in this Jewish boy with his face painted like a Southern Negro singing in the Negro dialect?" a critic asked. "No, there is not. Indeed, I detected again and again the minor key of Jewish music, the wail of the Chazan, the cry of anguish of a people who had suffered. The son of a line of rabbis well knows how to sing the songs of the most cruelly wronged people in the world's history."[20] African-American music, according to another article, "was born on the plantations of the South and in which one can hear the cracks of the slave-drivers' whips and the clanging of chains and the pain of expression."[21] Eastern Jews, many of whom had come from the bleak Russian Pale, believed they were uniquely qualified to interpret that music. Al Jolson himself made the shibboleth comparison of Jewish and African-American exiles in his film *Big Boy*. On the lawn of a plantation, dressed in overalls, burnt cork, a wig of wool, and a broken hat of straw, Jolson leads a group of recently freed slaves, played by African-American actors, through verses of the classic slave spiritual "Go Down Moses."

> When Israel was in Egypt land—
>   Let my people go!
> Oppressed so hard they could not stand—
>   Let my people go!

Go down Moses, way down in Egypt land,
Tell old Pharaoh to let my people go![22]

Exile was the content of the shared sacred history to which the *Kali-fornia Yidishe Shtime* referred in its praise of Jolson's blackface performance. "In every fluctuation of Jolson's voice, and in the smallest movement of his body, there is such religious tragedy that a shiver courses through the bones."[23]

That same newspaper saw more than just shared tragedy in minstrelsy, however. It posited something quite fantastic. "When one hears Jolson's jazz songs," the newspaper suggested, "one realizes that jazz is the new prayer of the American masses, and Al Jolson is their cantor. The Negro makeup in which he expresses his misery is the appropriate *talis* for such a communal leader."

Burnt cork as talis. The comparison merits reflection. A talis (or tallith) is a ritual prayer shawl first found in Israelite religion in the biblical injunction to wear fringes on one's garment. Upon placing the talis on the body for Sabbath, Yom Kippur, and Ninth of Av prayer services, the wearer recites the following blessing: "Blessed are you, Lord our God, King of the Universe who has sanctified us by your commandments and has commanded us to wrap ourselves in the fringed garment." According to the Talmud, in wearing the prayer shawl one envelops himself in the holiness of God's commandments and covenant with Israel. Thereby, the wearer of a talis subjects himself to the divine will and commits himself to the obligations of the Law. It is traditional for Jews to so remind themselves of their envelopment in the commandments at significant moments in the lifecycle. Jews marry beneath a talis; male Jews are buried in one, as was Al Jolson.[24]

Yet it is safe to assume that for the Yiddish journalist who compared burnt cork to a talis, envelopment in the Law was not what he had in mind. Rather, when he suggested the replacement of one ritual costume for another, he thought not of religious commandment, but of the "religious tragedy" of the Jewish people, and the reflection of that tragedy in African-American marginalization. If burnt cork was the new talis for the Jews in America, then *marginalization* had replaced *commandment* as the framework of Jewish identity: exile replaced covenant.

There is a second implication. According to our Yiddish journalist, "jazz is the new prayer of the American masses, and Al Jolson is their cantor." The Jewish mediation of the voice of "the people" and what was "typically American" had been suggested by the Jewish songwriters, but interpreters of *The Jazz Singer* induced a significantly more powerful version of this mediation. Jews were marginalized, blacks were marginalized, and somehow *Americans* were marginalized. When Al Jolson interpreted the African-American story to America, he served as America's religious leader. "Al Jolson is their cantor." With two thousand years of diaspora as their history, and jazz music as their voice, Jews imagined that no other group could better navigate for Americans their identity as a nation of outsiders.

That Jews imagined America as a place where all are marginalized may seem strange, but the feeling was not at all limited to Jews. As R. Laurence Moore has suggested, for many Americans perceiving oneself as marginalized had become a "characteristic way of inventing one's Americanness." This was particularly so in the midst of the Jazz Age and in the wake of everything that the Great War had churned together and torn apart—many Americans were feeling rudderless and lost. For Jewish Americans, the view dovetailed well with their 2,700-year-old theology of exile first codified in the book of Exodus. In the Jewish imagination, Jews, Blacks, and America all conjoined in their mutual marginalizations. By being in exile, Jews were finally at home in America.[25]

Yet the conjunction was not stable. Burnt cork could not replace the talis. The doctrine of exile released from the obligations of the covenant would be something short of Judaism, an empty ideology without an attendant structure of behavior. Ultimately, the Judaism suggested by *The Jazz Singer* looked to fill that identity with African-American cultural forms. But the Jewish imagination of African-American culture was also an empty set, a longing to incorporate that which was never really considered but only imagined. Burnt cork was a fiction. Perhaps even Al Jolson came to realize this as he interposed the following question in the final frames of *The Jazz Singer*:

"Mammy, don't you know me? It's your little *baby!*" But neither an antebellum Mammy nor a yidishe mama would recognize the jazz singer as her own. He is neither Jewish nor African-American, neither from the Russian Pale nor from Dixie. He is located nowhere but in his own imagination.

And, of course, on movie screens worldwide.

THE attitude of *The Jazz Singer* toward the traditions and commandments of Judaism was not confined to the film. In 1927, one day before *The Jazz Singer* premiered, Conservative Rabbi Mordecai Kaplan announced to his congregation that the kol nidre prayer was too mindful of the Law, too neglectful of Jewish emotions, and would be deleted from his Yom Kippur service. "No text could be more inappropriate and less in keeping with the spirit of Yom Kippur than the text of Kol Nidre," Kaplan told the Jewish press. "It is a dry, legalistic formula." Kaplan thought it was "poor religious taste, to say the least, to resort to a legalistic formula for the articulation of our emotions." For High Holiday services at his synagogue that year, Rabbi Kaplan decided that the authoritarian and commandment-centered prayer of kol nidre would be replaced by a more emotional Psalm 130.[26]

Compared to the blackface revision of Judaism, Kaplan's redraft was rather gentle. It had taken thirty years and three Jewish industries of song, stage, and screen to make *The Jazz Singer*. As a document of the American Jewish imagination, collectively written by Jews from all sectors of the Eastern European immigration and their children, it is a fundamental document in the history of world Jewry because it is the most elaborate and subtle fiction that American Jews have collectively made about themselves.

And Jewish audiences loved it. Though no major African-American newspaper even mentioned *The Jazz Singer*,[27] not one Jewish paper in America wrote a bad review of it. Not Yiddish or English. Not Reform, Conservative, or Orthodox. Some grumbled about imperfections in Jolson's screen acting but quickly forgave the handicap of an old stage dog forced to learn new tricks for film. But no negative word was written about the portrayal of the content of the Jewish imagination. There was no disparaging comment on the Jewish fascination with blackness, for instance. Moreover, someone might have contested the film's presentation of Judaism as fundamentally lacking both joy and liberatory possibility, and suggested that the songs of Purim or Klezmer music were readier comparisons to jazz. Someone might have mentioned the fact that kol nidre and its attending culture of commandments is only one component of Jewish culture. Nevertheless, the Jewish imagination presented in *The Jazz Singer* was accepted by all quarters who cared enough to comment on the depiction of their faith in the world's most celebrated film. The Jewish press had faltered initially in its acceptance of Rothstein's criminality and was delayed in recognizing their sympathies for Sacco and Vanzetti, but for Jolson they simply cheered. One Yiddish journalist suggested that he knew why: "*Heymishkayt,*" he thought, "the feeling of home is Al Jolson's charm."[28] By identifying with blacks, Jews were at home in America.

The Jazz Singer opened film to some Jewish papers as a legitimate subject for review, and then enjoyed the honor of being the first film reviewed in those papers. Many film reviews would follow, as would many motion pictures. Jolson did well in some, not so well in others. But no picture would ever capture the approval of the Jewish imagination as categorically as had Al Jolson's *The Jazz Singer*.

When Yom Kippur ended on the evening of October 6, 1927, and as fans rushed the Warner Theater where the first reel at *The Jazz Singer* premiere began to roll, Jolson must have sat back in his seat and smiled.[29] From the applause, he knew that he had been right all along. Jolie was the greatest. He would have told you that, too. He had come to represent the Jewish imagination of the Jazz Age to the Jews themselves, and he had entertained America doing it. But most momentous for the Jews, Al Jolson had come to embody what his people believed because he understood viscerally the symbol that Samson Raphaelson needed to spell out for the rest of us. "The singer of jazz is what Matthew Arnold said of the Jew," wrote Raphaelson, "'lost between two worlds, one dead, the other powerless to be born.'"[30]

Jazz Age Jews

IN PALESTINE of the 1920s, the greatest political and academic minds vied to establish beliefs and behaviors with which to forge Jewish identity. That is an amazing story in its own right, how those minds managed to resuscitate the government of Israel. But in America during the same period, similar attempts to organize Jewish personality simply failed.[1] Neither a Talmud-bound rabbinate nor a Jewish self-government (*kehilla*) took hold as an institution of complete moral authority. This terrified many leading Jewish-American intellectuals.[2]

But American Jewish identity did emerge. It sprang up from everywhere: from neighborhoods, newspapers, literature and theater, business and industry, philanthropy, material culture, kitchens in both homes and restaurants, picket lines and politics, Zionism, new rituals and holidays, nostalgia, and along countless other lanes so familiar that scholars of the Jews have only begun to notice them. We do well to note that for American Jewry, this ethnic identity comprised a large part of lived religion.[3]

Yet we also do well to remember what it is that living religions do. They manifest commonly held understandings of the way the world is, as well as one's right place in that world, into ideological and behavioral forms.

Among Jews, lived religion has been supported by the twin doctrines of a communal covenant with God and communal exile from both the world and Israel. These doctrines have acted as the lenses through which Jews see, believe, and behave traditionally. In choosing a life of commandment as the way to live rightly in the world, Jews have also recognized their incapacity to fulfill completely the lessons of those commandments, let alone truly understand them.

180

Thus, traditionally, the concepts of covenant and exile are immutably paired; combined, they have comprised the basis of Jewish identity in the diaspora.[4]

In nineteenth-century Eastern Europe, however, as Russian Jewry fell out from under the protection of the tsars and institutions of Jewish communal and religious authority deteriorated, the doctrine of communal exile came to take on special significance in the lived religion of the Jews. To be sure, Ashkenazic Jewish identity had long been fused with social alienation, but for some that status became the primary category of Jewish attachment—unhinged from the commandments. Those Jews who did not seek to fulfill the behavioral strictures of the covenant remained Jews simply by imagining themselves as marginalized. For them, identity replaced ritual observance. This continued in America in the 1920s, even though Eastern Jewry was no longer oppressed. I suggest, along with participants of the Jewish Jazz Age themselves, that outsider identification is a Jewish-American practice derived, in part, from the theology of exile, and is linked to discomfort with social success. In America of the 1920s, when Jews themselves were succeeding, they identified with those who were not. Thus Jews met the obligation of their own definition of themselves as a marginalized people.[5]

This phenomenon is just one theological aspect of ethnic Jewish identity and behavior in America. Theological expressions abide in all realms of Jewish culture, from the Talmud-Torah school of the most orthodox community to the syncopated songs of Tin Pan Alley. The increased understanding of material, commercial, racial, class, and gender aspects of Jewish behaviors and rituals has revealed worlds upon worlds of Jewish lived religion. These newly recognized expressions of Jewish identity, however, must be considered as part of a longer history of Jewish culture. Discussions of American Jewish behavior need to consider the theological life and its role in identity. We must note, for instance, that the Passover meal is the most practiced American Jewish ritual, bar none. Most American Jews, today as in the Jazz Age, sit at a table once a year and *voluntarily reenact their exile*. This says something powerful about what Jews believe themselves to be.

The Jazz Singer cannot be understood apart from either the doctrine of exile or its attendant Passover ritual, not least because much of Hollywood participated in that ritual. Moreover, not to consider the self-understandings of historical subjects shuns irreplaceable evidence. When Jews likened their social position to medieval usurers, anarchists, and African Americans, and explicitly understood these identifications within an historical and sociological context of marginalization and a theological context of exile, we must consider the possibility that they actually *believed* it and behaved accordingly. These beliefs are the content of the Jewish-American imagination, which is simply another way of saying that they are the content of the Jewish-American faith.[6]

In blackface, Al Jolson became a symbol through which Eastern Jewry in America understood itself. To a people who imagined itself fundamentally as Other, a Jew painted as an African American was an image of magisterial striking power. To the Jews in America, its symbolic power must have compared with that of the prophet Ezra, swallowing a Torah scroll in an age when to be a Hebrew meant to embody the Law.

That comparison is not made glibly or without the counsel of the Yiddish journalist who thought Jolson's burnt cork had superseded the talis. And it begs one further point. The people of the book have also become the people of the fringe. Marginalization has become a core component of American Jewish identity.

There have always been shufflings between the twin doctrines of covenant and exile. Given the extraordinary boom in the building and attendance of synagogues in America in the 1920s, the covenant seems to have been changing but secure.[7] Nevertheless, perhaps a slow cultural shift in favor of exile has occurred over the past two centuries in the imagination of the descendents of Eastern European Ashkenaz, a shift that is still in progress. The three subjects examined herein are only convenient exemplars of that shift in America. Today of course, Arnold Rothstein's fame has been replaced by that of businessmen of more recent marginal financial activity. Felix Frankfurter's Sacco-Vanzetti work has been copied many times by those who claim a Jewish propensity "to achieve justice."[8] Al Jolson's fascination with African-American culture hasn't vanished either. Exhaustive examples of outsider identification would go well beyond the 1920s. And so the projects of our three subjects continue to register as types in the contemporary American Jewish mind—as stereotypes to some, but as compelling categories in the Jewish imagination nevertheless. All of this leads me to suggest, as a closing thought, that perhaps American Jews today continue to be Jazz Age Jews as well.

NOTES

INTRODUCTION

1. This is the "second generation" described by Deborah Dash Moore in *At Home in America: Second Generation New York Jews* (New York: Columbia University Press, 1981). For success in the American economy, see Thomas Kessner, *The Golden Door: Italian and Jewish Immigrant Mobility in New York City, 1880–1915* (New York: Oxford University Press, 1977) and Moore, *At Home in America*, 61–87; for political success, see Moore, *At Home in America*, 201–230, as well as part II of this book, "Frankfurter among the Anarchists." For just one example of the Jewish place in cultural production, see Neal Gabler, *An Empire of Their Own: How the Jews Invented Hollywood* (New York: Crown Publishers, 1988).

2. There is little by way of scholarly literature on the concept of Jewish identification with outsiders. Several works treat the Jew *as* outsider, and find antisemitism to be a central factor. In the realm of politics for instance, see Robert A. Burt, *Two Jewish Justices: Outcasts in the Promised Land* (Berkeley: University of California Press, 1988). With respect to Jewish identification with African-American culture, Michael Rogin argues that it is not identification at all, but that whatever relation does exist is based upon antisemitism: "Anti-Semitism is *The Jazz Singer's* structuring absence." See Rogin, *Blackface, White Noise: Jewish Immigrants in the Hollywood Melting Pot* (Berkeley: University of California Press, 1996), 89. In his groundbreaking work on Jewish identification with Jewish criminality, Arthur Goren makes no claim to the cause of the identification; see Goren, *Saints and Sinners: The Underside of American Jewish History* (Cincinnati: American Jewish Archives, 1988). For a view that emphasizes the effects of antisemitism in the period, see Leonard Dinnerstein, *Antisemitism in America* (New York: Oxford University Press, 1994), 58–104.

3. In each case both the actions of the Jewish participants and the reactions of the larger Jewish public exemplify outsider identification. In this study the reaction of the second generation is found predominantly in Yiddish newspaper coverage of the described events. Rothstein, Frankfurter, and Jolson eventually became heroes to the whole Jewish press, both English (controlled by Western European Jews) and Yiddish (controlled by Eastern Jews). Yet the Yiddish press always became supportive earlier, so it is important to determine if the Yiddish press can be used to gauge the opinions of the second generation—again, children of immigrants or those who migrated while young. I think it is an appropriate source for the following reasons. According to a 1925 survey, the Yiddish press reached 550,000 Jews (about a fifth of American Jewry, which itself was close to 90 percent Eastern European at this point). It was usually read in tandem with English (mainstream) papers—77 percent of its readers did this. Over 70 percent of its readers had been in America for more than

eleven years, the majority of whom were between twenty-six and fifty, with good numbers at the younger end of the spectrum, between twenty-six and thirty-five. Granted, only 9 percent of its readers were born in America. Still, it is possible to conclude that there were many second generation Eastern Jews among the readers of the Yiddish press (naturalized while young—products of the American ghetto), and that the opinions of these readers are reflected in their pages, especially because the readers so loyally continued to read them, even in tandem with the regular American press. Moreover, the conformity of Yiddish coverage of the three cases, despite their usual bickering, does suggest a larger conformity of mind among Eastern Jewry in these three instances. About the survey, see Hasia R. Diner, *In the Almost Promised Land: American Jews and Blacks, 1915–1935* (Westport, Conn.: Greenwood Press, 1977), 30. For population estimates, see Jonathan D. Sarna, ed., *The American Jewish Experience* (New York: Holmes & Meier, 1986), 296ff.

4. Eli Lederhendler, "Did Russian Jewry Exist Prior to 1917?" in *Jews and Jewish Life in Russia and the Soviet Union*, ed. Yaacov Ro'i (Portland, Oreg.: Frank Cass and Co., 1995), 22, 25.

5. Jacob Katz, *Exclusiveness and Tolerance: Studies in Jewish-Gentile Relations in Medieval and Modern Times* (West Orange, N.J.: Behrman House, 1961), 13, 22.

6. See Katz, *Exclusiveness and Tolerance*. The demarcation of Jewish communal life was Katz's career-long project. On the social position of alienation as a sign of the covenant, see also Yehezkiel Kaufmann, *Golah v'Nekhar* [Hebrew: Exile and Alienation], Vol. 1 & 2 (Tel Aviv: Dvir Company, 1929). The Jewish doctrine of exile may be distinguished from the Islamic notion of the "stranger." In medieval Islam, as I understand it, a Muslim might be in an alien society (*dar al-Harb*), but that had no relation to his theological status. See Franz Rosenthal, "The Stranger in Medieval Islam," *Arabica* 44 (1997): 35–75.

See also Eli Lederhendler, "Modernity without Emancipation or Assimilation? The Case of Russian Jewry," in *Assimilation and Community: The Jews in Nineteenth-Century Europe*, eds. Jonathan Frankel and Steven J. Zipperstein (New York: Cambridge University Press, 1992), 324–333. In that essay, Lederhendler reminds us of "Jacob Katz's critique of the dominant Germanocentric tradition in modern Jewish historiography" and of how that critique has been accepted and modified by Todd Endelman in his work on English Jewry, Marsha Rozenblit and Robert S. Wistrich in their separate works on Vienna, and Hillel Kieval in his work on Prague. See the essays by Katz, Wistrich, and Kieval in Jacob Katz, ed., *Toward Modernity: The European Jewish Model* (New Brunswick, N.J.: Transaction Books, 1987); Todd M. Endelman, *The Jews of Georgian England: Tradition and Change in a Liberal Society* (Philadelphia: Jewish Publication Society of America, 1979); Marsha L. Rozenblit, *The Jews of Vienna, 1867–1914: Assimilation and Identity* (Albany: State University of New York Press, 1983).

7. Recent scholarship has framed the question of the Jew as outsider entirely within the context of Enlightenment and emancipation, and from the perspective of Western European Jewry. According to this interpretation, Jewish feelings of margin-

ality in America, including those of the descendents of Eastern European Jewry, are founded on the fact that "for two centuries, Jews have staked their position in Western society on the promise of the Enlightenment," meaning emancipation. But simultaneously the program of Enlightenment sought to assimilate Jews and to eliminate the Jewish group identity that had formed around Jewish communal status in the middle ages. "What the modern state gave to such groups with one hand it took away with the other." This is what some have called "the dialectic of the Jewish Enlightenment," in which Jews found themselves in ambivalent and contradictory relationships with the modern state and with mainstream society: sometimes Jews accepted emancipation and longed for individual acceptance by the majority, while sometimes they disdained such acceptance and longed for group identity. For advocates of this view, the Jewish Question of Western Europe frames the ambivalence of Jewish "insider/outsider" identity for all Jews in America. I do not take this view here, since almost 90 percent of American Jewry did not come from the emancipated West. See David Biale, Michael Galchinsky, and Susannah Heschel, "Introduction: The Dialectic of Jewish Enlightenment," in *Insider/Outsider: American Jews and Multiculturalism*, eds. David Biale, Michael Galchinsky, and Susannah Heschel (Berkeley: University of California Press, 1998), 1–16; see also David Biale, "The Melting Pot and Beyond: Jews and the Politics of American Identity," in *Insider/Outsider*, 17–33, in which the dialectic of Jewish Enlightenment becomes for Eastern Jewry a "double consciousness" of assimilative and separationist tendencies in America.

8. Lederhendler has found the same behavior in Russia. "Where community remained so central an issue, those who advocated Western-type accommodation combining integration and identity also articulated a strong commitment to community." See Lederhendler, "Modernity Without Emancipation and Assimilation?" 338.

9. See R. Laurence Moore, *Religious Outsiders and the Making of Americans* (New York: Oxford University Press, 1986), xi, 33, 73, in which Moore argues that America is a land where many groups consider themselves apart from an imagined mainstream; therefore, perceiving oneself as marginalized has become a "characteristic way of inventing one's Americanness." Outsider status, he thinks, is invented "by turning aspects of a carefully nurtured sense of separate identity against a vaguely defined concept of mainstream culture." Moore calls these "deliberate strategies of differentiation," and sees them among Mormons, Christian Scientists, African-American churches, Catholics, and Jews. He also suggests that the sacred history of the Jews has become a worldview with which many American religious groups identify.

10. Eleanor Roosevelt to Sara Delano Roosevelt, May 12, 1918, Franklin D. Roosevelt Library, cited in Joseph P. Lash, ed., *From the Diaries of Felix Frankfurter* (New York: W. W. Norton & Company, 1975), 24; E. Digby Baltzell, *The Protestant Establishment: Aristocracy & Caste in America* (New Haven: Yale University Press, 1987); John Higham, *Send These to Me: Immigrants in Urban America* (Baltimore: The Johns Hopkins University Press, 1984).

11. Several intriguing works have described a Catholic "ambiguity of success" among discrete portions of American Catholicism and link these feelings with the theological call to emulate Christ as a suffering servant. See David J. O'Brien, *The Renewal of American Catholicism* (New York: Oxford University Press, 1972), 80–108; James Terence Fisher, *The Catholic Counterculture in America, 1933–1962* (Chapel Hill: University of North Carolina Press, 1989). So far as I can tell, this has not translated into outsider identification as it has for Jews.

INTERLUDE: JAZZ AGE ECONOMICS

1. John D. Hicks, *Republican Ascendancy: 1921–1933* (New York: Harper & Brothers, 1960), 6; F. Scott Fitzgerald, "Echoes of the Jazz Age," *The Crack-Up*, ed. Edmund Wilson (New York: New Directions, 1945), 13–22.

2. *Abstract of the Census of Manufacturers, 1919* (Washington, D.C., 1923), 886; *Fourteenth Census of the United States, Population* (Washington, D.C., 1921), I, 76; President's Conference on Unemployment, *Recent Economic Changes in the United States*, 2 vols. (New York, 1929), I, 272–273. Also see the Henry Ford Museum & Greenfield Village website at: http://www.hfmgv.org/histories/fmc/fmc.chrono.html.

3. Arcadius Kahan, "Economic Opportunities and Some Pilgrims' Progress: Jewish Immigrants from Eastern Europe in the United States, 1890–1914," in *Essays in Jewish Social and Economic History* (Chicago: University of Chicago Press, 1986), 101–117. Though they were by no means the majority, by 1925 a Jewish newspaper could brag about "Our New Multi-Millionaires," and note with delighted surprise that "these new wizards come from Lithuania, Poland and Galicia." *American Israelite*, June 18, 1925, 3.

4. *Recent Economic Changes in the United States*, I, 80–82. Catherine Gudis, "The Road to Consumption: Outdoor Advertising and the American Cultural Landscape," Yale Ph.D. dissertation, 1999.

5. Fitzgerald, "Echoes," 21.

CHAPTER 1: ARNOLD ROTHSTEIN

1. Chicago *Herald and Examiner*, September 30, 1920, cited in Eliot Asinof, *Eight Men Out: The Black Sox and the 1919 World Series* (New York: Holt, Rinehart and Winston, 1963), 121.

2. The *Sporting News*, cited in Asinof, *Eight Men Out*, 135ff.

3. See "Jewish Wires Direct Tammany's Gentile Puppets," "Jewish Idea Molded Federal Reserve Plan," "Jewish Jazz Becomes Our National Music," "Jewish Gamblers Corrupt American Baseball," and "Jewish Degradation of American Baseball," in *The International Jew: The World's Foremost Problem*, vols. I–IV (Dearborn, Mich.: The Dearborn Independent, 1921).

4. I hope these chapters will stand as evidence. Also see Robert Lacey, *Little Man: Meyer Lansky and the Gangster Life* (Boston: Little, Brown and Company, 1991); Ed Reid and Ovid Demaris, *The Green Felt Jungle* (New York: Trident Press, 1963).

5. The New York *World* never mentions his first name. See *World*, May 5, 1920, 1.

6. See Kahan, "The Impact of Industrialization in Tsarist Russia on the Socioeconomic Conditions of the Jewish Population" and "Notes on Jewish Entrepreneurship in Tsarist Russia," in *Essays*, 1–69, 82–100; Kessner, *The Golden Door*.

CHAPTER 2: GAMBLING IN THE TIME
OF ROTHSTEIN'S YOUTH

1. Two of Sullivan's poolhalls were located on Center Street, one on Marion (now Lafayette), and the other at 116 Center, across from the Tombs Police Court. Alvin F. Harlow, *Old Bowery Days* (New York: D. Appleton and Company, 1931), 489. Daniel Czitrom wonders if Sullivan's illegal activities were inventions of muckrakers. See Czitrom, "Underworlds and Underdogs: Big Tim Sullivan," *Journal of American History* 78 (1991): 536–558.

2. Lloyd Morris, *Incredible New York: High Life and Low Life of the Last Hundred Years* (New York: Random House, 1951), 233.

3. Herbert Asbury, *Sucker's Progress: An Informal History of Gambling in America from the Colonies to Canfield* (New York: Dodd, Mead & Co., 1938), 455–458; "This City's Crying Shame," *New York Times*, March 9, 1900. Again, Czitrom wonders whether the "gambling commission" was a figment of the progressive imagination. See Czitrom, "Underworlds and Underdogs."

4. Scarne (who knew Rothstein) estimated that the dice are thrown 337 times per hour in a private game. See John Scarne, *Scarne on Dice* (North Hollywood: Melvin Powers Wilshire Book Company, 1980), 187.

5. Leo Katcher, *The Big Bankroll: The Life and Times of Arnold Rothstein* (New Rochelle, N.Y.: Arlington House, 1959), 28.

6. Asbury, *Sucker's Progress*, 442ff.

7. Alexander Garfield, *Canfield: The True Story of the Greatest Gambler* (Garden City, N.Y.: Doubleday, Doran and Co., 1930), 152.

8. Asbury, *Sucker's Progress* 441–451; Morris, *Incredible New York*, 226–229; "This City's Crying Shame," *New York Times*, March 9, 1900.

9. Ann Fabian, *Card Sharps, Dream Books, & Bucket Shops: Gambling in 19th-Century America* (Ithaca, N.Y.: Cornell University Press, 1990), 3. Fabian considers the use of ideas about gambling "both overtly and implicitly, to construct the ordered economic rationality so necessary to a liberal political economy" and does not seem to consider the practice of gambling to be a resistance to that order.

10. Clifford Geertz, "Deep Play: Notes on the Balinese Cockfight," in *The Interpretation of Cultures* (New York: Basic Books, 1973), 412–453.

11. Garfield, *Canfield*, 11, 158–163; Asbury, *Sucker's Progress*, 421–427.

12. Garfield, *Canfield*, 143; Richard Dormant and Margaret F. Macdonald, *James McNeill Whistler* (New York: Harry N. Abrams, Inc., 1995), 282.

13. Carolyn Rothstein, *Now I'll Tell* (New York: Vanguard Press, 1934), 26; Daniel Bell, *The End of Ideology* (New York: The Free Press, 1962), 127–150; Baltzell, *The Protestant Establishment*, 26–45.

14. *Morgen Zhurnal*, November 18, 1928, 2; see Jeffrey S. Gurock and Jacob J. Schacter, *A Modern Heretic and a Traditional Community: Mordecai M. Kaplan, Orthodoxy, and American Judaism* (New York: Columbia University Press, 1997).

15. Rothstein, *Now I'll Tell*, 44; *Morgen Zhurnal*, November 18, 1928, 2.

16. Rothstein, *Now I'll Tell*, 19.

17. Katcher, *Big Bankroll*, 20.

18. See, for instance, the classic statement of this theme in Anzia Yezierska's *Bread Givers: A Struggle between a Father of the Old World and a Daughter of the New* (New York: Doubleday, 1925).

19. Moore, *At Home in America*.

20. Mishnah Rosh Ha-Shanah 1:8, BT Rosh Ha-Shanah 22a; Mishnah Sanhedrin 3:3, BT Sanhedrin 24b-25a, Mishnah Avot 4:4.

21. Morris, *Incredible New York*, 220–230. Progressivism is here understood as the ideology and attending social movement of a particular social class, which Martin Sklar (following Digby Baltzell and Max Weber) considers to be both capitalist and largely Protestant. See Martin J. Sklar, *The Corporate Reconstruction of American Capitalism, 1890–1916* (New York: Cambridge University Press, 1988).

22. Czitrom, "Underworlds and Underdogs," 548–551; Asbury, *Sucker's Progress*, 460–464.

23. Hugh Bradley, *Such Was Saratoga* (New York: Doubleday, Doran and Company, 1940), 147.

24. Cited in Garfield, *Canfield*, 290.

CHAPTER 3: THE RISE OF ROTHSTEIN

1. Donald Henderson Clarke, *In the Reign of Rothstein* (New York: Vanguard Press, 1929), 20; Bradley, *Such Was Saratoga*, 316.

2. Pari-mutuel systems gather bets centrally and then divide the proceeds among the winners in proportion to their original wagers. Bookmakers collect and distribute bets individually.

3. Bradley, *Such Was Saratoga*, 282.

4. Rothstein, *Now I'll Tell*, 27ff.

5. Edward Hotaling, *They're Off! Horse Racing at Saratoga* (Syracuse, N.Y.: Syracuse University Press, 1995), 192.

6. Bradley, *Such Was Saratoga*, 285, 300.

7. Pearl Sieben, *Immortal Jolson: His Life and Times* (New York: Frederick Fell, Inc., 1962), 61; Clarke, *Reign of Rothstein*, 14ff.

8. Clarke, *Reign of Rothstein*, 20.

9. Morris, *Incredible New York*, 260, 262; Rothstein, *Now I'll Tell*, 32

10. Rothstein, *Now I'll Tell*, 149–151; The *Morgen Zhurnal* thought the show was *Keep Shufflin'*. See *Morgen Zhurnal*, November 15, 1928, 9. Recall the Lorenz Hart lyric from "Manhattan" (1925): "Our future babies we'll take to *Abie's Irish Rose* / I hope they'll live to see it close." Dorothy Hart and Robert Kimball, eds., *The Complete Lyrics of Lorenz Hart* (New York: Da Capo Press, 1995), 33.

11. Rothstein, *Now I'll Tell*, 46ff.

12. Ibid., 151; E. J. Kahn Jr., *The World of Swope* (New York: Simon and Schuster, 1965), 117.

13. Damon Runyon, "Social Error," *Guys and Dolls* in *The Damon Runyon Omnibus* (Garden City, N.Y.: Sun Dial Press, 1943), 37.

14. Katcher, *Big Bankroll*, 39.

15. Rothstein, *Now I'll Tell*, 72

16. Ibid., 31, 71ff.

17. Ibid., 49.

18. Ibid., 54.

19. Jonathan Root, *One Night in July: The True Story of the Rosenthal-Becker Murder Case* (New York: Coward-McCann, 1961), 16; Harlow, *Old Bowery Days*, 45, 485; Kahn, *The World of Swope*, 144; Scarne, *Scarne on Dice*, 20.

Twenty-two billion dollars are the gross gambling revenues for casinos in fiscal year 1998, according to the American Gaming Association. The figure does not include Indian reservation gaming ($8.2 billion) or state sponsored lotteries ($16.7 billion). This trade association also notes that forty-eight states recognize some sort of legal gambling. Source: Christiansen Capital Advisors, Inc., available at: http://www.americangaming.org/casino_entertainment/aga_facts/facts.cfm/id/7.

20. Bradley, *Such Was Saratoga*.

21. "Rosenthal Said 'Big Tim' Helped Him Start Gambling House," New York *World*, July 17, 1912. 4.

22. The band of four was Louis Seidensher, Louis Rosenzweig, Francesco Cirofici, and Harry Horowitz.

23. See Goren, *Saints and Sinners*; Root, *One Night*, 96.

24. Jenna Weissman Joselit, *Our Gang: Jewish Crime and the New York Jewish Community, 1900–1940* (Bloomington: Indiana University Press, 1983), 76; see *Yidishes Tageblat*, July 28, 1912.

25. Clarke, *Reign of Rothstein*, 34; Runyon, "Guys and Dolls;" Lacey, *Little Man*; Reid and Demaris, *Green Felt Jungle*. Casino locations are stated in Rothstein, *Now I'll Tell*, 55, 135.

26. Rothstein, *Now I'll Tell*, 73f, 134, 138.

27. Ibid., 156.

28. Stephen Birmingham, *"Our Crowd"* (New York: Berkley Books, 1984), 11–32, 57–62.

29. Cited in Kahn, *World of Swope*, 118.

30. Hotaling, *They're Off!*, 218; Bradley, *Such Was Saratoga*, 318ff.

31. Rothstein, *Now I'll Tell*, 102. For details, of the Seligman-Hilton affair, see Birmingham, *"Our Crowd,"* 141–150.

CHAPTER 4: FINANCIAL CRIME

1. William Gibbs McAdoo, *Crowded Years* (Boston: Houghton Mifflin, 1931), 374–379, cited in David M. Kennedy, *Over Here: The First World War and American Society* (New York: Oxford University Press, 1980), 105.

2. Newell Dwight Hillis, *The Atrocities of Germany: Buy LIBERTY BONDS and End Them Forever* (Second Federal Reserve District: Liberty Loan Committee, no date), 24.

3. Kennedy, *Over Here*, 103. The figures are for the years between 1916–1920.

4. John Cooney, *The Annenbergs* (New York: Simon and Schuster, 1982), 54; the biography of George Graham Rice comes from Watson Washburn and Edmund DeLong, *High and Low Financiers* (Indianapolis, Ind.: Bobbs-Merrill, 1932), 13–40.

5. George Graham Rice, *My Adventures with Your Money* (New York: Bookfinger, 1974 [1913]), 9ff. See also William Leavitt Stoddard, *Financial Racketeering and How to Stop It* (New York: Harper & Brothers, 1931), 1ff.

6. Katcher, *Big Bankroll*, 189.

7. These were different from the bucket shops described by Fabian, which were mock stock exchanges in which one bets on the movement of stocks without actually purchasing them at all. See Fabian, *Card Sharps*, 189.

8. Cited in Stoddard, *Financial Racketeering*, 10.

9. Washburn and DeLong, *High and Low Financiers*, 29.

10. Edwin Lefevre, *Reminiscences of a Stock Operator* (New York: John Wiley & Sons, 1994 [1923]), 47. For Rothstein's relationship to Fields, see Katcher, *Big Bankroll*, 192.

11. Nat Ferber, *I Found Out: A Confidential Chronicle of the Twenties* (New York: Dial Press, 1939), 201; Clarke, *Reign of Rothstein*, 126.

12. For the perspective of Arthur Garfield Hays, the Jewish lawyer who defended the bucket shops of Edward M. Fuller for Rothstein, sat with the defense team for the Scopes trial, and assisted Felix Frankfurter in the defense of Sacco and Vanzetti, see part III of this book, as well as Arthur Garfield Hays, *City Lawyer: The Autobiography of a Law Practice* (New York: Simon and Schuster, 1942), and Hays, *Let Freedom Ring* (New York: Boni and Liveright, 1928).

13. Katcher, *Big Bankroll*, 166f; Gene Fowler, *The Great Mouthpiece: A Life Story of William J. Fallon* (New York: Covici Friede, 1932), 163.

14. Lefevre, *Reminiscences*, 49ff.

15. New York *World*, February 21, 1920, 5.

16. Clarke, *Reign of Rothstein*, 78.

17. Barbara W. Grossman, *Funny Woman: The Life and Times of Fanny Brice* (Indianapolis: Indiana University Press, 1991), 60ff.

18. *New York Times*, May 2, 1920, 1, 18.

19. See *New York Times*, February 21, 1920, 1, 2; May 2, 1920, 1, 18; May 5, 1920, 1, 3; New York *World*, February 21, 1920, 5; February 22, 1920, 1; May 5, 1920, 1, 2. See also Ferber, *I Found Out*, 201. Ferber investigated the bucket shops for Hearst's New York *American*. Ferber was a Jew, born on Cherry Street in 1889; his father left Russia in 1887.

20. Grossman, *Funny Woman*, 61.

21. See *New York Times*, February 6, 1924, 29.

22. *American Hebrew*, March 26, 1920, 554.

CHAPTER 5: THE BLACK SOX AND
THE JEWS

1. Rothstein, *Now I'll Tell*, 139; Clarke, *Reign of Rothstein*, 17. Meyer Lansky and "Bugsy" Siegel preferred Ratner's on Delancey Street.

2. The structure of Italian-American organized crime parallels this Jewish one, although it only emerges definitively under Charles "Lucky" Luciano, Rothstein's protégé, toward the end of the 1920s. Rothstein's separation of political office from underworld power continues, as the Gambino crime family parodied the authority of the U.S. government by referring to the home of family boss Paul Castellano as "The White House." And when Sammy Gravano decided to turn state's evidence, he informed authorities by saying: "I want to switch governments." See Peter Maas, *Underboss: Sammy the Bull Gravano's Story of Life in the Mafia* (New York: HarperCollins, 1997), 113, 461. For the best treatment of the organization of American crime, see Stephen Fox, *Blood and Power: Organized Crime in Twentieth-Century America* (New York: William Morrow and Company, 1989).

3. Charles C. Alexander, *John McGraw* (Lincoln: University of Nebraska Press, 1988), 209f; Katcher, *Big Bankroll*, 159.

4. Rothstein, *Now I'll Tell*, 117.

5. In his popular history of the Black Sox scandal, Eliot Asinof offers the intriguing suggestion that Rothstein eventually paid Sullivan and fixed the Series. Unfortunately, that suggestion is ambiguously and contradictorily developed. Asinof based his conclusion on certain affidavits said to be found in Rothstein's files after his murder. According to Asinof, the affidavits, taken by the Chicago Grand Jury, somehow had been lost at the time of the Black Sox trial in 1921, bought by Rothstein, and miraculously kept by him—rather than immediately destroyed. These affidavits claimed Rothstein made a payment of eighty thousand dollars to the ballplayers. They were signed both by Abe Attell and Sullivan, the two men most interested in passing along responsibility for the fix and whose credibility one must question. If these affidavits did exist—and I have been unable to find any record of them—they still would not substantiate Asinof's claim that Rothstein fixed the Series. Because of these ambiguities and inconsistencies, and because Arnold Rothstein was an exceedingly cautious man, I tend to agree with Carolyn Rothstein: "If . . . it were charged that

Arnold had been sounded out on the subject of bribing baseball players, that he had declined to have a part in the transaction, but had used his inside knowledge that they were going to be bribed to make winning bets, I would believe it. As a matter of fact, I do believe it." Rothstein, *Now I'll Tell*, 170. See Asinof, *Eight Men Out*, 286.

6. Rothstein actually used this alibi. In 1923, Rothstein was called as a hostile witness in an unrelated case against the bucket shop of Fuller and McGee, in which Rothstein had a large financial interest. The attorney for the receivers of the bankrupt bucket shop, William M. Chadbourne, hounded Rothstein about his connection to the World Series fix. Note how ably Rothstein acted as his own legal counsel, and how comfortably he sat in the witness stand:

> CHADBOURNE: Did you wager on the 1919 World Series?
>
> ROTHSTEIN: I object on the ground that the question is irrelevant and immaterial. . . .
>
> CHADBOURNE: I am seeking to prove that the witness had full knowledge that the Series was fixed and that, with this knowledge, he won various wagers including some from Mr. Fuller.
>
> ROTHSTEIN: This baseball thing has been the sore spot of my career. I faced a Grand Jury and was vindicated. . . . I object and I want this objection in the record.
>
> CHADBOURNE: Didn't you hire counsel to appear in your behalf in the investigation?
>
> ROTHSTEIN: You ought to be ashamed to ask me that. This is no place to ask that kind of question. You ought to be ashamed. Before I'd be a tool like you, I'd jump in the Hudson River. . . .
>
> CHADBOURNE: Did you bet with Fuller on the 1919 Series?
>
> ROTHSTEIN: I made a lot of bets. It's a long time. I'm not sure I remember.
>
> CHADBOURNE: Check your records.
>
> ROTHSTEIN: [checks records] Yes.
>
> CHADBOURNE: How much did you bet with Fuller?
>
> ROTHSTEIN: The bet was $25,000.
>
> CHADBOURNE: Then you won $25,000 from Fuller on a Series that was fixed?
>
> ROTHSTEIN: I didn't win. I lost.

Katcher, *Big Bankroll*, 199ff. See also Ferber, *I Found Out*.

Incidentally, the character of Jay Gatsby was based on Edward Fuller, and the Fuller/Rothstein relationship was the foundation of the one between Gatsby and Meyer Wolfsheim. See Fitzgerald's letter of December 20, 1924, to Maxwell Perkins, in *F. Scott Fitzgerald: A Life in Letters*, ed. Matthew J. Bruccoli (New York: Charles Scribner's Sons, 1994), 91.

7. Asinof, *Eight Men Out*, 219. Grand Jury testimony is sealed, so it is unclear how Asinof might have found this quote. Nevertheless, it captures the gist of Rothstein's defense as it was repeated in the press.

8. Ibid.

9. Alexander, *McGraw*, 229; Rothstein, *Now I'll Tell*, 41.

10. New York *World*, September 26, 1920, 1.

11. Asinof, *Eight Men Out*, 200.

12. *American Review of Reviews* 63 (April 1921): 418, 420.

13. "Jewish Gamblers Corrupt American Baseball," in *The International Jew*, 49.

14. Police Commissioner Theodore A. Bingham had accused Jewry of extraordinary criminal behavior in 1908. See Theodore A. Bingham, "Foreign Criminals in New York," *North American Review* 187 (September 1908): 383–394; Arthur A. Goren, *New York Jews and the Quest for Community: The Kehilla Experiment, 1908–1922* (New York: Columbia University Press, 1970); Joselit, *Our Gang*, 23–53.

15. *American Hebrew*, September 2, 1921, 568.

16. See John T. Gilchrist, *The Church and Economic Activity in the Middle Ages* (New York: Macmillan, 1969); Benjamin Nelson, *The Idea of Usury* (Chicago: University of Chicago Press, 1969); Kenneth R. Stow, "Papal and Royal Attitudes Toward Jewish Lending in the Thirteenth Century," *AJS Review* 6 (1981): 161–184.

17. F. Scott Fitzgerald, *The Great Gatsby* (New York: Simon & Schuster, 1925), 73–78.

18. Clarke, *Reign of Rothstein*, 20.

19. See Fitzgerald's letter to Corey Ford of July 1937, in *Letters of F. Scott Fitzgerald*, 551.

20. Ernest Lockridge, ed., *Twentieth Century Interpretations of The Great Gatsby* (Englewood Cliffs, N.J.: Prentice-Hall, 1968), 106f (emphasis original). See also Willa Cather's character, Louie Marcellus, in *The Professor's House* (1925), cited in Higham, *Send These to Me*, 168.

21. On the continuing project to place baseball in the American memory, see Charles Fruehling Springwood, *Cooperstown to Dyersville: A Geography of Baseball Nostalgia* (Boulder, Colo.: Westview, 1996).

CHAPTER 6: THE JEWS REACT

1. *Forverts*, August 6, 1903, cited in Peter Levine, *Ellis Island to Ebbets Field* (New York: Oxford University Press, 1992), 87.

2. Levine, *Ellis Island*, 87–99.

3. David A. Jasen, *Tin Pan Alley: The Composers, the Songs, the Performers and Their Times: The Golden Age of American Popular Music from 1886–1956* (New York: Donald I. Fine, 1988), 51; Charles Hamm, *Irving Berlin: Songs from the Melting Pot* (New York: Oxford University Press, 1997), 46, 54.

4. *Yidishes Tageblat*, September 29, 1920, 2; *Forverts*, September 30, 1920, 5.

5. For the debate over reporting Jewish crime, see "Should the Jewish Press Report Crime?" *American Israelite*, May 28, 1925, 3. For complete discussions of the strategy of the German-Jewish community to deal with Eastern European Jewish criminality, see Goren, *New York Jews and the Quest for Community*, and Joselit, *Our Gang*.

6. *Forverts*, September 30, 1920, 5.

7. *Forverts*, October 7, 1920, 3.

8. Fabian, *Card Sharps*, 3.

9. *Forverts*, July 22, 1921, 5.

10. *Der Tog*, August 19, 1927, 5.

11. *Der Tog*, November 7, 1928, 8.

12. *Morgen Zhurnal*, November 12, 1928, 9.

13. *Forverts*, November 7, 1928, 1.

14. *Der Amerikaner*, November 16, 1928, 3.

15. *Morgen Zhurnal*, November 12, 1928, 9.

16. *Der Tog*, November 5, 1928, 1.

17. *Forverts*, November 6, 1928, 1, 7, 10.

18. Their names were Jacob Orgen and John T. Nolan. See David Dubinsky and A. H. Raskin, *David Dubinsky: A Life With Labor* (New York: Simon and Schuster, 1977), 69.

19. *Morgen Zhurnal*, November 18, 1928, 2.

20. *Der Tog*, November 7, 1928, 8. This is Arthur Goren's translation, from *Saints and Sinners* 9.

21. *American Israelite*, September 23, 1923, 1.

22. *Der Amerikaner*, November 16, 1928, 3.

23. New York *World*, October 1, 1920, 1.

24. William Chester Jordan, "An Aspect of Credit in Picardy in the 1240s: The Deterioration of Jewish-Christian Financial Relations," *Revue des études juives* 142 (1983): 141–152; Jordan, "Women and Credit in the Middle Ages: Problems and Directions," *The Journal of European Economic History* 17, no. 1 (1988): 33–62; Aaron Kirschenbaum "Jewish and Christian Theories of Usury in the Middle Ages," *Jewish Quarterly Review* 75 (1985): 270–289; Gavin I. Langmuir, "Tanguam servi: The Change in Jewish Status in French Law about 1200," in *Les Juifs dans l'histoire de France*, ed. M. Yardeni (Leiden: 1980), 24–54; Joseph Shatzmiller, *Shylock Reconsidered: Jews, Moneylending, and Medieval Society* (Los Angeles: University of California Press, 1990).

25. See Selma Stern, *The Court Jew*, trans. Ralph Weinman (New Brunswick, N.J.: Transaction Books, 1985); Jonathan I. Israel, *European Jewry in the Age of Mercantilism 1550–1750* (Oxford, U.K.: Clarendon Press, 1991), 123–144.

26. See Gershon David Hundert, *The Jews in a Polish Private Town* (Baltimore: The Johns Hopkins University Press, 1992); Kahan, *Essays in Jewish Social and Economic History*.

27. See Reid and Demaris, *The Green Felt Jungle*; Lacey, *Little Man*.

28. The story of the master Jewish thief who becomes king through deception is considered a type by folklorists. See Beatrice Silverman Weinreich and Leonard Wolf, eds. *Yiddish Folktales* (New York: Pantheon Books/YIVO Institute, 1988), 89–92.

29. Kessner, *Golden Door*.

30. Kahan, "Impact of Industrialization," in *Essays*, 101–117.

31. On the difficulty of understanding the categories of "covenant" and "exile" in America, see Arnold Eisen, *The Chosen People in America* (Bloomington: Indiana

University Press, 1983). Moreover, there has been no attempt on the part of Eastern Jewry to remove either the doctrines of covenant or exile, as Western Jewry had in the fifth section of the Pittsburgh Platform of 1885. See Jacob Rader Marcus, ed., *The Jew in the American World: A Source Book* (Detroit, Mich.: Wayne State University, 1996), 241–243.

32. *Der Amerikaner*, November 16, 1928, 3.

33. Rothstein, *Now I'll Tell*, 116.

34. Cited in Tom Clark, *The World of Damon Runyon* (New York: Harper & Row, 1978), 182.

35. Clarke, *Reign of Rothstein*, 29.

36. *Der Amerikaner*, November 16, 1928, 3.

INTERLUDE: JAZZ AGE POLITICS

1. Paul Sann, *The Lawless Decade* (New York: Crown, 1957), 53.

2. *New York Times*, September 17, 1920, 1.

3. John D. Hicks, *Republican Ascendancy: 1921–1933* (New York: Harper & Brothers, 1960), 14.

4. Alice Roosevelt Longworth, *Crowded Hours* (1933), cited in Sann, *Lawless*, 55.

5. Sann, *Lawless*, 86.

6. Ibid., 202.

7. Ibid., 62.

CHAPTER 7: FELIX FRANKFURTER

1. Paul Avrich, *Sacco and Vanzetti: The Anarchist Background* (Princeton, N.J.: Princeton University Press, 1991), 94, 142ff. The epigraph comes from Walter Lippmann, *Public Opinion* (New York: The Free Press, 1949 [1922]), 10.

2. Robert K. Murray, *Red Scare: A Study in National Hysteria, 1919–1920* (Minneapolis: University of Minnesota Press, 1955), 190–209.

3. J. H. Wigmore "Freedom of Speech and Freedom of Thuggery," *Illinois Law Review* 19 (1925), 496–497, cited in William R. Roalfe, *John Henry Wigmore: Scholar and Reformer* (Evanston, Ill.: Northwestern University Press, 1977), 151; Avrich, *Sacco and Vanzetti*, 137ff.

4. Felix Frankfurter, "Kàrolyi, Kellog, and Coolidge," *New Republic*, December 2, 1925, cited in Felix Frankfurter, *Law and Politics*, eds. Archibald MacLeish and E. F. Prichard, Jr. (New York: Harcourt, Brace and Company, 1939), 137.

5. Avrich, *Sacco and Vanzetti*, 81.

6. Ibid., 28.

7. Ibid., 64–66, 157–159, 160.

8. Some treatments of Frankfurter are very fine, though none emphasizes the Sacco-Vanzetti case: Michael E. Parrish, *Felix Frankfurter and His Times: The Reform Years* (New York: The Free Press, 1982), 176–196; Liva Baker, *Felix Frankfurter*

(New York: Coward-McCann, 1969), 121–138; H. N. Hirsch treats Frankfurter's Sacco-Vanzetti work, indeed all of his work, in the light of his understanding of Frank-furter as "a textbook case of a neurotic personality"; see H. N. Hirsch, *The Enigma of Felix Frankfurter* (New York: Basic Books, 1981), 90–94. Robert A. Burt does not treat Sacco and Vanzetti extensively. Moreover, while Burt sees Brandeis and Frank-furter as "outcasts in the promised land" and frames Frankfurter's behaviors as re-sulting from a mentality of "diaspora," he frames the discussion along a "Dialectic of Jewish Enlightenment" discussed above in Introduction, note 6. Burt claims that "Frankfurter can easily be seen in [Hannah] Arendt's terms as parvenu: always charm-ing, cajoling, seducing the widest possible circle of admirers, but never quite success-ful in finding the right chord." I suggest that Frankfurter struck the right chord in-deed, as is evidenced by his categorical approval by the Eastern Jewish press, and that Back Bay Boston was not cajoled in the least. As Frankfurter moved ever more into the American political order, I suggest, he continued to identify out. But see Burt, *Two Jewish Justices*, 57f, 62.

CHAPTER 8: THE YOUNG PROGRESSIVE

1. Rozenblit, *Jews of Vienna*, 2.

2. Columbia Oral History Project: Felix Frankfurter, 37 (henceforth COHP).

3. Leonard Baker, *Brandeis and Frankfurter: A Dual Biography* (New York: Harper & Row, 1984), 41.

4. COHP, 15.

5. Felix Frankfurter, *Felix Frankfurter Reminisces*, ed. Harlan B. Phillips (New York: Reynal & Company, 1960), 11, 199.

6. Stephan F. Brumberg, *Going to America, Going to School* (New York: Praeger, 1986), 71–94, 111–147, 175–198.

7. See Sherry Gorelick, *City College and the Jewish Poor* (New York: Schocken Books, 1982); Kessner, *The Golden Door*, 98; Irving Howe, *World of Our Fathers* (New York: Harcourt Brace Jovanovich, 1976), 280–286.

8. Baker, *Felix Frankfurter*, 21; Frankfurter, *Reminisces*, 17, 19; Jerold S. Auer-bach *Unequal Justice: Lawyers and Social Change in Modern America* (New York: Oxford University Press, 1976), 29.

9. Frankfurter, *Reminisces*, 19.

10. Lewis J. Paper, *Brandeis* (Secaucus, N.J.: Citadel Press, 1983), 16, 55–68.

11. Louis D. Brandeis, "The Opportunity in the Law," *American Law Review* 39 (July/August 1905): 559; see Joel Seligman, *The High Citadel: The Influence of Har-vard Law School* (Boston: Houghton Mifflin Company, 1978).

12. Brandeis, "The Opportunity in the Law," 558ff.

13. Ibid., 562ff.

14. See Melvin I. Urofsky, *Louis D. Brandeis and the Progressive Tradition* (Bos-ton: Little, Brown and Company, 1981); for a view that sees Brandeis as an advocate of deeper reform, see Philippa Strum, *Brandeis: Beyond Progressivism* (Lawrence:

University Press of Kansas, 1993). For an overview of German-Jewish philanthropy, see Hasia R. Diner, *A Time for Gathering: The Second Migration 1820–1880. The Jewish People in America*, ed. Henry L. Feingold (Baltimore: The Johns Hopkins University Press, 1992), 100–106.

15. For a glowing interview with Samuel Untermyer concerning the opportunities for Jews in the legal profession at the turn of the century and three decades after, see the *Jewish Tribune*, March 16, 1928, 5.

16. Frankfurter, *Reminisces*, 43.

17. For the development of progressivism from Roosevelt to Taft to Wilson, see Sklar, *Corporate Reconstruction*, 333–430.

18. Henry L. Stimson to Felix Frankfurter, June 28, 1913, Felix Frankfurter Papers in the Library of Congress (hereafter FFPLC). Cited in Parrish, *Felix Frankfurter*, 60.

19. Frankfurter, *Reminisces*, 107.

20. Frankfurter, "Herbert Croly and American Political Opinion," reprinted in *Law and Politics*, 306.

21. Felix Frankfurter to Henry L. Stimson, November 2, 1916, FFPLC. Cited in Lash, *Diaries*, 20.

22. Frankfurter to Stimson, June 28, 1913, FFPLC. Cited in Lash, *Diaries*, 12.

23. *Muller v. Oregon*, 208 U.S. 412, 419-421 (1908).

24. Cited in Baker, *Brandeis and Frankfurter*, 87.

25. Ibid., 57; Paper, *Brandeis*, 161.

26. *Stettler v. O'Hara*, 139 P. 743 (Or. 1914), aff'd, 243 U.S. 629 (1917); *Simpson v. O'Hara*, 141 P. 158 (Or. 1914), aff'd, 243 U.S. 629; *State v. Bunting*, 139 P. 731 (Or. 1914), aff'd sub nom., *Bunting v. Oregon*, 243 U.S. 426 (1917).

27. Frankfurter, *Reminisces*, 114.

28. Ibid., 115.

29. Ibid., 138.

30. Parrish, *Felix Frankfurter*, 81–101.

31. "Report on the Mooney Dynamite Cases in San Francisco Submitted by President Wilson's Mediation Commission," *Official Bulletin of the United States Committee on Public Information* (Pamphlet), January 18, 1918.

32. Theodore Roosevelt to Felix Frankfurter, December 19, 1917, reprinted in the *Boston Evening Transcript*, April 27, 1927, II: 2.

33. Felix Frankfurter to Theodore Roosevelt, reprinted in the *Boston Evening Transcript*, April 29, 1927, II: 1.

34. Cited in Parrish, *Felix Frankfurter*, 121. See also Baker, *Felix Frankfurter*, 91.

CHAPTER 9: ZION AND CAMBRIDGE

1. For a treatment of this struggle, see Goren, *New York Jews*.

2. See Sarah Schmidt, *Horace M. Kallen: Prophet of American Zionism* (Brooklyn, N.Y.: Carlson Publishing, 1995), 62.

3. Philippa Strum, *Louis D. Brandeis: Justice for the People* (Cambridge, Mass.: Harvard University Press, 1984), 232.

4. My colleague and friend David Levy, editor of the Brandeis papers, tells me he knows of no statement Brandeis ever made on Zionism before 1912. See Louis D. Brandeis, *Letters of Louis D. Brandeis*, eds. Melvin Urofsky and David Levy (Albany: State University of New York Press, 1971–1978), 5 vols.

5. Horace M. Kallen, "Democracy *Versus* the Melting-Pot," in *Culture and Democracy in the United States* (New York: Boni and Liverright, 1924), 67–125; Schmidt, *Horace M. Kallen*, 63–64

6. Cited in Schmidt, *Horace M. Kallen*, 60. The phrase was first used in a speech to Cleveland, Ohio, Zionists sometime between October 13 and October 17, 1914, and repeated very often after that.

7. Harry Barnard, *The Forging of An American Jew: The Life and Times of Judge Julian W. Mack* (New York: Herzl Press, 1974).

8. Schmidt, *Horace M. Kallen*, 89.

9. For a different view of Brandeis's and Mack's Zionism, see Jerold S. Auerbach, *Rabbis and Lawyers: The Journey from Torah to Constitution* (Bloomington: Indiana University Press, 1993), 123–167. Auerbach makes the intriguing argument that Zionism became a means by which Jews of the old German-Jewish establishment could assuage their festering outcast identities by linking their Jewish origins with a vision of true American democracy. In seeing Zionism as the ultimate form of democracy (according to Kallen's conception), Brandeis found a way to feel connected to the American Pilgrim fathers rather than to the Jewish patriarchs. I suggest that Brandeis and Mack used Zionism to embrace the difference of their Jewish selves for the first time.

10. Felix Frankfurter, "The Palestine Situation Restated," *Foreign Affairs*, April 1931, cited in Baker, *Brandeis and Frankfurter*, 162.

11. Although it would appear that Frankfurter complied with the model of assimilation that Milton Gordon called "Anglo-American conformity," Frankfurter's political leanings and defense of radicals complicates the meaning of that identification. Milton M. Gordon, *Assimilation in American Life: The Role of Race, Religion, and National Origins* (New York: Oxford University Press, 1964).

12. Cited in Lash, *Diaries*, 19.

13. Seligman, *The High Citadel*, 59. Lawrence Lowell to Julian Mack, March 14, 1922, FFPLC 81/49-415 (numbers refer to container/reel-frame).

14. Mark DeWolfe Howe, ed. *Holmes-Laski Letters* (Cambridge, Mass.: Harvard University Press, 1953), April 4, 1919, 193 (hereafter *Holmes-Laski*).

15. Holmes to Frankfurter, December 4, 1919. Robert M. Mennel and Christine L. Compston, eds. *Holmes & Frankfurter: Their Correspondence, 1912–1934* (Hanover, N.H.: University Press of New England, 1996), 78.

16. Lash, *Diaries*, 33. Frankfurter worked on a deportation case in Boston in May 1920: *Colyer v. Skeffington*, 265 F. 17 (D. Mass. 1920); he represented the National Consumers League in *Adkins v. Children's Hospital* 261 U.S. 525 (1923).

17. A. Lawrence Lowell to Alfred A. Benesch, June 9, 1922, in Raphael, *Jews and Judaism in the United* States, 294ff. See Marcia Graham Synnott, *The Half-Opened Door: Discrimination and Admissions at Harvard, Yale, and Princeton, 1900–1970* (Westport, Conn.: Greenwood Press, 1979), 26–124; Penny Hollander Feldman, *Recruiting an Elite* (New York: Garland, 1988).

18. Lowell to Mack, June 14, 1922, FFPLC 81/49-427.

19. Frankfurter to Lowell, June 19, 1922, FFPLC 126/77-649.

20. Lowell to Frankfurter, June 20, 1922, FFPLC 126/77-649.

21. Frankfurter to Lowell, June 21, 1922, FFPLC 126/77-650. Lowell to Frankfurter, June 24, 1922, FFPLC 126/77-650.

22. Frankfurter to Lowell, June 29, 1922, FFPLC 126/77-651.

23. Walter Lippmann, "Public Opinion and the American Jew," *American Hebrew*, April 14, 1922, 575.

24. See Heinz Eulau, "From Public Opinion to Public Philosophy," *American Journal of Economics and Sociology* 15 (1956): 442–446.

CHAPTER 10: SACCO AND VANZETTI

1. Avrich, *Sacco and Vanzetti*, 205.

2. Parrish, *Felix Frankfurter*, 177.

3. Brandeis, "The Opportunity in the Law," 562.

4. *The Sacco-Vanzetti Case: Transcript of the Record of the Trial of Nicola Sacco and Bartolomeo Vanzetti in the Courts of Massachusetts and Subsequent Proceedings, 1920–1927*, 5 Vols., with a supplemental volume on the Bridgewater Case (New York: Holt, 1927–1929), Vol. 4, 3641–3643 (hereafter *Holt*).

5. See James E. Starrs, "Once More Unto the Breech: The Firearms Evidence in the Sacco and Vanzetti Case Revisited," *Journal of Forensic Science* (April 1986, July 1986): 630–654, 1050–1078, see especially 644–646. Starrs notes that none of the four expert witnesses called on behalf of the prosecution and defense of Sacco and Vanzetti used ballistic evidence considered even remotely viable today. For a contemporary example of how courts may accept expert testimony with the ambiguous language "consistent with," see *Florey v. State*, 720 A.2d 1132, 1136 (Del. 1998). I thank Joel E. Friedlander for bringing this case to my attention, and for his many insights, criticisms, and suggestions.

6. Frankfurter, *Reminisces* 212. See also Felix Frankfurter to Julian Mack, October 15, 1927, Felix Frankfurter Papers at the Harvard Law School, 34-946 (numbers refer to reel-frame—all citations from Part III of that collection) (hereafter FFPHLS).

7. Frankfurter to Mack, October 15, 1927, FFPHLS 34-946. Brandeis to Frankfurter, December 7, 1924: "Auntie B. seems much relieved by what you did re W. G. Thompson. But the size of the fee is a bit like Julius Henry C." Louis D. Brandeis, *"Half Brother, Half Son": The Letters of Louis D. Brandeis to Felix Frankfurter*, eds. Melvin I. Urofsky and David W. Levy (Norman: University of Oklahoma Press, 1991), 183 (Letter 172). For the fee, see Louis Joughin and Edmund M. Morgan, *The Legacy*

of Sacco & Vanzetti (Princeton, N.J.: Princeton University Press, 1976), 237. For Elizabeth Glendower Evans's relationship to Brandeis, see Paper, *Brandeis*, 28–30. See also Elizabeth Glendower Evans, *Outstanding Features of the Sacco-Vanzetti Case* (Boston: New England Civil Liberties Committee, 1924).

8. Rabbi Stephen Wise to Frankfurter, May 13, 1927, FFPHLS 26-45. Stephen S. Wise, "Law Versus Justice: A Challenge to America," *Boston Herald*, May 2, 1927.

9. Brandeis to Frankfurter, October 29, 1926, *Half Brother*, 258 (letter 244); *Boston Herald*, October 26, 1926.

10. Ronald Steel, *Walter Lippmann and the American Century* (Boston: Little, Brown and Company, 1980), 205–206.

11. Walter Lippmann, "Al Smith: Man of Destiny," in *Men of Destiny* (New York: Macmillan, 1927), 2–9. Frankfurter agreed that Smith should be elected as a move in the symbolic struggle between old and new America. As President "Alfred E. Smith will serve as a symbol," Frankfurter thought. "The lowliness of his origin, his lack of cultural opportunities, and his esthetic limitation will fall into their proper places in the perspective of his whole personality. More and more it will become manifest that his character is an achievement and not a gift of circumstances." "Why I Am For Smith," *New Republic*, October 31, 1928, reprinted in *Law and Politics*, 320–328. Remarkably, Frankfurter felt comfortable noting the lowliness of Smith's origins, although Smith's Irish-American family had been in America since 1841. See also Alfred E. Smith, "Catholic and Patriot," *Atlantic Monthly* 139 (May 1927): 721–728.

12. See *World*, April 11, 1927, and Frankfurter's notes, FFPHLS 24-684.

13. See Brandeis, *Half Brother*, 338f, note 1.

14. David Felix, *Protest: Sacco-Vanzetti and the Intellectuals* (Bloomington: Indiana University Press, 1965), 204.

15. Hays, *City Lawyer*, xi, 48, 238.

16. Frankfurter to Mack, October 15, 1927, FFPHLS 34-946. See also a series of letters between Frankfurter and Stoughton Bell, a Boston lawyer, who had claimed publicly that Frankfurter was serving as counsel to Sacco and Vanzetti. Frankfurter to Bell, April 6, 1927: "I learned with regret that you have made yourself the vehicle of the wholly false statement that I was one of the lawyers for Sacco and Vanzetti," FFPHLS 33-159. Bell to Frankfurter, April 8, 1927: "Mr. W.G. Thompson . . . informs me that you have rendered valuable assistance to defense counsel in the Sacco and Vanzetti case, but without compensation. Whether or not in view of this you are 'one of the lawyers for Sacco and Vanzetti' would seem to be a matter of opinion," FFPHLS 33-160. Frankfurter to Bell, April 9, 1927: "I repeat to you—and Mr. Thompson will state it no less emphatically—that in no sense in which language can be responsibly used have I been 'one of the lawyers for Sacco and Vanzetti.' That is not a 'matter of opinion.' It is an unequivocal fact and anyone who states that I have been 'one of the lawyers for Sacco and Vanzetti' states something that is not true," FFPHLS 33-161. Eventually Bell relented.

17. Frankfurter, *Reminisces*, 204.

18. Frankfurter to unknown recipient, December 17, 1927, FFPHLS 34-977.

19. Wiretappings available from the Massachusetts Department of Public Safety, Frankfurter-Gardiner Jackson telephone conversation, August 20, 1927, cited in Parrish, *Felix Frankfurter*, 194.

20. Reprinted in Felix Frankfurter, *Law and Politics*, 140–188. Sylvester G. Gates, a young Commonwealth Fellow from London, wrote the *Atlantic Monthly* piece, which Frankfurter edited, as well as an earlier piece for the *New Republic* on June 9, 1926. Felix Frankfurter, "The Case of Sacco and Vanzetti," *Atlantic Monthly* 139 (March 1927): 409–432. See also Baker, *Felix Frankfurter*, 119.

21. Frankfurter, *The Case of Sacco and Vanzetti: A Critical Analysis for Lawyers and Laymen* (Boston: Little, Brown, 1927), 159.

22. Ibid., 160, 164.

23. *Holt*, Vol. V., 47–48

24. Frankfurter, *Reminisces*, 201.

25. Frankfurter, *The Case of Sacco and Vanzetti*, 171, 186.

26. Felix Frankfurter, *The Case of Sacco and Vanzetti*, 106. "The courageous stand taken by the *Boston Herald* has enlisted the support of some of the most distinguished citizens of Massachusetts. President Comstock of Radcliffe College; Dr. Samuel M. Crothers; Mrs. Margaret Deland, the novelist; Professor W. E. Hocking, the philosopher; Mr. John F. Moors; Professor Samuel E. Morison, the historian; President Neilson of Smith College; Mr. Reginald H. Smith, author of *Justice and the Poor*; Dean Sperry of the Harvard Theological School; Professor Frank W. Taussig, the economist, are among those who have asked for a dispassionate hearing on all the facts."

27. Frankfurter, *The Case of Sacco and Vanzetti*, 140.

28. For Joughin and Morgan, Frankfurter's article marked the beginning of the development of international opinion. Before this, Sacco and Vanzetti had been merely a labor issue. See Joughin and Morgan, *Legacy*, 233.

29. *New York Times*, April 11, 1927, interview with Judge Thayer.

30. Wigmore, *Boston Evening Transcript*, April 25, 1927.

31. Frankfurter, *Boston Evening Transcript*, April 26, 1927, II:3. The *Boston Herald* of that day carried an identical version of Frankfurter's response.

32. Wigmore, *Boston Evening Transcript*, April 25, 1927.

33. Theodore Roosevelt to Felix Frankfurter, December 19, 1917, reprinted in the *Boston Evening Transcript*, April 27, 1927, II:2.

34. Sanford H. E. Freund to Frankfurter, February 1, 1928, FFPHLS 25-149.

35. Frankfurter to Lippmann, July 25, 1927, FFPLC 77/47–320. Frankfurter was well aware that nonviolence was far from Vanzetti's avowed political position: "If we have to die for a crime of which we are innocent, we ask for revenge, revenge in our names and in the names of our living and dead. . . . I will make a list of honor of the perjurers who murdered us. I will try to see Thayer death. . . . I will put fire into the human breaths." From Marion D. Frankfurter and Gardner Jackson, eds. *The Letters of Sacco and Vanzetti* (New York: Penguin Books, 1997 [1928]), 119–120, 151, 315, culled by Avrich, *Sacco and Vanzetti*, 212.

36. Frankfurter to "Eustace," May 14, 1927, FFPHLS 35-112. Most likely this is Eustace Percy, English diplomat and educational reformer. Thank you, David Levy.

37. See *Holmes-Laski*, Vol. I, 230–232, 255–257.

38. *Holmes-Laski*, June 5, 1927, 952.

39. A. Lawrence Lowell to Robert W. Hale, August 15, 1927, FFPHLS 25–287.

40. Mack to Frankfurter, August 4, 1927, FFPLC 81/49-454.

41. New York *World* August 19, 1927, 12. See Mack to Frankfurter, August 8, 1927, FFPLC 81/49-455.

42. Hays, *Let Freedom Ring*, 324.

43. Ibid., 329.

44. *Holmes-Laski*, August 24, 1927, 974–975. See Holmes's denial of habeas corpus in *Holt*, V, 5532. See Holmes's dissent in *Frank v. Magnum*, 237 U.S. 309, 245 (1914).

45. See *Holmes-Laski*, April 15, 1927, 934; May 29, 1927, 947; August 19, 1927, 972.

46. *Holmes-Laski*, August 24, 1927, 974.

47. *Holmes-Laski*, September 1, 1927, 975.

48. *Holmes-Laski*, July 10, 1930, 1266.

49. Brandeis, *Half Brother*, March 9, 1927, 278 (letter 264).

50. Brandeis, *Half Brother*, April 14, 1927, 284 (letter 270).

51. Vanzetti to H.W.L. Dana, August 22, 1927, in Frankfurter and Jackson, *Letters of Sacco and Vanzetti*, 324.

52. Kallen to Frankfurter, September 2, 1927, FFPLC 71/43-531.

53. Kallen to Mack, September 14, 1927, FFPHLS 34-870.

54. Mack to Kallen, September 20, 1927, FFPHLS 34-891 (emphasis original).

55. Frankfurter to Kallen, September 15, 1927, FFPHLS 34-872.

56. *Forverts*, April 11, 1927, 1, 12; *Yidishes Tageblat*, April 11, 1927, 1. Einstein had been a celebrity in the pages of the Jewish press since his first trip to America in 1921. See "Jewish Brains in Goyishe Places," *Forverts*, July 23, 1921, 3; "So Says Einstein!" *Der Amerikaner*, July 29, 1921, 6; "Einstein Does Work from His Sickbed," *Der Tog*, October 6, 1928, 1; "The World's Greatest Man," *The Southern Israelite*, November 9, 1928, 1.

57. *Forverts*, August 10, 1927, 4, 7. See also *Forverts*, August 22, 1927, 1, 8; August 24, 1927, 4, 5.

58. *Yidishes Tageblat*, August 5, 1927, 4; August 12, 1927, 4.

59. *Yidishes Tageblat*, August 14, 1927, 4.

60. *Yidishes Tageblat*, August 24, 1927, 2.

61. *Der Tog*, August 5, 1927, 4.

62. *Der Amerikaner*, August 19, 1927, 3. That *Der Amerikaner* had decidedly placed Jews in the camp of "non-Nordics" and other ethnics is treated in part III of this book, "'Mammy, Don't You Know Me?': Al Jolson and the Jews."

63. *Morgen Zhurnal*, August 23, 1927, 4. Nevertheless, when the death sentence was carried out, the *Morgen Zhurnal* stood by what it considered "the Talmudic rule:

'after the court has acted, there is no complaint.'" *Morgen Zhurnal*, August 24, 1927. The *Chicago Sentinel*, September 1, 1927, 10, and the *Jewish Daily Bulletin*, August 24, 1927, 2–3, noted in their reports that even the usually stolid *Morgen Zhurnal* had joined in with the rest of the Jewish press on the Sacco-Vanzetti case.

64. See "Circumstantial Evidence," *Jewish Tribune*, September 2, 1927, 28; Maurice G. Hindus, "The Jew as a Radical," *Menorah Journal* 13:4 (August 1927): 367–379; The Chicago *Sentinel*, September 1, 1927, 10; *American Hebrew*, April 5, 1929, 755.

65. *Holmes-Laski*, December 16, 1928, 1121.

66. Brandeis, "*Half Brother*," August 24, 1927, 306 (Letter 293).

Chapter 11: Aftermath

1. Frankfurter, "America and the Immigrant," in *Law and Politics*, 198.

2. Frankfurter, "Why I Am For Smith," in *Law and Politics*, 324.

3. Hays, *City Lawyer*, xi, 52.

4. Frankfurter, *Reminisces* 189. Frankfurter was fanatically interested in upholding the law, even when justice was denied. Helen Shirley Thomas describes how Frankfurter was against a progressive child labor law from a legal standpoint: "He finds the identification of 'justice' and 'legality' false. . . . When the Court in 1922 struck down the Federal Child Labor Tax Law, many people were outraged. Frankfurter pointed out, however, that 'humanity' is not the test of constitutionality. Recognition that a law enacted by Congress seeks to redress monstrous wrongs and to promote the highest good does not dispose of the Supreme Court's duty when the validity of such a law is challenged.'" Helen Shirley Thomas, *Felix Frankfurter: Scholar on the Bench* (Baltimore: The Johns Hopkins University Press, 1960), 110, citing Frankfurter "Child Labor Law and the Constitution," *New Republic* 31 (July 26, 1922): 248. This even applied to his belief about the Congressional Act of June 5, 1920, which greatly limited the rights of certain immigrants and certain political beliefs. As much as he hated the legislation, he considered it the law. See Frankfurter, "Kàrolyi, Kellog, and Coolidge," *New Republic*, December 2, 1925, reprinted in Frankfurter, *Law and Politics*, 137.

5. Frankfurter to unknown "Bob," September 16, 1927, FFPHLS 34-878 (emphasis added).

6. Ibid., 202–203.

7. Ibid., 205.

8. Ibid., 205–206.

9. Frankfurter to Ferris Greenslet, January 2, 1946, FFPHLS 34-0199.

10. Frankfurter to Ferris Greenslet, January 2, 1946, FFPHLS 34-0199.

11. Frankfurter to Mack October 25, 1927, FFPHLS 34-952–957.

12. Frankfurter to Hans Zinsser, December 17, 1927, FFPHLS 34-976–977.

13. Nechemias Zucker, *In nomen fun gerekhtikeyt—tragedye in dray aktn: zeks bilder mit a prolog un epilog* (Buenos Aires: N. Tsunker, 1935); Martin H. Bush, *Ben*

Shahn: The Passion of Sacco and Vanzetti (Syracuse, N.Y.: Syracuse University Press, 1968); see Ann Pinchot, "Champion of Unpopular Causes," *American Hebrew*, April 5, 1929, 755; Abraham Silverstein, "An Outstanding American Liberal: Arthur Garfield Hays Has Defended Numerous Unpopular Causes," *Jewish Tribune*, June 1, 1928, 3.

14. Comment by David Montgomery at the "Sacco & Vanzetti and the American Dream" Conference at Yale Law School, October 13, 1997; see also Montgomery, *The Fall of the House of Labor* (New York: Cambridge University Press, 1987), 463–464.

15. Frankfurter to unknown "Richard," September 4, 1927 FFPHLS 34-858.

16. Frankfurter to Lippmann, January 5, 1929, FFPHLS 35-373.

17. Massachusetts State Police Firearm Examination Panel: Henry C. Lee et. al. *Examination of Firearm-related Evidence: The Nicola Sacco and Bartolomeo Vanzetti Case* (Boston: Westinghouse Broadcasting and Cable Corp., 1983); Starrs, "Once More Unto the Breech"; Francis Russel, *Sacco and Vanzetti: The Case Resolved* (New York: Harper & Row, 1986); Joseph B. Kadane and David A. Schum, *A Probabilistic Analysis of the Sacco and Vanzetti Evidence* (New York: John Wiley, 1996); for a rather unbelievable conspiracy theory that the Boston police planted this bullet into the evidence, see William Young and David E. Kaiser, *Postmortem: New Evidence in the Case of Sacco and Vanzetti* (Amherst: University of Massachusetts Press, 1985).

INTERLUDE: JAZZ AGE CULTURE

1. Cited in Michael G. Kammen, *The Lively Arts* (New York: Oxford University Press, 1996), 54.

2. Cited in Kammen, *Lively Arts*, 88.

3. New York *World*, January 7, 1923.

4. Robert Sklar, *Movie-Made America* (New York: Vintage, 1994), 141–157.

5. Gilbert Seldes *The 7 Lively Arts* (New York: Sagamore Press, 1957 [1924]), 181ff.

CHAPTER 12: AL JOLSON

1. *Time*, July 30, 1973, cited in William Torbert Leonard, *Masquerade in Black* (Metuchen, N.J.: Scarecrow Press, 1986), 270. The epigraph comes from the album *Irving Berlin—A Hundred Years* (Columbia CGK 40035, 1988).

2. *New York Times*, October 7, 1927, 24.

3. Berkeley began in Hollywood by choreographing Eddie Cantor's *Whoopee!* (1930) another blackface production. See Martin Rubin, *Showstoppers: Busby Berkeley and the Tradition of Spectacle* (New York: Columbia University Press, 1993), 229ff.

4. Cited in Howe, *World of Our Fathers*, 562.

5. Jon W. Finson, *The Voices that Are Gone: Themes in Nineteenth-Century American Popular Song* (New York: Oxford University Press, 1994), 159–239.

6. Ken Emerson, *Doo-dah!: Stephen Foster and the Rise of American Popular Culture* (New York: Simon & Schuster, 1997), 178–183, 269; Hamm, *Irving*, 97; *That's Entertainment*, dir. Jack Haley Jr. (MGM, 1974). There are thirty-three recorded performances of Judy Garland singing "Swanee" and forty-eight recordings of her singing "Rock-a-Bye Your Baby With a Dixie Melodie." See Emily R. Coleman, *The Complete Judy Garland* (New York: Harper & Row, 1990). The Back-to-Dixie theme was still used by African-American writers, even in the early twentieth century, but in a different way. The African-American ragtime team of James Weldon Johnson, J. Rosamund Johnson, and Bob Cole (1898–1906) wrote tunes about returning to the South, but their themes were of the loss of simpler, more bucolic times—the plantation and the people now stand in tatters. Theirs was a lament of times irrevocably gone by. The Jews imagined those times as real, as upbeat, as Edenic, and as presently located in the South. For this information, I thank Lori Brooks.

7. *A Plantation Act*, dir. Philip Roscoe (Warner Bros., 1926).

8. *The Singing Kid*, dir. William Keighley (Warner Bros., 1936).

9. Seldes, *7 Lively Arts*, 182.

10. Eric Lott, *Love & Theft: Blackface Minstrelsy and the American Working Class* (New York: Oxford University Press, 1995), 234.

11. See Ann Douglas, *Terrible Honesty: Mongrel Manhattan in the 1920s* (New York: Noonday Press, 1995).

12. Al Jolson "'I Become a Movie Star': In Which the World's Greatest Black-Face Comedian Tells Some of His Thoughts About the Not-So-Silent Movies," *Jewish Tribune*, January 20, 1928, 3.

CHAPTER 13: ASA YOELSON DISCOVERS THE THEATER

1. Herbert G. Goldman, *Jolson: The Legend Comes to Life* (New York: Oxford University Press, 1988), 11ff.

2. Sieben, *Immortal Jolson*, 32; Goldman, *Jolson*, 21ff.

3. Jolson, "'I Become a Movie Star,'" 3.

4. Michael Stanislawski, *Tsar Nicholas I and the Jews* (Philadelphia: Jewish Publication Society of America, 1983), 123–154; Gerald Sorin, *A Time for Building: The Third Migration 1880–1920* in The Jewish People In America, series ed. Henry L. Feingold (Baltimore: The Johns Hopkins University Press, 1992), 176.

5. Samson Raphaelson, *The Jazz Singer* (New York: Brentano's Publishers, 1925). See Robert C. Allen, *Horrible Prettiness: Burlesque and American Culture* (Chapel Hill: University of North Carolina Press, 1991).

6. A. Bryan and B. Hanlon, "O-Hi-O (O!-My!-O!)," charted 4/9/21; weeks: 7; peak #1 (4 weeks). Introduced by Eddie Cantor in 1920, lyrics by Jack Yellen. Also sung by Lou Holtz, Ted Lewis, and Van and Schenck, and eventually by the Andrew Sisters in 1947 under the name "Down by the Ohio." It can be heard on the album

Al Jolson: You Ain't Heard Nothin' Yet: Jolie's Finest Columbia Recordings (Columbia CK/CT 53419, 1994).

7. "Melting pot" was popularized by the aforementioned Israel Zangwill, Jewish playwright and personality, in his play *The Melting Pot* (New York: Macmillan, 1909). Both the Jewish gang the Eastmans, led by Monk Eastman, and the Italian gang the Five Pointers claimed the Pelham Cafe as part of its territory. For leisure, Monk Eastman kept a bird and animal store on Broome Street. See Harlow, *Old Bowery Days*, 501–502.

8. Hamm, *Irving Berlin*, 22–67.

9. Harry Jolson, "Under the Burnt Cork, Part I & II," *Saturday Evening Post*, December 7 and 28, 1929, 64.

CHAPTER 14: JEWISH MINSTRELSY EMERGES

1. Examples here are limited to Jewish performers, although accounts of serendipity are general. Will Rogers, the man who invented the modern comedy monologue with its emphasis on the daily news—still a staple technique of late-night television comedy—claimed he was so shy that his lasso routine included no spoken words except for a necessary few to explain the more complicated tricks. According to legend, these few words, with their hilarious Western twang, "accidently" won audiences. See Gregory Koseluk, *Eddie Cantor: A Life in Show Business* (Jefferson, N.C.: McFarland & Company, 1995), 61.

2. Cited in Alec Wilder, *American Popular Song: The Great Innovators, 1900–1950* (New York: Oxford University Press, 1972), 191.

3. Cited in Grossman, *Funny Woman*, 34.

4. The Irish comedians were no different in their constructions of brogue. John T. Kelly, born in the Chelsea section of Boston, told the *Cleveland Leader* (June 12, 1906) about his learned brogue:

> I was from Boston, where I heard spoken every kind of Irish brogue that ever was imported. When I first went on the stage I tried being a Dutchman and a lot of other things, but I soon found out that I had to specialize, so I took up the Irish, and went in for clog dancing, becoming the champion of the east. It was a brogue that blended in one all the old country brogues that I had heard in Boston in my childhood days. It was a brogue that battled description, as the writer of the Boston paper found out when he tried to tell his readers how it sounded. After using up a lot of space saying nothing, he ended in despair by saying that I was "nothing more or less than a flannel-mouthed Mick." That phrase went over the country like wild fire and the flannel-mouthed brogue had many imitators years afterward.

Cited in Paul A Distler, "The Rise and Fall of the Racial Comics in American Vaudeville" (Ph.D. dissertation, Tulane University, 1963), 116.

5. Cited in Grossman, *Funny Woman*, 28. Of course, "I'm an Indian" became one of Brice's biggest hits ("Oy yoy yoy," she sang, "I'm a yiddishe squaw"), and

vaudeville already had songs such as "Solomon Cohen, Indian Chief." The stage Indian, however, was only a transitory character in vaudeville. Red paint was used for a particular skit and was removed by the performer for the next one. Minstrels and other ethnic comics tended to base entire careers on one persona, and Brice's was decidedly Jewish.

6. Cited in Grossman, *Funny Woman*, 91.

7. Cited in Grossman, *Funny Woman*, 102. See Distler, "Rise and Fall." Although Distler claims "their personal racial or ethnic backgrounds did not necessarily play any part in their stage representations" (8) his examples contradict him. The great Irish comedians, namely John T. Kelly, Maggie Cline, Thomas J. Ryan, and the Russell Brothers, were all second generation Irish-American, and most were born in Boston. The great stage Jews, Joe Welch, Barney Bernard (of Potash and Perlmutter fame), and David Warfield, were Jewish. The exception seems to be the "Dutch" or German comedians, who were often German or Eastern and Jewish (Weber and Fields, and Jospeh Kline Emmett, *née* Kleinfeller).

Robert W. Snyder is right to note, however, that "according to the conventions of the period, anyone could play any nationality. All that was needed was a convincing presentation of stock traits (down to skin color: sallow greasepaint for Jews, red for Irishmen, and olive for Sicilians)." See Snyder, *The Voice of the City: Vaudeville and Popular Culture in New York* (New York: Oxford University Press, 1989), 64. For example, the Jewish Marx Brothers started with Groucho as the Dutch comic, Harpo as the slapstick Irishman, and Chico as the Italian. See David Nasaw, *Going Out: The Rise and Fall of Public Amusements* (New York: Basic Books, 1993), 51ff. Generally, however, in the twentieth century, ethnic groups represented themselves.

8. On the stage Jew, see Harley Erdman, *Staging the Jew: The Performance of an American Ethnicity, 1860–1920* (New Brunswick, N.J.: Rutgers University Press, 1997).

9. *Jewish Tribune*, April 6, 1928, 38.

10. *Jewish Tribune*, September 11, 1925, 2.

11. *Morgen Zhurnal*, October 8, 1928, 8, cited and translated in Hasia R. Diner, *In the Almost Promised Land*, 69.

12. Koseluk, *Eddie Cantor*, 21–24, 63.

13. Goldman, *Jolson*, 35ff. Jolson had other versions of his first encounter with blackface. *The Jewish Tribune* reported the following just before the release of *The Jazz Singer*:

> He was still a white face comedian . . . and perhaps he would have been to this day if not for the old Negro who sometimes helped him in dressing. He was not able to employ a regular dresser then. "Boss, if your skin's black, they always laugh," the darkey said. Jolson decided to try it. He blackened up with some burnt cork and rehearsed before the old negro. "You's jus' as funny as me, Mistah Jolson," chuckled the old man. Al Jolson in white face was just a vaudeville performer. Al Jolson in black face was an overnight hit.

Jewish Tribune, September 30, 1927, 5. The toenail explanation is reported in Sieben, *Immortal Jolson*, 78.

14. Al Greason, "New Acts," *Variety*, February 22, 1909, cited in Goldman, *Jolson*, 52, as the most important review in Jolson's career.

CHAPTER 15: BLACKFACE ARRIVES ON BROADWAY

1. Goldman, *Jolson*, 48–55.
2. Sieben, *Immortal Jolson*, 61.
3. Cited in Goldman, *Jolson*, 61.
4. Ibid., 50ff.
5. According to Sieben, *Immortal Jolson*, 68–69.
6. Al Jolson "'I Become a Movie Star,'" 3.
7. *New York Herald*, March 21, 1911, cited in Goldman, *Jolson*, 63.
8. "The Decay of Vaudeville," *American Magazine*, April 1910, cited in Goldman, *Jolson*, 50.
9. Their self-sufficiency may be demonstrated by their economic strength. Independent producers, who were mainly Jewish, stood outside of the Theatrical Syndicate, a monopoly of mainstream producers of the legitimate theater. The enormous success of such independents as the Shuberts and David Belasco eventually broke the Theatrical Syndicate in 1913. See Jack Poggi, *Theater in America: The Impact of Economic Forces, 1870–1967* (Ithaca, N.Y.: Cornell University Press, 1968), 20, 33, and Jerry Stagg, *The Brothers Shubert* (New York: Random House, 1968), chapter 6.

CHAPTER 16: THE JEWS ON TIN PAN ALLEY

1. Cited in Sieben, *Immortal Jolson*, 75.
2. *Jewish Tribune*, May 18, 1928, 2.
3. *Jewish Tribune*, September 14, 1928, 75.
4. Fitzgerald, *The Great Gatsby*, 96ff.
5. See Nahma Sandrow, *Vagabond Stars: A World History of Yiddish Theatre* (New York: Harper & Row, 1986); Mark Slobin, *Tenement Songs: The Popular Music of the Jewish Immigrants* (Chicago: University of Illinois Press, 1982); Irene Heskes, *Passport to Jewish Music* (Westport, Conn.: Greenwood Press, 1994).
6. Charles K. Harris, *After the Ball: Forty Years of Melody* (New York: Frank Maurice, 1926), 257.
7. Ibid., 54ff.
8. Cited in Jasen, *Tin Pan Alley*, 39.
9. Ibid., 41.

10. Kenneth Aaron Kanter, *The Jews on Tin Pan Alley: The Jewish Contribution to American Popular Music, 1830–1940* (New York: Ktav Publishing House, 1982), 35.

11. *American Israelite*, May 4, 1922, 1.

12. Ibid. For the critics, see "Ethics of Ragtime," *Literary Digest* (August 10, 1912): 223, and "Can Popular Songs be Stamped Out?" *Literary Digest* (August 14, 1920): 31–32.

13. All quotations are from an article by Arthur Farwell in *Musical America* magazine, as cited in "Ethics of Ragtime," 223.

14. Harris, *After the Ball*, 15.

15. Alexander Wollcott, *The Story of Irving Berlin* (New York: Putnam, 1925), 37.

16. All quotations from an article by Kenneth S. Clark in *Musical America* magazine, as cited in "Can Popular Songs be Stamped Out?" 31–32.

17. *Al Jolson: You Ain't Heard Nothin' Yet* (Columbia CK/CT 53419, 1994).

18. From the aforementioned article by Arthur Farwell in *Musical America* magazine, as cited in "Ethics of Ragtime," 223.

19. *American Israelite*, May 4, 1922, 1.

20. Cited in Hamm, *Irving Berlin*, 10.

21. *American Israelite*, May 4, 1922, 1.

22. See chapter 8 of this book.

23. Laurence Bergreen, *As Thousands Cheer: The Life of Irving Berlin* (New York: Penguin Books, 1991), 154–164.

24. *American Israelite*, May 4, 1922, 1.

25. Gilbert Seldes, for instance, considered this the first ragtime song. See Seldes, *7 Lively Arts*, 71. See also Hamm, *Irving Berlin*, 102–136.

26. Cited in Hamm, *Irving Berlin*, 103 (emphasis original).

27. Hamm, *Irving Berlin*, 107–108. Hamm has written the definitive historical and musicological work on the origins of "Alexander" and its surrounding controversies in his chapter "Alexander and His Band," 102–136.

28. From an interview in the *New York Dramatic Mirror*, 1925, cited in Kanter, *Jews on Tin Pan Alley*, 137ff.

29. By Joseph H. McLeon, Harry M. Piano, and W. Raymond Walker (1909).

30. Hamm, *Irving Berlin*, 86–88, 101.

31. *American Israelite*, May 4, 1922, 1.

32. Cited in Charles Schwartz, *Gershwin: His Life & Music* (New York: Da Capo Press, 1973), 35.

33. Hart, *Complete Lyrics of Lorenz Hart*, 97.

34. Irving Berlin with Justus Dickinson, "'Love-Interest' As a Commodity," *Green Book Magazine* 13 (April 1916): 698, cited in Hamm, *Irving Berlin*, 107.

35. Cited in Jasen, *Tin Pan Alley*, epigraph.

36. Cited in Hamm, *Irving Berlin*, 3.

37. Goldman, *Jolson*, 109ff.

CHAPTER 17: *THE JAZZ SINGER*

1. *American Hebrew*, October 14, 1927, 812.

2. Robert L. Carringer, ed. *The Jazz Singer* (Wisconsin/Warner Bros. Screenplay Series. Madison: University of Wisconsin Press, 1979), 12; Gabler, *An Empire of Their Own*, 139.

3. See reviews in The *New York Post*, September 15, 1925, and the *New York Times*, September 25, 1925.

4. *Jewish Tribune*, August 3, 1928, 25.

5. Harry Austryn Wolfson, "Escaping Judaism," *Menorah Journal* (June, 1921): 71–83, and (August 1921): 155–168.

6. Raphaelson, *The Jazz Singer*, 18.

7. The construction of *The Jazz Singer* suggested other conflicts of opposites. For example: Father/Mother as competing gendered representatives of sacred wrath/mercy; Cantor/Entertainer as competing mediators of sacred song, as when Jack Robin confronts his father: "We in show business have our religion too—on every day—the *show must go on!*" and "My songs mean as much to my audience as yours do to your congregation." There are others. For the purpose of this analysis, however, I stick to the conflict of opposites that is the central and explicit conflict of the plot, that between Jewish and African-American musics.

8. Theodore Dreiser's brother, Paul Dresser, who wrote "My Gal Sal" (1905), which was performed in *The Jazz Singer*, was not a Jew. I cannot determine whether Edgar Leslie, who wrote "Dirty Hands Dirty Face," was a Jew.

9. He continued: "As the Greeks would say, 'it is *methetic* rather than *mimetic.*' It is 'a helping-out of the action.'" Johan Huizinga, *Homo Ludens: A Study of the Play Element in Culture* (Boston: Beacon Press, 1955), 14ff (emphasis original).

10. Rogin, *Black Face, White Noise*, 100, 102, 116.

11. This has been shown in the works of Sander Gilman. See Sander L. Gilman, *Jewish Self-Hatred* (Baltimore: The Johns Hopkins University Press, 1986).

12. Moore, *At Home in America*, 19–58.

13. Rogin, *Blackface, White Noise*, 89.

14. Matthew F. Jacobson, *Whiteness of a Different Color* (Cambridge: Harvard University Press, 1998), 118–122. See also Jeffrey Melnick who "above all, [is] interested in tracing how Jewish musicians ... learned to use their access *as Jews* to African Americans and Black music as evidence of their racial health—that is, of their whiteness." Jeffrey Melnick, *A Right to Sing the Blues* (Cambridge, Mass.: Harvard University Press, 1999), 12.

15. Jean-Paul Sartre, *Anti-Semite and Jew*, trans. George J. Becker (New York: Schocken, 1995).

16. See Jacob Katz, *Tradition and Crisis: Jewish Society at the End of the Middle Ages*, trans. Bernard Dov Cooperman (New York: Schocken Books, 1993).

17. One scholar who has noted this is W. T. Lhamon Jr., in his book about the history of minstrelsy in America. Lhamon suggests "that we conceive the 'exchange' of cultural tokens as *transactions*: they do not replace the parts of one's identity but, instead, compound who one is" (91). Therefore Lhamon sees Jolson's blackface work as "nakedly earnest and poignant," (103) a legitimate attempt to incorporate African-American tropes into his own identity; therefore Lhamon denies the reading that blackface is about the "replacement of ethnicity or Jewishness with whiteness. 'Replacement' is simply insufficient to describe what is happening in any of these black or blackface performances. Rather, they all stage continual transactions of assimilation," (107) by which Lhamon means something less ominous than Rogin's assimilation. Still, because Lhamon is not a historian of the Jews, he neglects the Eastern European sources of Jewish identity, and mistakes basic facts about Jewish culture: "*The Jazz Singer* celebrates *April Follies* instead of the Jewish springtime ritual of kol nidre" (109). Al Jolson, the Warner Brothers, and everyone else involved with the picture were well aware of the autumn date of Yom Kippur when they scheduled the debut of *The Jazz Singer* for the evening after the holiday, October 6, 1927, to catch the Jewish audiences they so desperately courted after their ritual breakfast. Jewish culture must be considered by those who study Jewish behavior. W. T. Lhamon Jr., *Raising Cain: Blackface Performance from Jim Crow to Hip Hop* (Cambridge, Mass.: Harvard University Press, 1998).

18. *Jewish Tribune*, February 3, 1928, 16.

19. See Ruth Frankenburg, *The Social Construction of Whiteness: White Women, Race Matters* (Minneapolis: University of Minnesota Press, 1993).

20. *Morgen Zhurnal*, October 8, 1927, 8, translated by Diner, *In the Almost Promised Land*, 69.

21. *Forverts*, October 21, 1926, 6. Cited in Diner, *In the Almost Promised Land*, 61.

22. *Big Boy*, dir. Alan Crosland (Warner Bros., 1930).

23. *Kalifornia Yidishe Shtime*, January 2, 1928, 3.

24. Numbers 15:38–41; BT Rosh Ha-Shanah, 17b.

25. Moore, *Religious Outsiders*, xi.

26. See *Jewish Daily Bulletin*, October 7, 1927, 1f; Mordecai M. Kaplan, "Judaism as a Civilization: Religion's Place in It," *Menorah Journal*, 15:6 (December 1928), 501–514. Samson Raphael Hirsh, an Orthodox reformer in mid-nineteenth-century Germany, had removed Kol Nidre from his service in 1840 for similar reasons, but pressure from his congregation in Oldenburg forced him to reinstate it. See Noah H. Rosenbloom, *Tradition in an Age of Reform: The Religious Philosophy of Samson Raphaelson Hirsch* (Philadelphia: Jewish Publication Society, 1976), 69–70.

27. This may not have been a snub. Generally, the African-American press didn't mention cultural events that did not include African-American performers, which *The Jazz Singer* did not. But African-American responses to the Jewish radio team of Amos 'n' Andy may provide some insight into what African-Americans thought of a performer like Jolson. In the case of Amos 'n' Andy in the late 1920s, black opinion

was divided between fans and detractors. See Melvin Patrick Ely, *The Adventures of Amos 'n' Andy* (New York: Free Press, 1991), 160–193.

28. *Kalifornia Yidishe Shtime*, January 2, 1928, 3.

29. The *American Hebrew* reported Jolson's words in response to calls of bravo: "My god, I think you're really on the level about it. I feel good!" *American Hebrew*, October 14, 1927, 823.

30. Raphaelson, *The Jazz Singer*, 10.

Conclusion: Jazz Age Jews

1. See Goren, *New York Jews and the Quest for Community*; see also Eisen, *The Chosen People in America*.

2. See David N. Myers, *Re-Inventing the Jewish Past* (New York: Oxford University Press, 1995).

3. See Paula E. Hyman, *Gender and Assimilation in Modern Jewish History: The Roles and Representation of Women* (Seattle: University of Washington Press, 1995); Jenna Weissman Joselit, *The Wonders of America: Reinventing Jewish Culture 1880–1950* (New York: Hill and Wang, 1994); Moore, *At Home in America*; Moore, *To the Golden Cities: Pursuing the American Jewish Dream in Miami and L.A.* (Cambridge, Mass.: Harvard University Press, 1994).

4. Arnold Eisen, *Galut: Modern Jewish Reflection on Homelessness and Homecoming* (Bloomington: Indiana University Press, 1986); David Novak, *The Election of Israel: The Idea of the Chosen People* (Cambridge, U.K.: Cambridge University Press, 1995); Daniel H. Frank, ed., *A People Apart: Chosenness and Ritual in Jewish Philosophical Thought* (Albany: State University of New York Press, 1993).

5. Scholars of Judaica have been known to participate in the same propensity for marginalization. See Salo W. Baron's call to end the "lachrymose conception" of Jewish history in "Emphases in Jewish History" in *History and Jewish Historians: Essays and Addresses by Salo W. Baron*, eds. Arthur Hertzberg and Leon A. Feldman (Philadelphia: Jewish Publication Society of America, 1964), 65–89.

6. What Max Weber called *Verstehen*, or sympathetic understanding, may be in order. See Weber's notes in *Economy and Society* (Berkeley: University of California Press, 1978), 8ff. My own preference is for the sociological idealism of Charles Horton Cooley. See *Human Nature and the Social Order* in *Two Major Works of Charles H. Cooley* (Glencoe, Ill.: The Free Press, 1956).

7. The 1920s was a decade of unprecedented synagogue growth. From 1916 to 1926, the number of American synagogues doubled, from 1,619 to 3,118. See Beth S. Wenger, *New York Jews and the Great Depression* (New Haven, Conn.: Yale University Press, 1996), 168.

8. Alan M. Dershowitz, *The Vanishing American Jew* (New York: Simon & Schuster, 1997), 262.

BIBLIOGRAPHY

Newspapers and Magazines

American Hebrew
American Israelite
American Review of Reviews
Der Amerikaner un Froyen Magazin
Atlantic Monthly
B'nai B'rith Magazine
Boston Evening Transcript
Boston Herald
Chicago Defender
Chicago Sentinel
Crisis
Forverts
Jewish Daily Bulletin
Jewish Tribune
Kalifornia Yidishe Shtime

Literary Digest
Menorah Journal
Morgen Zhurnal
New Republic
New York Amsterdam News
New York Post
New York Times
New York World
Opportunity
Pittsburgh Courier
Saturday Evening Post
Scribner's Magazine
Southern Israelite
Der Tog
Yidishes Tageblat

Archives

Columbia Oral History Project (COHP)
Felix Frankfurter Papers at Harvard Law School (FFPHLS)
Felix Frankfurter Papers at the Library of Congress (FFPLC)
Yeshiva University Archives

CDs

Al Jolson—You Ain't Heard Nothin' Yet: Jolie's Finest Columbia Recordings (Columbia CK/CT 53419, 1994).
Irving Berlin—A Hundred Years (Columbia CGK40035, 1988).

Films

Big Boy, directed by Alan Crosland (Warner Bros., 1930).
The Jazz Singer, directed by Alan Crosland (Warner Bros., 1927).
A Plantation Act, directed by Philip Roscoe (Warner Bros., 1926).
The Singing Kid, directed by William Keighley (Warner Bros., 1936).

That's Entertainment, directed by Jack Haley Jr. (MGM, 1974).

Wonder Bar, directed by Lloyd Bacon (Warner Bros., 1934).

GOVERNMENT PUBLICATIONS

Abstract of the Census of Manufacturers, 1919. Washington, D.C., 1923.

Fourteenth Census of the United States. Washington, D.C., 1921.

Hillis, Newell Dwight. *The Atrocities of Germany: Buy LIBERTY BONDS and End Them Forever.* Second Federal Reserve District: Liberty Loan Committee, no date.

President's Conference on Unemployment, *Recent Economic Changes in the United States.* 2 Volumes. New York, 1929.

"Report on the Mooney Dynamite Cases submitted by President Wilson's Mediation Commission," Official Bulletin of the United States Committee on Public Information. Washington, D.C., 1918.

BOOKS AND ARTICLES

Alexander, Charles C. *John McGraw.* Lincoln: University of Nebraska Press, 1988.

Allen, Robert C. *Horrible Prettiness: Burlesque and American Culture.* Chapel Hill: University of North Carolina Press, 1991.

Asbury, Herbert. *Sucker's Progress: An Informal History of Gambling in America from the Colonies to Canfield.* New York: Dodd, Mead & Co., 1938.

Asinof, Eliot. *Eight Men Out: The Black Sox and the 1919 World Series.* New York: Holt, Rinehart and Winston, 1963.

Auerbach, Jerold S. *Rabbis and Lawyers: The Journey from Torah to Constitution.* Bloomington: Indiana University Press, 1993.

———. *Unequal Justice: Lawyers and Social Change in Modern America.* New York: Oxford University Press, 1976.

Avrich, Paul. *Sacco and Vanzetti: The Anarchist Background.* Princeton, N.J.: Princeton University Press, 1991.

Baker, Liva. *Felix Frankfurter.* New York: Coward-McCann, 1969.

Baker, Leonard. *Brandeis and Frankfurter: A Dual Biography.* New York: Harper & Row, 1984.

Baltzell, E. Digby. *The Protestant Establishment: Aristocracy & Caste in America.* New Haven: Yale University Press, 1987.

Barnard, Harry. *The Forging of an American Jew: The Life and Times of Judge Julian W. Mack.* New York: Herzl Press, 1974.

Baron, Salo W. "Emphases in Jewish History." In *History and Jewish Historians: Essays and Addresses by Salo W. Baron*, 65–89, edited by Arthur Hertzberg and Leon A. Feldman. Philadelphia: Jewish Publication Society of America, 1964.

Bell, Daniel. *The End of Ideology.* New York: Free Press, 1967.

Berger, Peter L. *The Sacred Canopy.* New York: Doubleday, 1967.

Bergreen, Laurence. *As Thousands Cheer: The Life of Irving Berlin*. New York: Penguin Books, 1991.

Biale, David, Michael Galchinsky, and Susannah Heschel, eds. *Insider/Outsider: American Jews and Multiculturalism*. Berkeley: University of California Press, 1998.

Birmingham, Stephen. *"Our Crowd."* New York: Berkley Books, 1984.

Bradley, Hugh. *Such Was Saratoga*. New York: Doubleday, Doran and Company, 1940.

Brandeis, Louis D. *"Half Brother, Half Son": The Letters of Louis D. Brandeis to Felix Frankfurter*, edited by Melvin I. Urofsky and David W. Levy. Norman: University of Oklahoma Press, 1991.

———. *Letters of Louis D. Brandeis*. 5 vols., edited by Melvin Urofsky and David Levy. Albany: State University of New York Press, 1971–1978.

———. "The Opportunity in the Law." *American Law Review* 39 (July/August 1905): 555–563.

Brumberg, Stephan F. *Going to America, Going to School*. New York: Praeger, 1986.

Burt, Robert A. *Two Jewish Justices: Outcasts in the Promised Land*. Berkeley: University of California Press, 1988.

Bush, Martin H. *Ben Shahn: The Passion of Sacco and Vanzetti*. Syracuse, N.Y.: Syracuse University Press, 1968.

Carringer, Robert L., ed. *The Jazz Singer*. Wisconsin/Warner Bros. Screenplay Series. Madison: University of Wisconsin Press, 1979.

Clarke, Donald Henderson. *In the Reign of Rothstein*. New York: Vanguard Press, 1929.

Clark, Tom. *The World of Damon Runyon*. New York: Harper & Row, 1978.

Coleman, Emily R. *The Complete Judy Garland*. New York: Harper & Row, 1990.

Cooley, Charles Horton. *Human Nature and the Social Order*, in *Two Major Works of Charles H. Cooley*. Glencoe, Ill.: Free Press, 1956.

Cooney, John. *The Annenbergs*. New York: Simon and Schuster, 1982.

Czitrom, Daniel. "Underworlds and Underdogs: Big Tim Sullivan." *Journal of American History* 78 (1991): 536–558.

Dershowitz, Alan M. *The Vanishing American Jew*. New York: Simon & Schuster, 1997.

Diner, Hasia R. *In the Almost Promised Land: American Jews and Blacks, 1915–1935*. Westport, Conn.: Greenwood Press, 1977.

———. *A Time for Gathering: The Second Migration 1820–1880*. The Jewish People in America, Vol. 2, ed. Henry L. Feingold. Baltimore: The Johns Hopkins University Press, 1992.

Dinnerstein, Leonard. *Antisemitism in America*. New York: Oxford University Press, 1994.

Distler, Paul A. "The Rise and Fall of the Racial Comics in American Vaudeville." Ph.D. dissertation. Tulane University, 1963.

Dormant, Richard, and Margaret F. Macdonald. *James McNeill Whistler*. New York: Harry N. Abrams, Inc., 1995.

Douglas, Ann. *Terrible Honesty: Mongrel Manhattan in the 1920s*. New York: Noonday Press, 1995.

Dubinsky, David, and A. H. Raskin. *David Dubinsky: A Life With Labor*. New York: Simon and Schuster, 1977.

Eisen, Arnold. *The Chosen People in America*. Bloomington: Indiana University Press, 1983.

——. *Galut: Modern Jewish Reflection on Homelessness and Homecoming*. Bloomington: Indiana University Press, 1986.

Ely, Melvin Patrick. *The Adventures of Amos 'n' Andy*. New York: Free Press, 1991.

Emerson, Ken. *Doo-dah!: Stephen Foster and the Rise of American Popular Culture*. New York: Simon & Schuster, 1997.

Endelman, Todd M. *The Jews of Georgian England: Tradition and Change in a Liberal Society*. Philadelphia: Jewish Publication Society of America, 1979.

Erdman, Harley. *Staging the Jew: The Performance of an American Ethnicity, 1860–1920*. New Brunswick, N.J.: Rutgers University Press, 1997.

Eulau, Heinz. "From Public Opinion to Public Philosophy." *American Journal of Economics and Sociology* 15 (1956): 442–446.

Evans, Elizabeth Glendower. *Outstanding Features of the Sacco-Vanzetti Case*. Boston: New England Civil Liberties Committee, 1924.

Fabian, Ann. *Card Sharps, Dream Books, & Bucket Shops: Gambling in 19th-Century America*. Ithaca, N.Y.: Cornell University Press, 1990.

Feldman, Penny Hollander. *Recruiting an Elite*. New York: Garland, 1988.

Felix, David. *Protest: Sacco-Vanzetti and the Intellectuals*. Bloomington: Indiana University Press, 1965.

Ferber, Nat. *I Found Out: A Confidential Chronicle of the Twenties*. New York: Dial Press, 1939.

Finson, Jon W. *The Voices that Are Gone: Themes in Nineteenth-Century American Popular Song*. New York: Oxford University Press, 1994.

Fisher, James Terence. *The Catholic Counterculture in America, 1933–1962*. Chapel Hill: University of North Carolina Press, 1989.

Fitzgerald, F. Scott. *The Crack-Up*, edited by Edmund Wilson. New York: New Directions, 1945.

——. *F. Scott Fitzgerald: A Life in Letters*, edited by Matthew J. Bruccoli. New York: Charles Scribner's Sons, 1994.

——. *The Great Gatsby*. New York: Charles Schribner's Sons, 1925.

——. *The Letters of F. Scott Fitzgerald*, edited by Andrew Turnbull. New York: Charles Scribner's Sons, 1963.

Ford, Henry, ed. *The International Jew*. Dearborn Independent, 1921.

Fowler, Gene. *The Great Mouthpiece: A Life Story of William J. Fallon*. New York: Covici Friede, 1932.

Fox, Stephen. *Blood and Power: Organized Crime in Twentieth-Century America*. New York: William Morrow and Company, 1989.

Frank, Daniel H., ed. *A People Apart: Chosenness and Ritual in Jewish Philosophical Thought*. Albany: State University of New York Press, 1993.

Frankenburg, Ruth. *The Social Construction of Whiteness: White Women, Race Matters*. Minneapolis: University of Minnesota Press, 1993.

Frankfurter, Felix. *The Case of Sacco and Vanzetti: A Critical Analysis for Lawyers and Laymen*. Boston: Little, Brown, 1927.

———. *Felix Frankfurter Reminisces*, edited by Harlan B. Phillips. New York: Reynal & Company, 1960.

———. *From the Diaries of Felix Frankfurter*, edited by Joseph P. Lash. New York: W. W. Norton & Company, 1975.

———. *Law and Politics: Occasional Papers of Felix Frankfurter 1913–1938*, edited by Archibald MacLeish and E. F. Prichard, Jr. New York: Harcourt, Brace and Company, 1939.

Frankfurter, Marion D., and Gardner Jackson, eds. *The Letters of Sacco and Vanzetti*. New York: Penguin Books, 1997 [1928].

Gabler, Neal. *An Empire of Their Own: How the Jews Invented Hollywood*. New York: Crown Publishers, 1988.

Garfield, Alexander. *Canfield: The True Story of the Greatest Gambler*. Garden City, N.Y.: Doubleday, Doran and Co., 1930.

Geertz, Clifford. "Deep Play: Notes on the Balinese Cockfight," in *The Interpretation of Cultures*, 412–453. New York: Basic Books, 1973.

Gilchrist, John T. *The Church and Economic Activity in the Middle Ages*. New York: Macmillan, 1969.

Gilman, Sander. *Jewish Self-Hatred*. Baltimore: The Johns Hopkins University Press, 1986.

Goldman, Herbert G. *Jolson: The Legend Comes to Life*. New York: Oxford University Press, 1988.

Gordon, Milton M. *Assimilation in American Life: The Role of Race, Religion, and National Origins*. New York: Oxford University Press, 1964.

Gorelick, Sherry. *City College and the Jewish Poor*. New York: Schocken Books, 1982.

Goren, Arthur A. *New York Jews and the Quest for Community: The Kehilla Experiment, 1908–1922*. New York: Columbia University Press, 1970.

———. *Saints and Sinners: The Underside of American Jewish History*. Cincinnati: American Jewish Archives, 1988.

Grossman, Barbara W. *Funny Woman: The Life and Times of Fanny Brice*. Bloomington: Indiana University Press, 1991.

Gudis, Catherine. "The Road to Consumption: Outdoor Advertising and the American Cultural Landscape." Ph.D. dissertation, Yale University, 1999.

Gurock, Jeffrey S., and Jacob J. Schacter. *A Modern Heretic and a Traditional Community: Mordecai M. Kaplan, Orthodoxy, and American Judaism*. New York: Columbia University Press, 1997.

Hamm, Charles. *Irving Berlin: Songs from the Melting Pot*. New York: Oxford University Press, 1997.

Harlow, Alvin F. *Old Bowery Days*. New York: D. Appleton and Company, 1931.

Harris, Charles K. *After the Ball: Forty Years of Melody*. New York: Frank Maurice, 1926.

Hart, Dorothy, and Robert Kimball, eds. *The Complete Lyrics of Lorenz Hart*. New York: Da Capo Press, 1995.

Hays, Arthur Garfield. *City Lawyer: The Autobiography of a Law Practice*. New York: Simon and Schuster, 1942.

———. *Let Freedom Ring*. New York: Boni and Liveright, 1928.

———. *Trial By Prejudice*. New York: Covici Friede, 1933.

Heskes, Irene. *Passport to Jewish Music*. Westport, Conn.: Greenwood Press, 1994.

Hicks, John D. *Republican Ascendancy: 1921–1933*. New York: Harper & Brothers, 1960.

Higham, John. *Send These to Me: Immigrants in Urban America*. Baltimore: The Johns Hopkins University Press, 1984.

Hirsch, H. N. *The Enigma of Felix Frankfurter*. New York: Basic Books, 1981.

Hotaling, Edward. *They're Off! Horse Racing at Saratoga*. Syracuse, N.Y.: Syracuse University Press, 1995.

Howe, Irving. *World of Our Fathers*. New York: Harcourt Brace Jovanovich, 1976.

Howe, Mark DeWolfe, ed. *Holmes-Laski Letters*. Cambridge, Mass.: Harvard University Press, 1953.

Huizinga, Johan. *Homo Ludens: A Study of the Play Element in Culture*. Boston: Beacon Press, 1955.

Hundert, Gershon David. *The Jews in a Polish Private Town*. Baltimore: The Johns Hopkins University Press, 1992.

Hyman, Paula E. *Gender and Assimilation in Modern Jewish History: The Roles and Representation of Women*. Seattle: University of Washington Press, 1995.

Israel, Jonathan I. *European Jewry in the Age of Mercantilism 1550–1750*. Oxford, U.K.: Clarendon Press, 1991.

Jacobson, Matthew F. *Whiteness of a Different Color*. Cambridge, Mass.: Harvard University Press, 1998.

Jasen, David A. *Tin Pan Alley: The Composers, the Songs, the Performers and Their Times: The Golden Age of American Popular Music From 1886–1956*. New York: Donald I. Fine, 1988.

Jordan, William Chester. "An Aspect of Credit in Picardy in the 1240s: The Deterioration of Jewish-Christian Financial Relations." *Revue des études juives* 142 (1983): 141–152.

———. "Women and Credit in the Middle Ages: Problems and Directions." *Journal of European Economic History* 17 (1988): 33–62.

Joselit, Jenna Weissman. *Our Gang: Jewish Crime and the New York Jewish Community, 1900–1940*. Bloomington: Indiana University Press, 1983.

————. *The Wonders of America: Reinventing Jewish Culture 1880–1950*. New York: Hill and Wang, 1994.

Joughin, Louis, and Edmund M. Morgan. *The Legacy of Sacco & Vanzetti*. Princeton, N.J.: Princeton University Press, 1976.

Kadane, Joseph, B., and David A. Schum. *A Probabilistic Analysis of the Sacco and Vanzetti Evidence*. New York: John Wiley, 1996.

Kahan, Arcadius. *Essays in Jewish Social and Economic History*. Chicago: University of Chicago Press, 1986.

Kahn Jr., E. J. *The World of Swope*. New York: Simon and Schuster, 1965.

Kallen, Horace M. *Culture and Democracy in the United States*. New York: Boni and Liverright, 1924.

Kammen, Michael G. *The Lively Arts*. New York: Oxford University Press, 1996.

Kanter, Kenneth Aaron. *The Jews on Tin Pan Alley: The Jewish Contribution to American Popular Music*. New York: Ktav Publishing House, 1982.

Katcher, Leo. *The Big Bankroll: The Life and Times of Arnold Rothstein*. New Rochelle, N.Y.: Arlington House, 1959.

Katz, Jacob. *Exclusiveness and Tolerance: Studies in Jewish-Gentile Relations in Medieval & Modern Times*. West Orange, N.J.: Behrman House, 1961.

————. *Tradition and Crisis: Jewish Society at the End of the Middle Ages*, translated by Bernard Dov Cooperman. New York: Schocken Books, 1993.

Katz, Jacob, ed. *Toward Modernity: The European Jewish Model*. New Brunswick, N.J.: Transaction Books, 1987.

Kaufmann, Yehezkiel. *Golah V'Nekhar* [Hebrew: Exile and Alienation], vol. 1 & 2. Tel Aviv: Dvir Company, 1929.

Kennedy, David M. *Over Here: The First World War and American Society*. New York: Oxford University Press, 1980.

Kessner, Thomas. *The Golden Door: Italian and Jewish Immigrant Mobility in New York City, 1880–1915*. New York: Oxford University Press, 1977.

Kirschenbaum, Aaron. "Jewish and Christian Theories of Usury in the Middle Ages." *Jewish Quarterly Review* 75 (1985): 270–289.

Koseluk, Gregory. *Eddie Cantor: A Life in Show Business*. Jefferson, N.C.: McFarland & Company, 1995.

Lacey, Robert. *Little Man: Meyer Lansky and the Gangster Life*. Boston: Little, Brown and Company, 1991.

Langmuir, Gavin I. "Tanguam servi: The Change in Jewish Status in French Law about 1200," in *Les Juifs dans l'histoire de France*, edited by M. Yardeni, 24–54. Leiden: 1980.

Lederhendler, Eli. "Did Russian Jewry Exist Prior to 1917?" in *Jews and Jewish Life in Russia and the Soviet Union*, edited by Yaacov Ro'I, 15–27. Portland, Oreg.: Frank Cass and Co., 1995.

————. "Modernity Without Emancipation or Assimilation? The Case of Russian Jewry," in *Assimilation and Community: The Jews in Nineteenth-Century*

Europe, edited by Jonathan Frankel and Steven J. Zipperstein, 324–333. New York: Cambridge University Press, 1992.

Lee, Henry C., et. al. for the Massachusetts State Police Firearm Examination Panel. *Examination of Firearm-related Evidence: The Nicola Sacco and Bartolomeo Vanzetti Case*. Boston: Westinghouse Broadcasting and Cable Corp., 1983.

Lefevre, Edwin. *Reminiscences of a Stock Operator*. New York: John Wiley & Sons, 1994 [1923].

Leonard, William Torbert. *Masquerade in Black*. Metuchen, N.J.: Scarecrow Press, 1986.

Levine, Peter. *Ellis Island to Ebbets Field*. New York: Oxford University Press, 1992.

Lhamon Jr., W. T. *Raising Cain: Blackface Performance from Jim Crow to Hip Hop*. Cambridge, Mass.: Harvard University Press, 1998.

Lippmann, Walter. *Men of Destiny*. New York: Macmillan, 1927.

———. *Public Opinion*. New York: Free Press, 1949 [1922].

Lockridge, Ernest, ed. *Twentieth Century Interpretations of The Great Gatsby*. Englewood Cliffs, N.J.: Prentice-Hall, 1968.

Lott, Eric. *Love & Theft: Blackface Minstrelsy and the American Working Class*. New York: Oxford University Press, 1995.

Maas, Peter. *Underboss: Sammy the Bull Gravano's Story of Life in the Mafia*. New York: HarperCollins, 1997.

Marcus, Jacob Rader, ed. *The Jew in the American World: A Source Book*. Detroit: Wayne State University Press, 1996.

Melnick, Jeffrey. *A Right to Sing the Blues*. Cambridge, Mass.: Harvard University Press, 1999.

Mennel, Robert M., and Christine L. Compston, eds. *Holmes & Frankfurter: Their Correspondence, 1912–1934*. Hanover, N.H.: University Press of New England, 1996.

Montgomery, David. *The Fall of the House of Labor*. New York: Cambridge University Press, 1987.

Moore, Deborah Dash. *At Home in America: Second Generation New York Jews*. New York: Columbia University Press, 1981.

———. *To the Golden Cities: Pursuing the American Jewish Dream in Miami and L.A.* Cambridge, Mass.: Harvard University Press, 1994.

Moore, R. Laurence. *Religious Outsiders and the Making of Americans*. New York: Oxford University Press, 1986.

Morris, Lloyd. *Incredible New York: High Life and Low Life of the Last Hundred Years*. New York: Random House, 1951.

Murray, Robert K. *Red Scare: A Study in National Hysteria, 1919–1920*. Minneapolis: University of Minnesota Press, 1955.

Myers, David N. *Re-Inventing the Jewish Past*. New York: Oxford University Press, 1995.

Nasaw, David. *Going Out: The Rise and Fall of Public Amusements*. New York: Basic Books, 1993.

Nelson, Benjamin. *The Idea of Usury*. Chicago: University of Chicago Press, 1969.

Novak, David. *The Election of Israel: The Idea of the Chosen People*. Cambridge, U.K.: Cambridge University Press, 1995.

O'Brien, David J. *The Renewal of American Catholicism*. New York: Oxford University Press, 1972.

Paper, Lewis J. *Brandeis*. Secaucus, N.J.: Citadel Press, 1983.

Parrish, Michael E. *Felix Frankfurter and His Times: The Reform Years*. New York: Free Press, 1982.

Poggi, Jack. *Theater in America: The Impact of Economic Forces, 1870–1967*. Ithaca, N.Y.: Cornell University Press, 1968.

Raphael, Marc Lee, ed. *Jews and Judaism in the United States: A Documentary History*. New York: Behrman House, 1983.

Raphaelson, Samson. *The Jazz Singer*. New York: Brentano's, 1925.

Reid, Ed, and Ovid Demaris. *The Green Felt Jungle*. New York: Trident Press, 1963.

Rice, George Graham. *My Adventures With Your Money*. New York: Bookfinger, 1974 [1913].

Roalfe, William R. *John Henry Wigmore: Scholar and Reformer*. Evanston, Ill.: Northwestern University Press, 1977.

Rogin, Michael. *Blackface, White Noise: Jewish Immigrants in the Hollywood Melting Pot*. Berkeley: University of California Press, 1996.

Root, Jonathan. *One Night in July: The True Story of the Rosenthal-Becker Murder Case*. New York: Coward-McCann, 1961.

Rosenbloom, Noah H. *Tradition in an Age of Reform: The Religious Philosophy of Samson Raphaelson Hirsch*. Philadelphia: Jewish Publication Society, 1976.

Rosenthal, Franz. "The Stranger in Medieval Islam." *Arabica* 44 (1997): 35–75.

Rothstein, Carolyn. *Now I'll Tell*. New York: Vanguard Press, 1934.

Rozenblit, Marsha L. *The Jews of Vienna, 1867–1914*. Albany: State University of New York Press, 1983.

Rubin, Martin. *Showstoppers: Busby Berkeley and the Tradition of Spectacle*. New York: Columbia University Press, 1993.

Runyon, Damon. *The Damon Runyon Omnibus*. Garden City, N.Y.: Sun Dial Press, 1943.

The Sacco-Vanzetti Case: Transcript of the Record of the Trial of Nicola Sacco and Bartolomeo Vanzetti in the Courts of Massachusetts and Subsequent Proceedings, 1920–1927. 5 vols., with a supplemental volume on the Bridgewater Case. New York: Holt, 1927–1929.

Sandrow, Nahma. *Vagabond Stars: A World History of Yiddish Theater*. New York: Harper & Row, 1986.

Sann, Paul. *The Lawless Decade*. New York: Crown, 1957.

Sarna, Johathan D., ed. *The American Jewish Experience*. New York: Holmes & Meier, 1986.

Sartre, Jean-Paul. *Anti-Semite and Jew*, translated by George J. Becker. New York: Schocken, 1995.

Scarne, John. *Scarne on Dice*. North Hollywood: Melvin Powers Wilshire, 1980.

Schmidt, Sarah. *Horace M. Kallen: Prophet of American Zionism*. Brooklyn, N.Y.: Carlson, 1995.

Schwartz, Charles. *Gershwin: His Life and Music*. New York: Da Capo Press, 1973.

Seldes, Gilbert. *The 7 Lively Arts*. New York: Sagamore Press, 1957 [1924].

Seligman, Joel. *The High Citadel: The Influence of Harvard Law School*. Boston: Houghton Mifflin Company, 1978.

Shatzmiller, Joseph. *Shylock Reconsidered: Jews, Moneylending, and Medieval Society*. Los Angeles: University of California Press, 1990.

Sieben, Pearl. *Immortal Jolson: His Life and Times*. New York: Frederick Fell, Inc., 1962.

Sklar, Martin J. *The Corporate Reconstruction of American Capitalism, 1890–1916*. New York: Cambridge University Press, 1988.

Sklar, Robert. *Movie-Made America*. New York: Vintage Books, 1994.

Slobin, Mark. *Tenement Songs: The Popular Music of the Jewish Immigrants*. Chicago: University of Illinois Press, 1982.

Snyder, Robert W. *The Voice of the City: Vaudeville and Popular Culture in New York*. New York: Oxford University Press, 1989.

Sorin, Gerald. *A Time For Building: The Third Migration 1880–1920*. The Jewish People In America, ed. Henry L. Feingold. Baltimore: The Johns Hopkins University Press, 1992.

Stagg, Jerry. *The Brothers Shubert*. New York: Random House, 1968.

Stanislawski, Michael. *Tsar Nicholas I and the Jews*. Philadelphia: Jewish Publication Society of America, 1983.

Starrs, James E. "Once More Unto the Breech: The Firearms Evidence in the Sacco and Vanzetti Case Revisited." *Journal of Forensic Science* (April 1986): 630–654, and (July 1986): 1050–1078.

Steel, Ronald. *Walter Lippmann and the American Century*. Boston: Little, Brown and Company, 1980.

Stern, Selma. *The Court Jew*, translated by Ralph Weinman. New Brunswick, N.J.: Transaction Books, 1985.

Stewart, James B. *Den of Thieves*. New York: Simon & Schuster, 1991.

Stoddard, William Leavitt. *Financial Racketeering and How to Stop It*. New York: Harper & Brothers, 1931.

Stow, Kenneth R. "Papal and Royal Attitudes toward Jewish Lending in the Thirteenth Century." *AJS Review* 6 (1981): 161–184.

Strum, Philippa. *Brandeis: Beyond Progressivism*. Lawrence: University Press of Kansas, 1993.

———. *Louis D. Brandeis: Justice for the People*. Cambridge, Mass.: Harvard University Press, 1984.

Synnott, Marcia Graham. *The Half-Opened Door: Discrimination and Admissions at Harvard, Yale, and Princeton, 1900–1970*. Westport, Conn.: Greenwood Press, 1979.

Thomas, Helen Shirley. *Felix Frankfurter: Scholar on the Bench*. Baltimore: The Johns Hopkins University Press, 1960.

Urofsky, Melvin, I. *Louis D. Brandeis and the Progressive Tradition*. Boston: Little, Brown and Company, 1981.

Washburn, Watson and Edmund DeLong. *High and Low Financiers*. Indianapolis, Ind.: Bobbs-Merrill, 1932.

Weber, Max. *Economy and Society*. Berkeley: University of California Press, 1978.

——. *The Protestant Ethic and the Spirit of Capitalism*. New York: Charles Scribner's Sons, 1958.

Weinreich, Beatrice Silverman, and Leonard Wolf, eds. *Yiddish Folktales*. New York: Pantheon Books/YIVO Institute, 1988.

Wenger, Beth S. *New York Jews and the Great Depression*. New Haven, Conn.: Yale University Press, 1996.

Wilder, Alec. *American Popular Song: The Great Innovators, 1900–1950*. New York: Oxford University Press, 1972.

Wollcott, Alexander. *The Story of Irving Berlin*. New York: Putnam, 1925.

Yezierska, Anzia. *Bread Givers: A Struggle between a Father of the Old World and a Daughter of the New*. New York: Doubleday, 1925.

Young, William, and David E. Kaiser. *Postmortem: New Evidence in the Case of Sacco and Vanzetti*. Amherst: University of Massachusetts Press, 1985.

Zangwill, Israel. *The Melting Pot*. New York: Macmillan, 1909.

Zucker, Nechemias. *In nomen fun gerekhtikeyt—tragedye in dray aktn: zeks bilder mit a prolog un epilog*. Buenos Aires: N. Tsunker, 1935.

MANY friends helped me by reading and commenting on select portions of this work. I wish to thank Michael Cohen, Frank Friedwald, Bob Glasser, Sam Hecht, O. B. Karp, Nancy Kopans, Brian Kopell, Bob Lichtman, Jason Miller, Ken Moon, Mark Oppenheimer, Adam Sachs, Sanjay Sharma, Dorothy Stefanczyk, Ellen Sweeney, Daniel Rubin, Jonathan Taylor, Scott Villa, and Amy Wruble.

Several scholars were particularly giving of their time and comments. Thank you Jere Bacherach, Arnold Eisen, Aryeh Goren, Kathryn Hellerstein, Martin Jaffee, Jenna Weissman Joselit, Ben Keppel, Eli Lederhendler, David Levy, Kathryn Miller, Deborah Dash Moore, Regina Morantz-Sanchez, David Stern, Norman Stillman, and David Waldstreicher. A special thanks to George Lindbeck and Philip Rieff who can never retire as my teachers.

At times, I consulted attorneys for help in areas well beyond my knowledge. Thank you Noah Feldman for incalculable insight, and Irving J. Pinsky for incalculable encouragement. I also wish to thank the following two gentlemen for their hospitality and their memories: Leo Lewis of the Barbary Coast Hotel, Las Vegas, and Donny Weinstein—Hawthorne School, class of 1956—formerly of Ratner's Delicatessen, New York.

Thanks to Joel Friedlander for matters of theory, and to Norman Watkins for problems of method and practice.

Several fellowships sponsored this work: the Holtzman Fellowship in Jewish Studies at Yale, the Pew Fellowship in American Religious History, the Cole Fellowship at the University of Washington, the Behrend Summer Fellowship from the Center for American Jewish History at Temple University, and the Chai Society Summer Scholarship.

My research was greatly aided by the collections and staffs of the following libraries: the Manuscript Division of the Library of Congress, the Yale libraries, the University of Washington libraries, the

227

Schomburg Center for Research in Black Culture, the Dorot Jewish Division of the New York Public Library, and the Sacco-Vanzetti Collection at the Boston Public Library. A special thanks to Shulamith Z. Berger, archivist at Yeshiva University.

I offer my permanent gratitude to Thomas LeBien who leaves this book so much better than how he found it. I am also in debt to Tim Sullivan for his keen and elegant copyediting, to Jan Lilly for the text design, and to the rest of the team at Princeton University Press, including Maura Roessner and Susan Chernesky.

I thank my wife, Catherine Gudis, who read every page, heard every complaint, always tempered justice with mercy, and helped me reach a place that is best shared.

And finally, I gladly thank my teachers who oversaw this project when it was a dissertation: Ivan Marcus, who infixed in me the weight of the old; Jon Butler, who introduced me to the weight of the new; and, most of all, Paula Hyman, who took every step along the way with me.

INDEX

Abie's Irish Rose, 31
acculturation, 6–7, 38–39, 164–65
Act of June 5, 1920, 72, 73
Adler, Sam, 17, 29
African Americans, 3, 149, 165, 175, 178, 213n.27; Rothstein's attitude toward, 31; shows of, 31. *See also* stereotypes
"After the Ball," 157
Agnew-Hart law, 29–30
"Alexander, Don't You Want Your Baby No More?" 158
"Alexander's Ragtime Band," 158, 162–63, 165
alienation. *See* marginalization
A. L. Libman, Inc., 49
Amalgamated Clothing Workers, 93
American Civil Liberties Union, 93
American Horse Exchange, 152
American Jewish Committee, 90
American Jewish Congress, 90–91
Americanization, 7, 38, 80, 88, 160–63, 164–65, 168, 177
Amos 'n' Andy, 213n.27
anarchism, 65, 85, 103; literature of, 73; slogan of, 73; terrorist acts of, 71–72
Annenberg, Moses, 41
Anti-Defamation League, 146
antisemitism, 5, 8, 16, 51–54, 61, 116, 163, 172, 173, 185n.2. *See also* stereotypes
arendators, 60
Arnold Rothstein Realty Corporation, 49
Arnstein, Nicky, 17, 44–47, 144; description of Rothstein, 31–32
Asinof, Eliot, 50, 51–52, 193n.5
assimilation, 6–7, 38–39, 90, 172–73, 200n.11
Attell, Abe, 28, 49, 55
Auerbach, Jerold S., 200n.9

authority, institutions of, 5, 7, 25, 140, 180
"*Avot*", 25
Avrich, Paul, 73

Back-To-Dixie songs, 135–36. *See also* song industry
Baker, Newton D., 84
"Bald" Jack Rose recipe, 33
Baltzell, Digby, 190n.21
Baron, Salo W., 214n.5
baseball commissioner, 51–52
baseball, 15, 54, 55. *See also* World Series fix
Becker, Charles, 34
Becker-Rosenthal affair, 34–35
Bedini and Arthur, 147
Belasco, David, 210n.9
Belmont Park, 37, 57. *See also* racetracks
Belmont, August I, 37
Belmont, August II, 37–38, 62
Benjamin, Judah P., 6
Berkeley, Busby, 134
Berkman, Alexander, 73, 85
Berlin, Irving, 55, 128, 136, 142, 145, 157, 158–59, 165; on Americanization, 164; self-criticism of, 160–164
Bernard, Barney, 209n.7
Bessarabian Landsmanschaft, 23
Beth Israel Hospital, 23
B. H. Sheftels and Company, 41
Biale, David, 187n.7
Big Boy, 175
Bingham, Theodore A., 195n.14
black books, 32, 36
Black Sox. *See* Chicago White Sox, World Series fix
blackness. *See* stereotypes
Blackwell's Island Prison, 41